Serene Seas

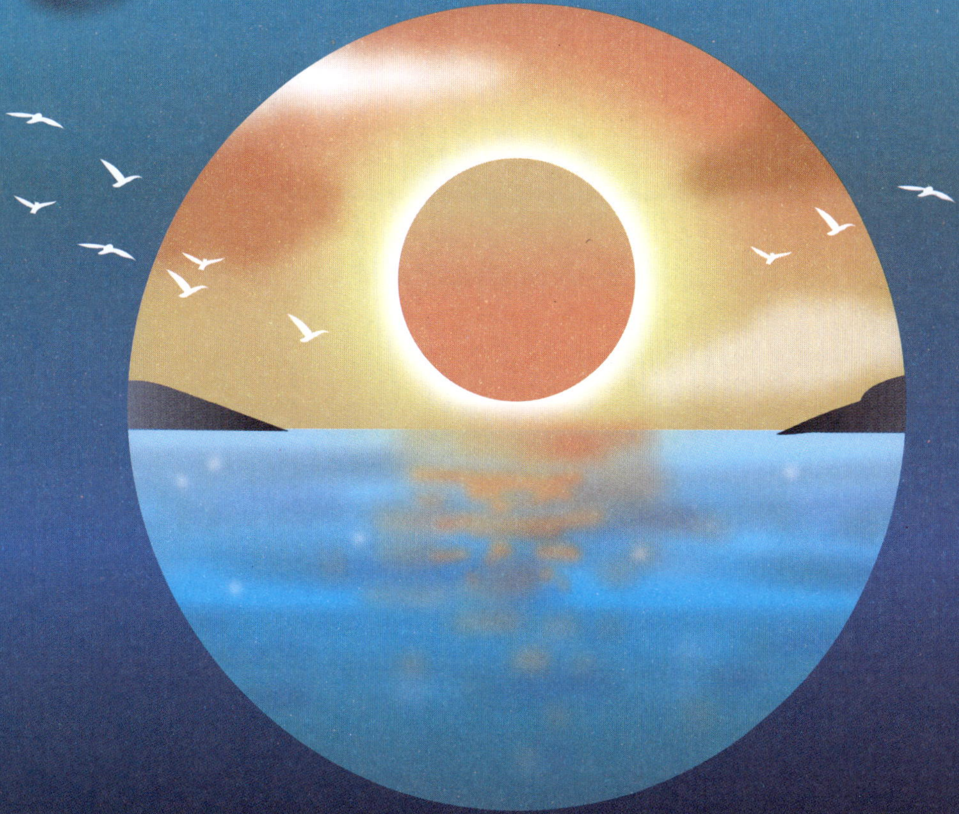

COLORING BOOK

MW01366152

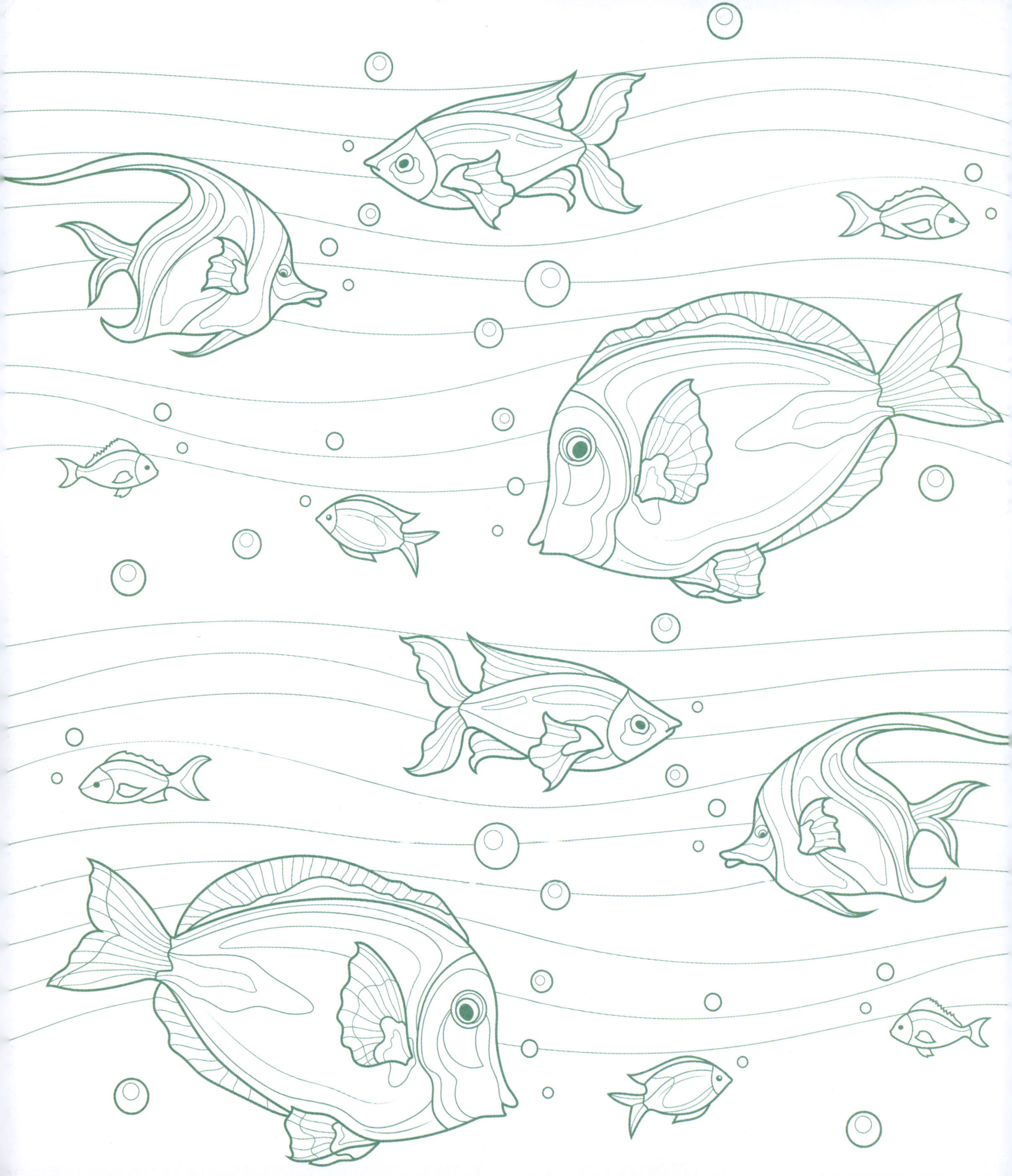

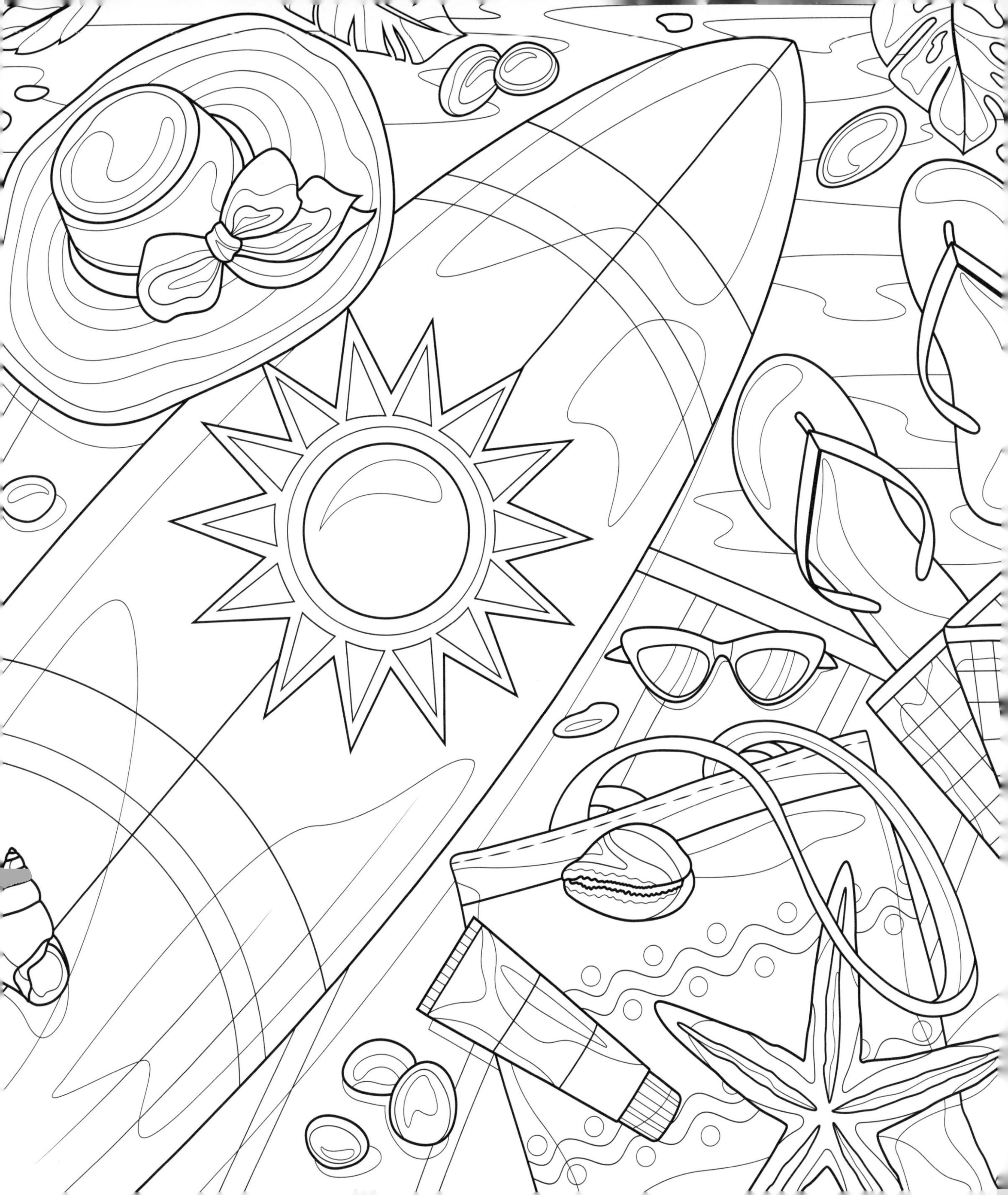

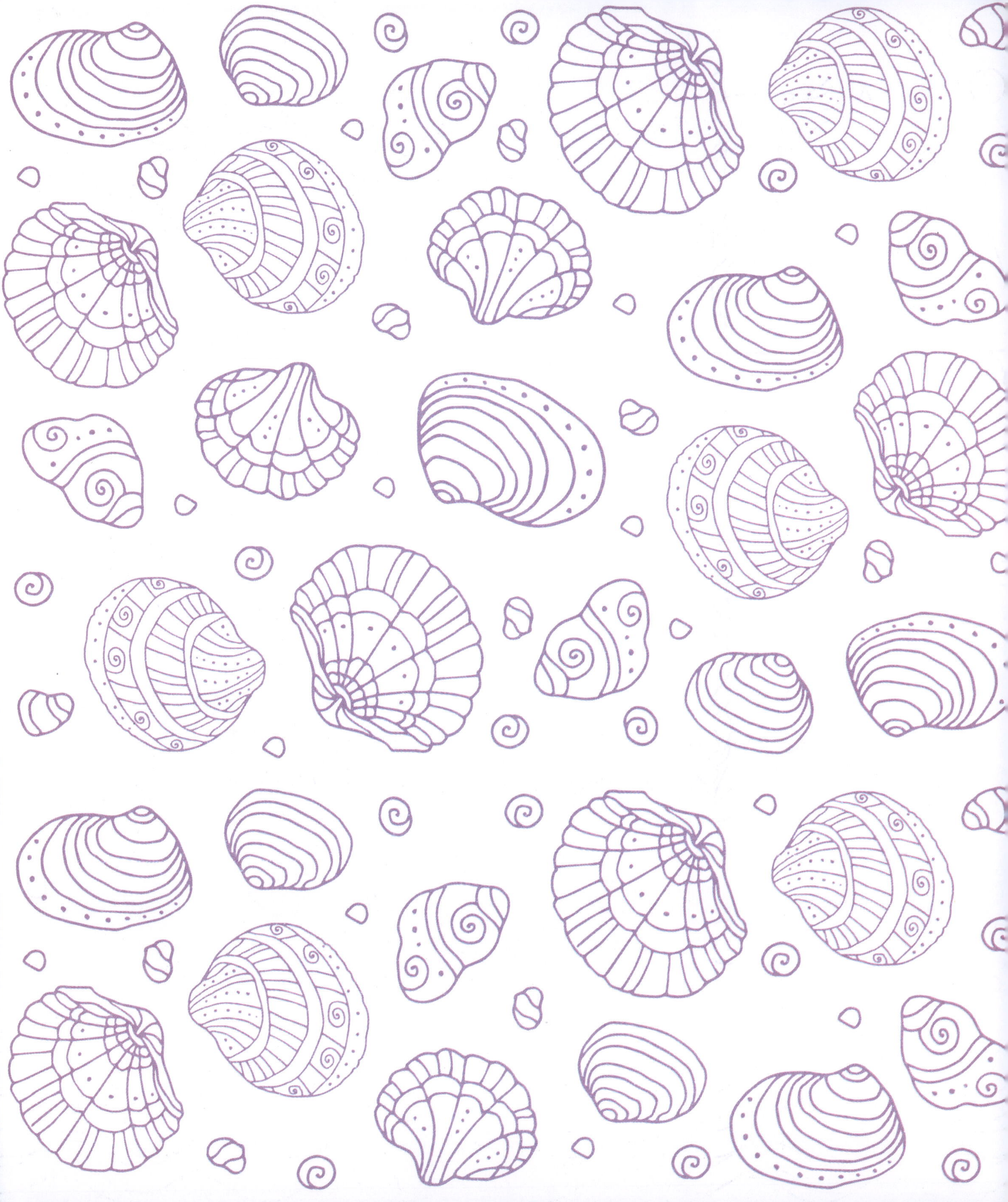

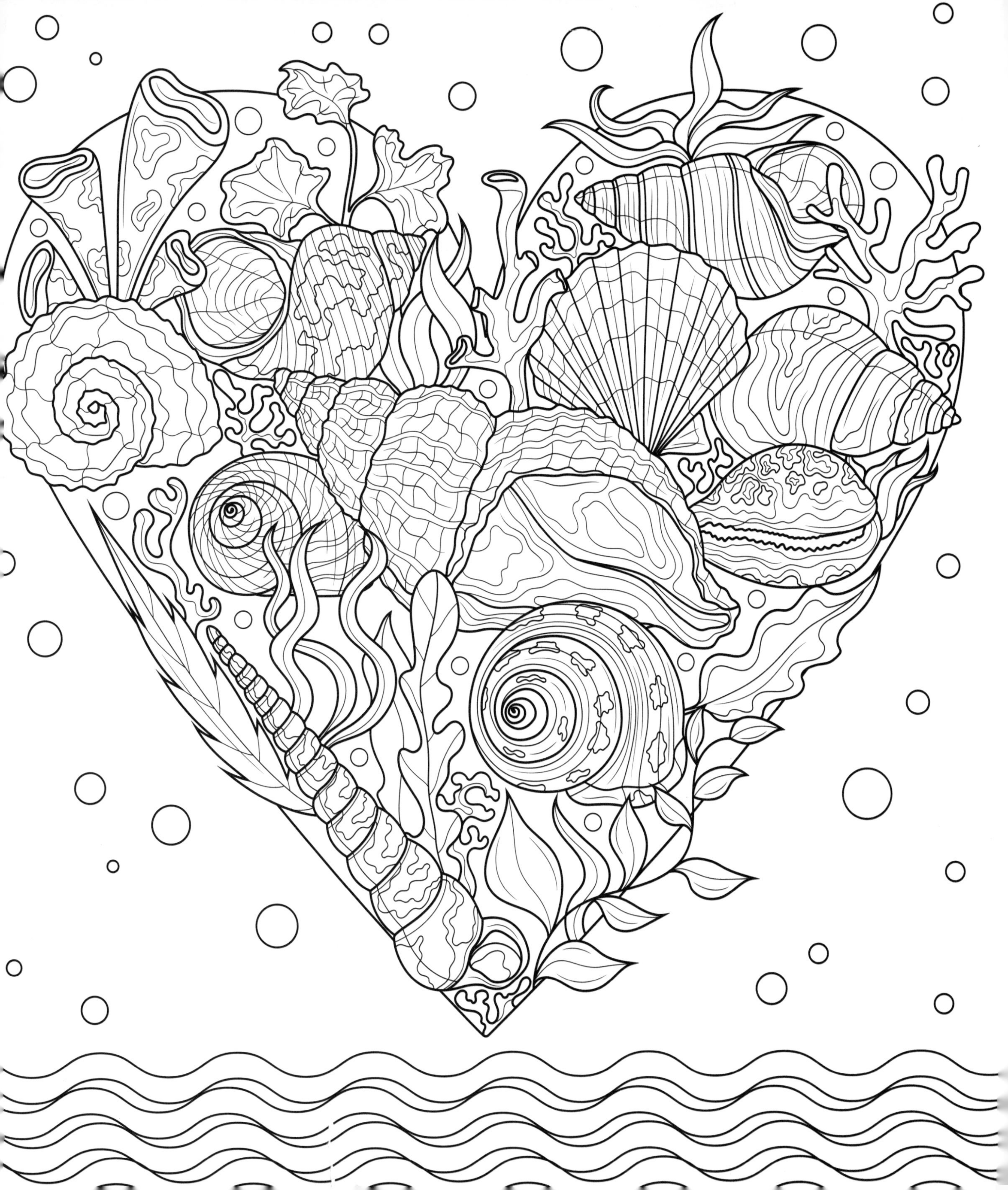

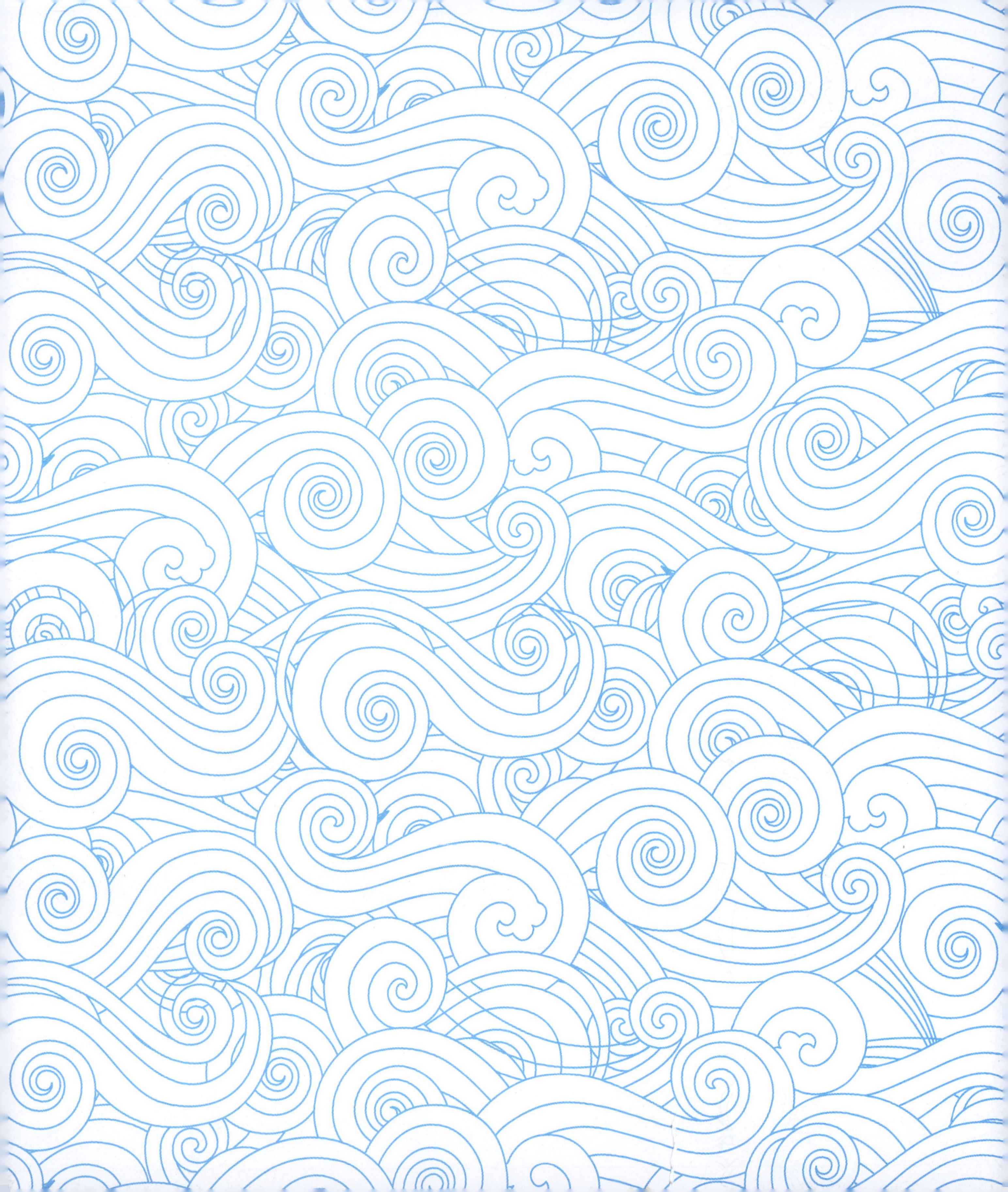

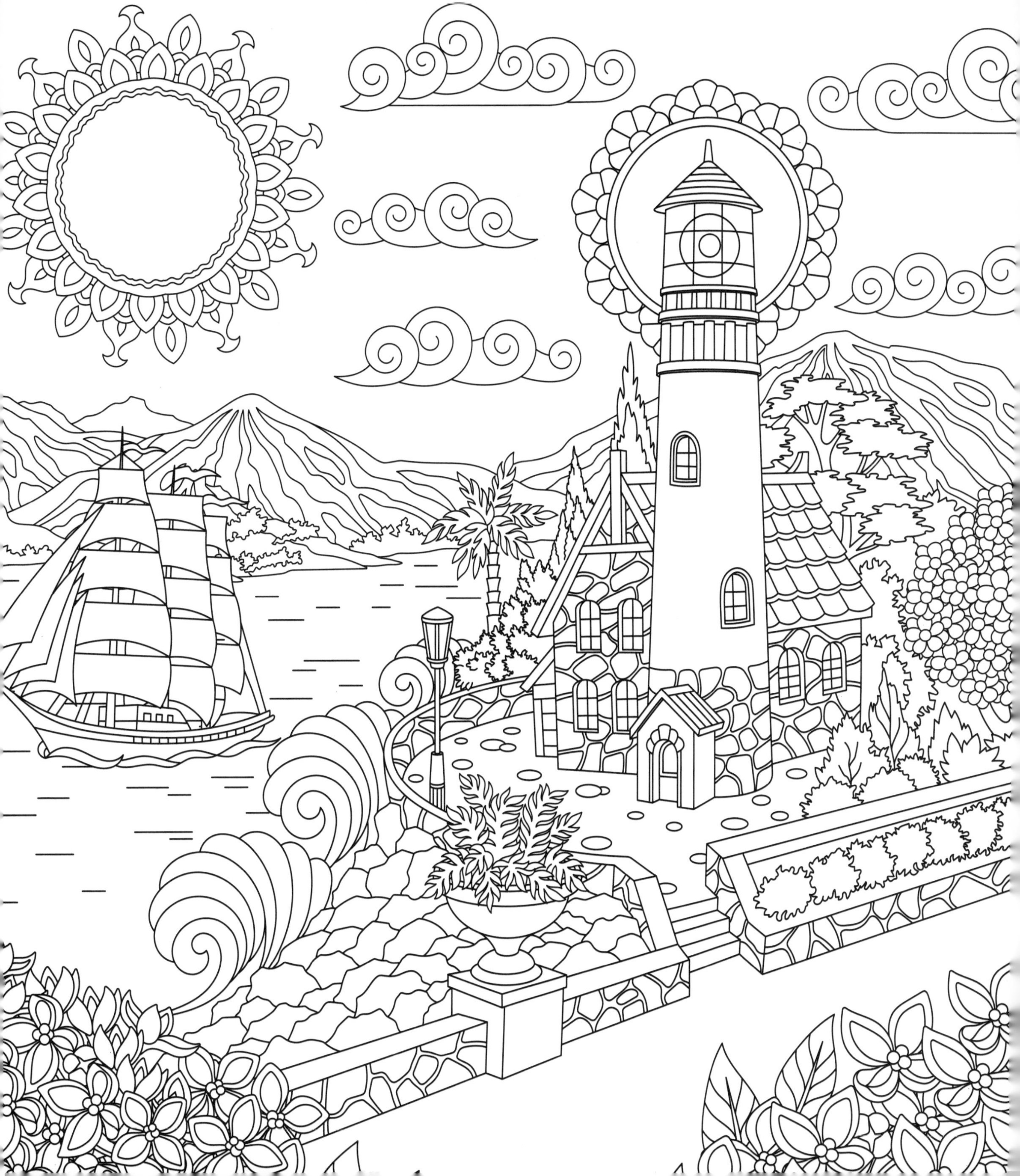

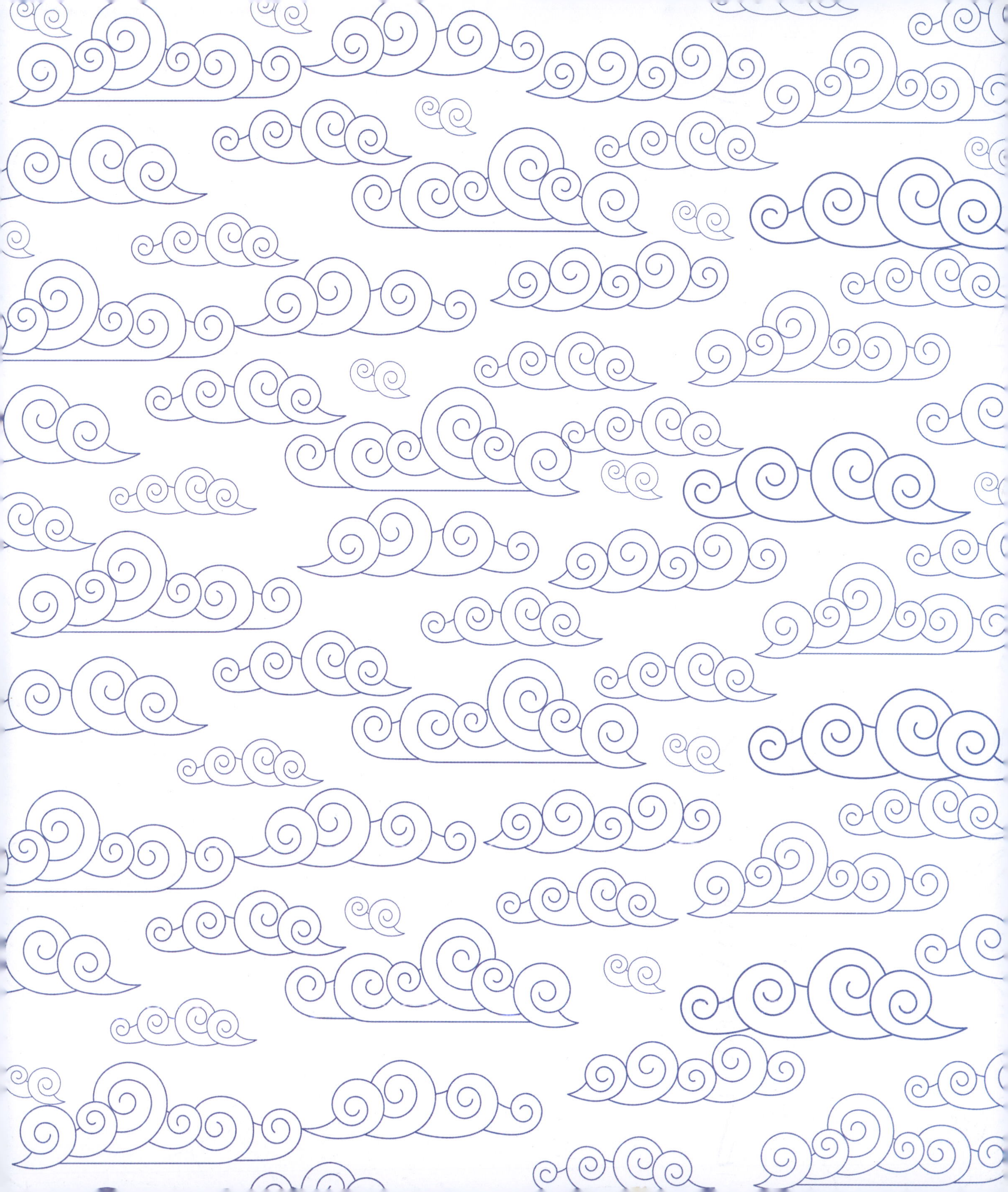

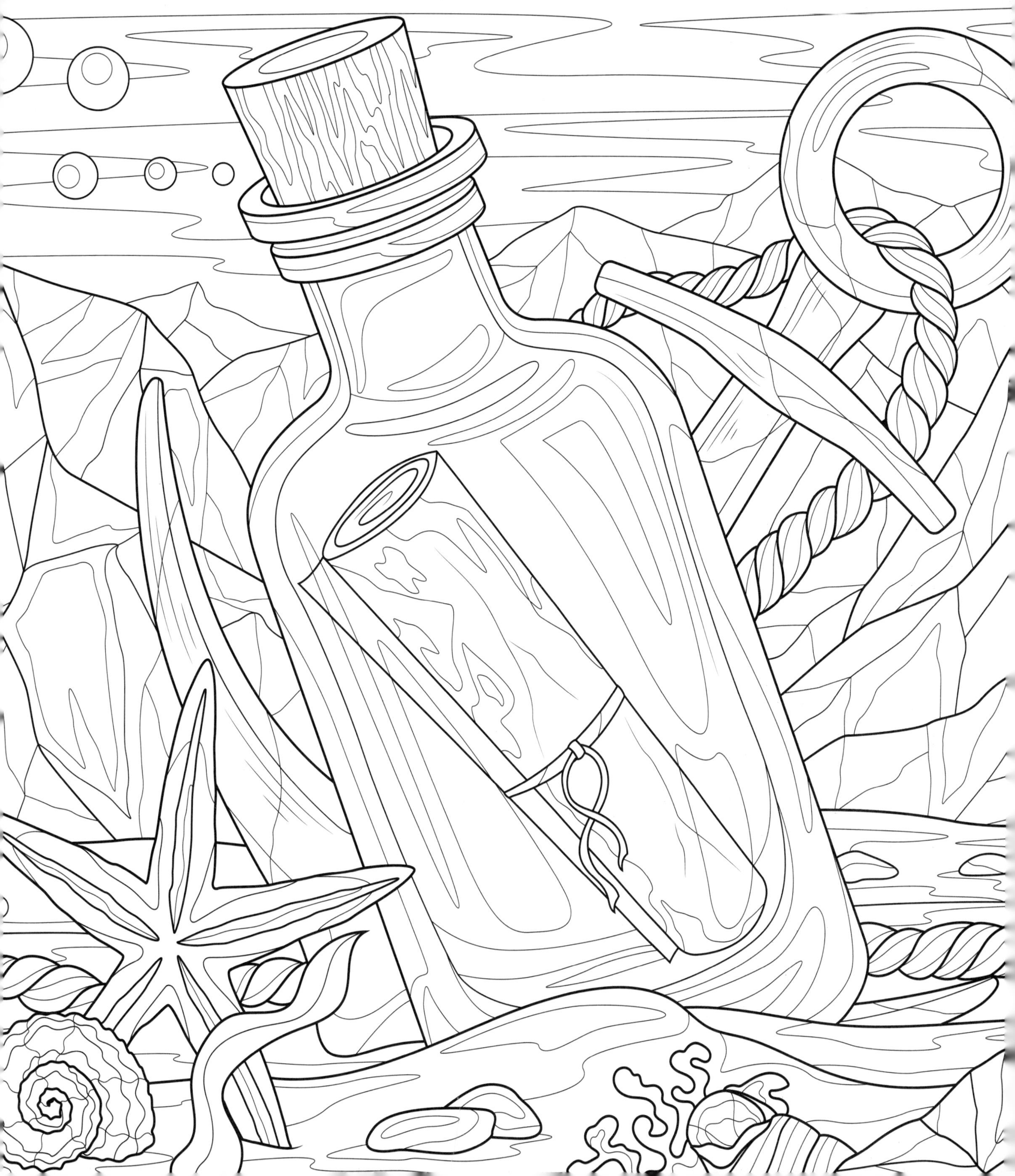

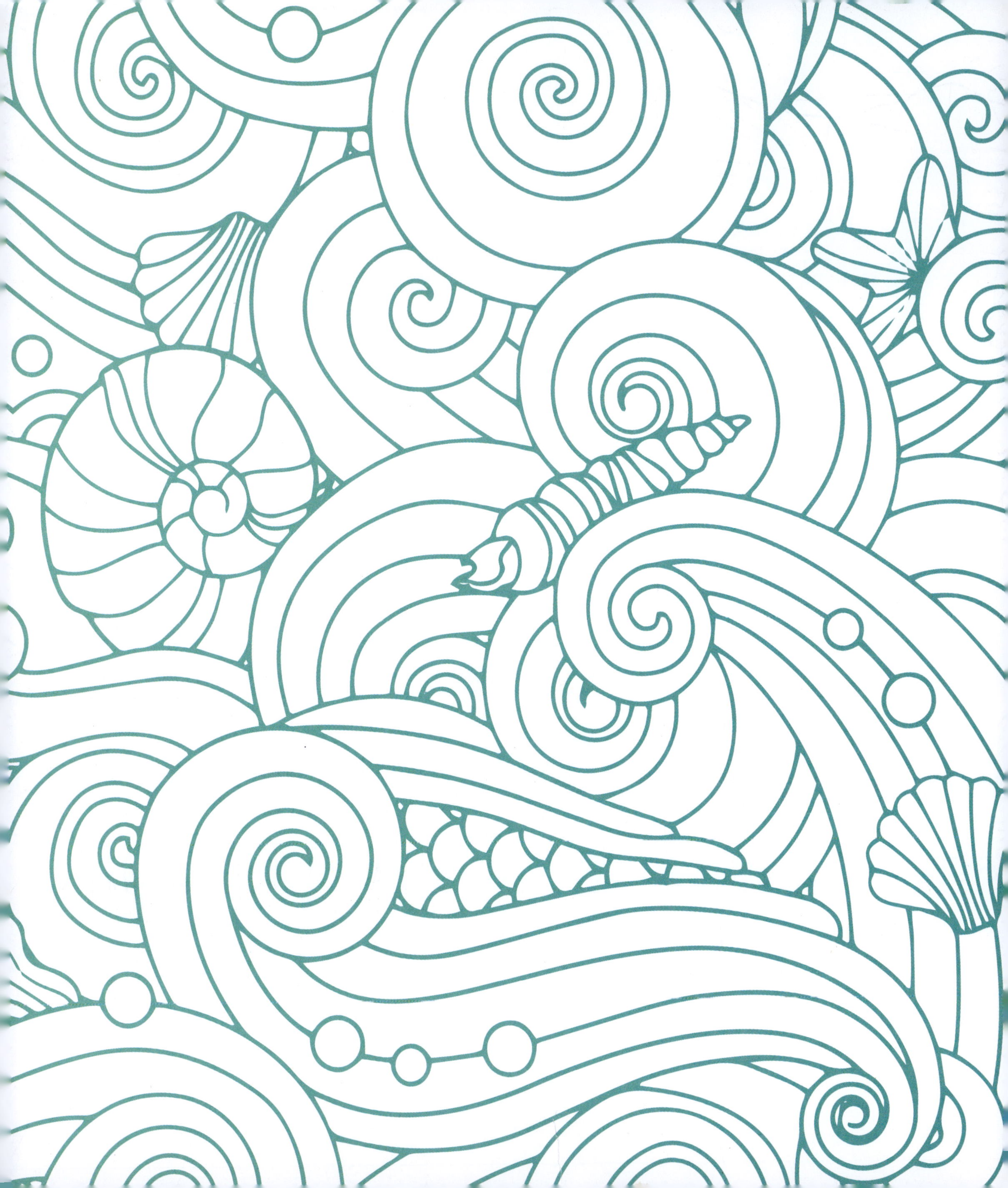

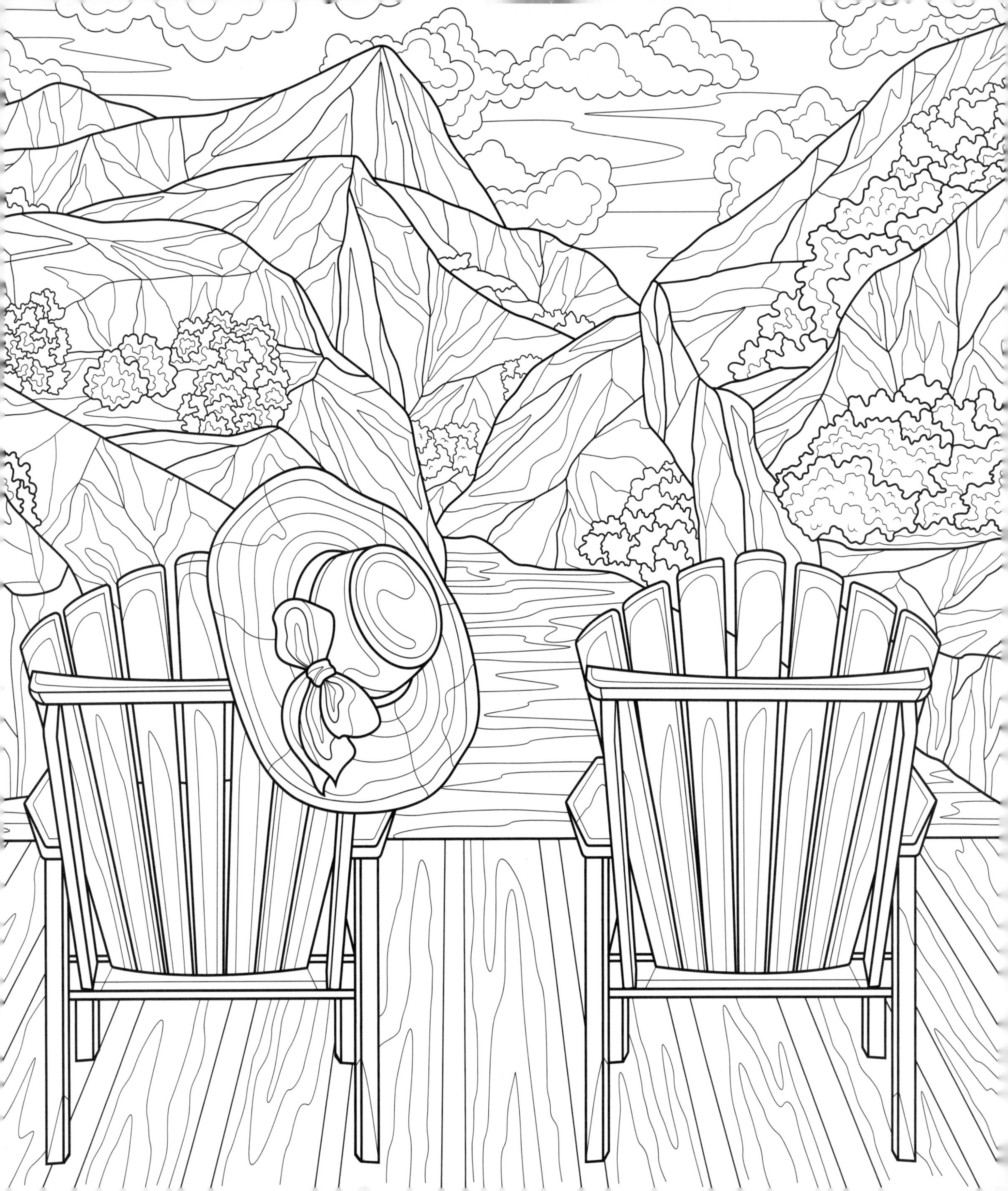

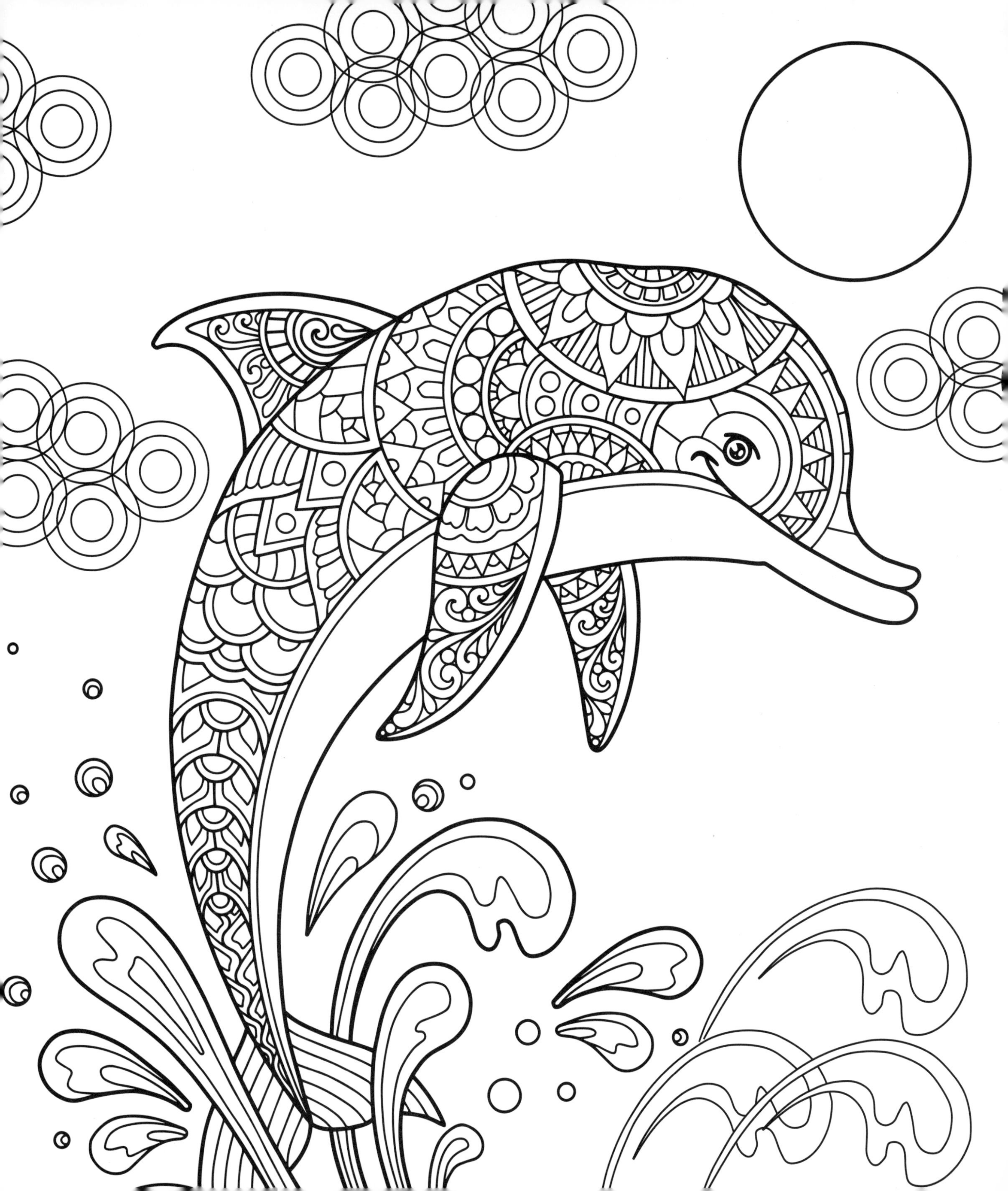

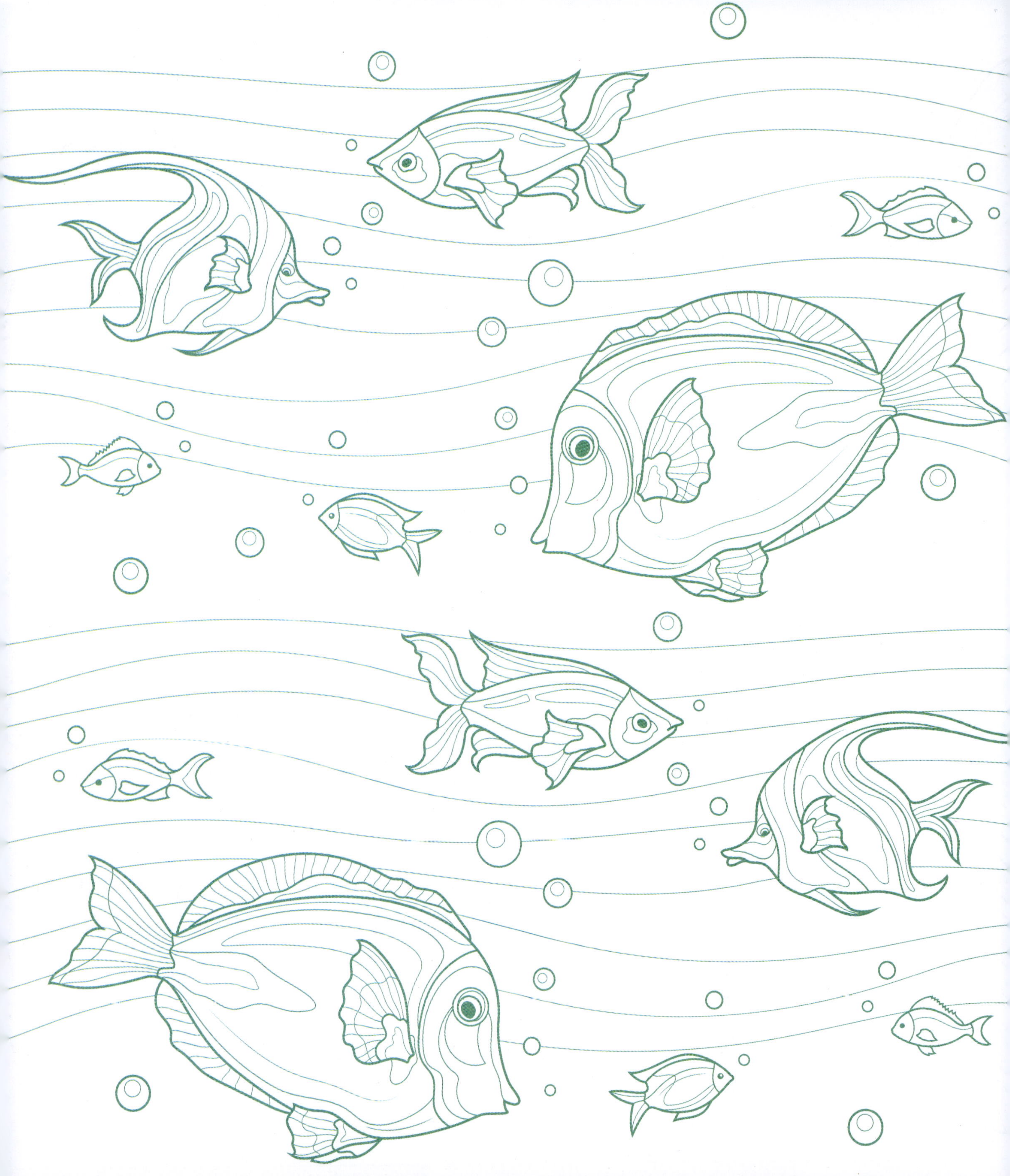

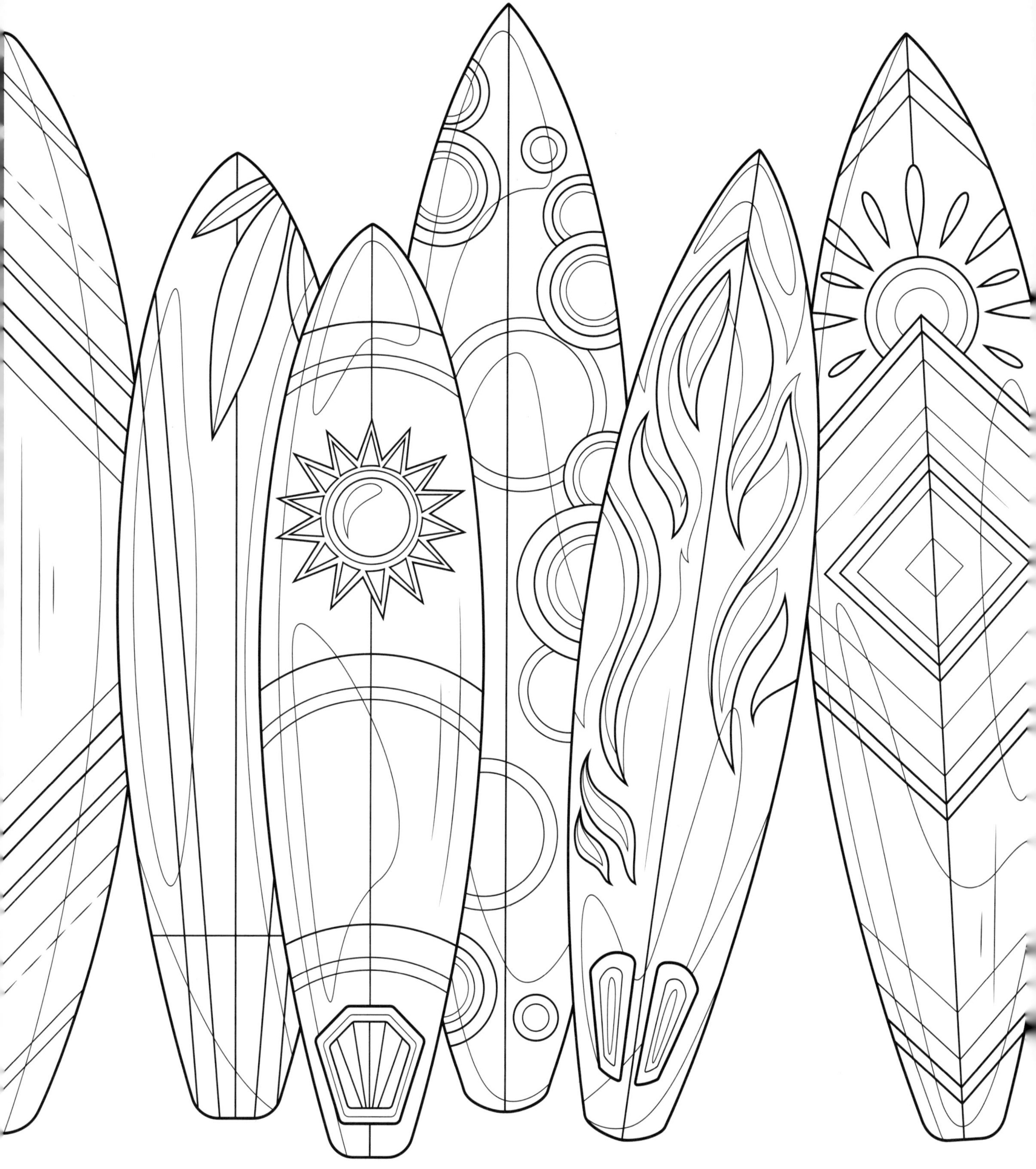

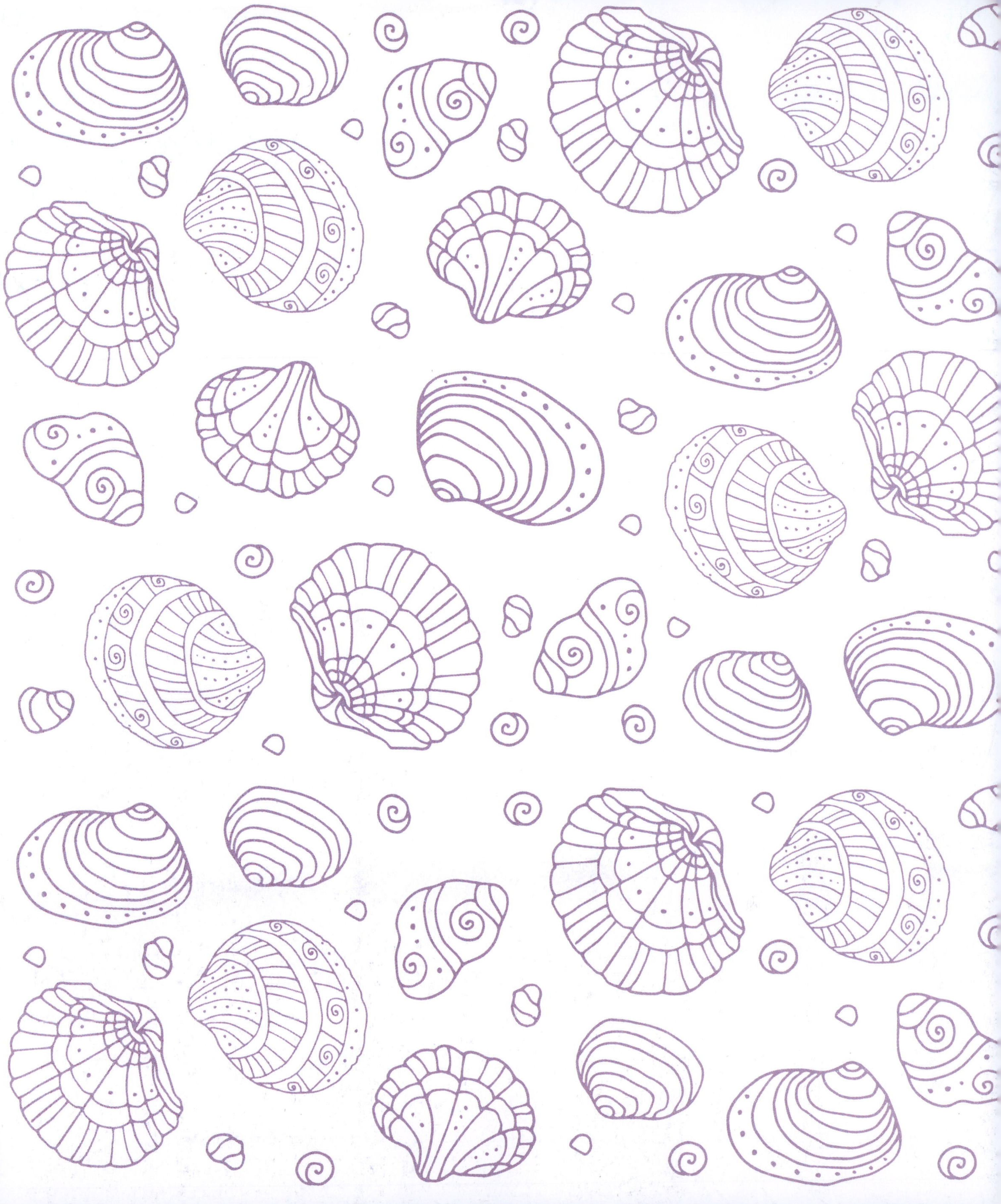

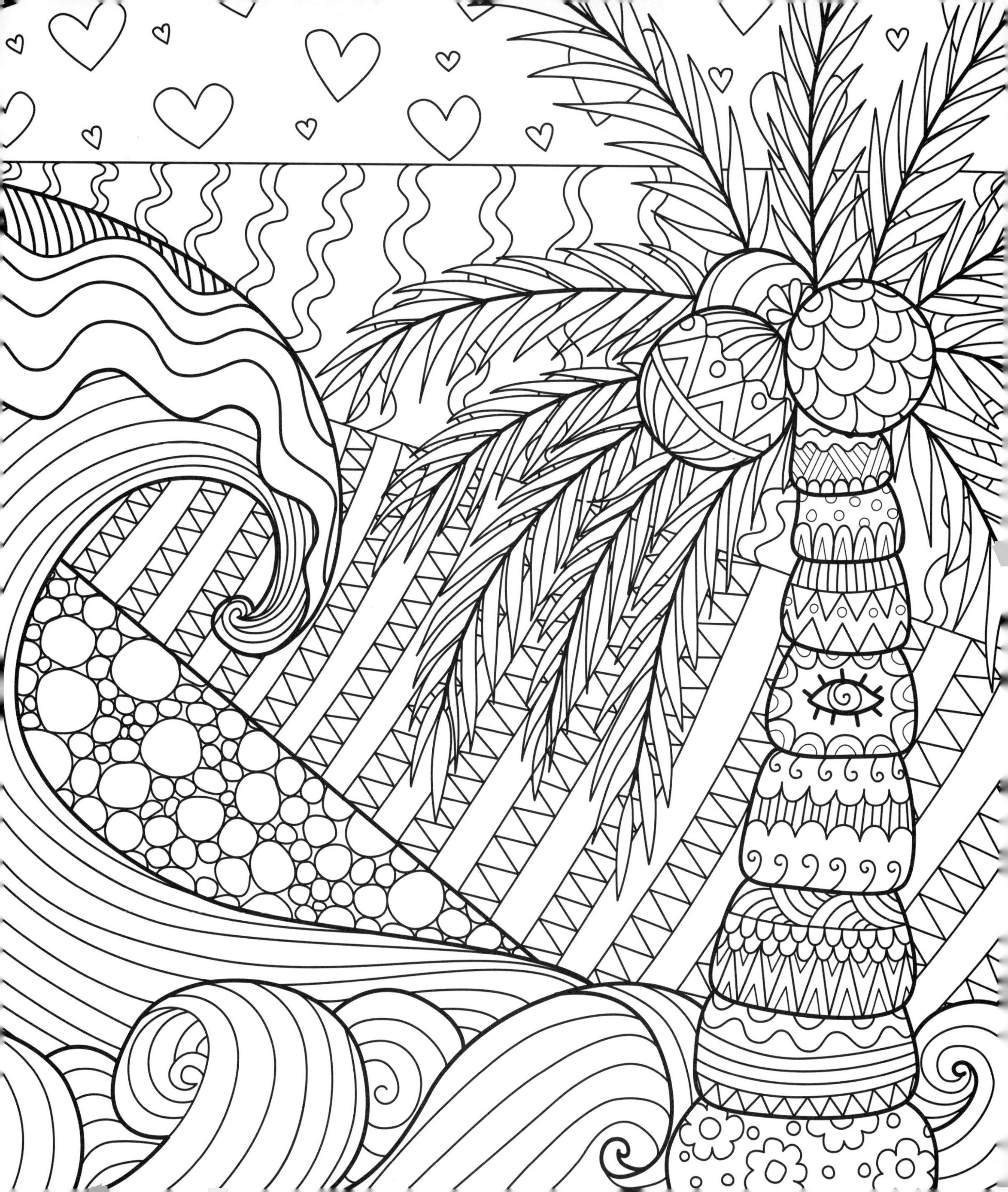

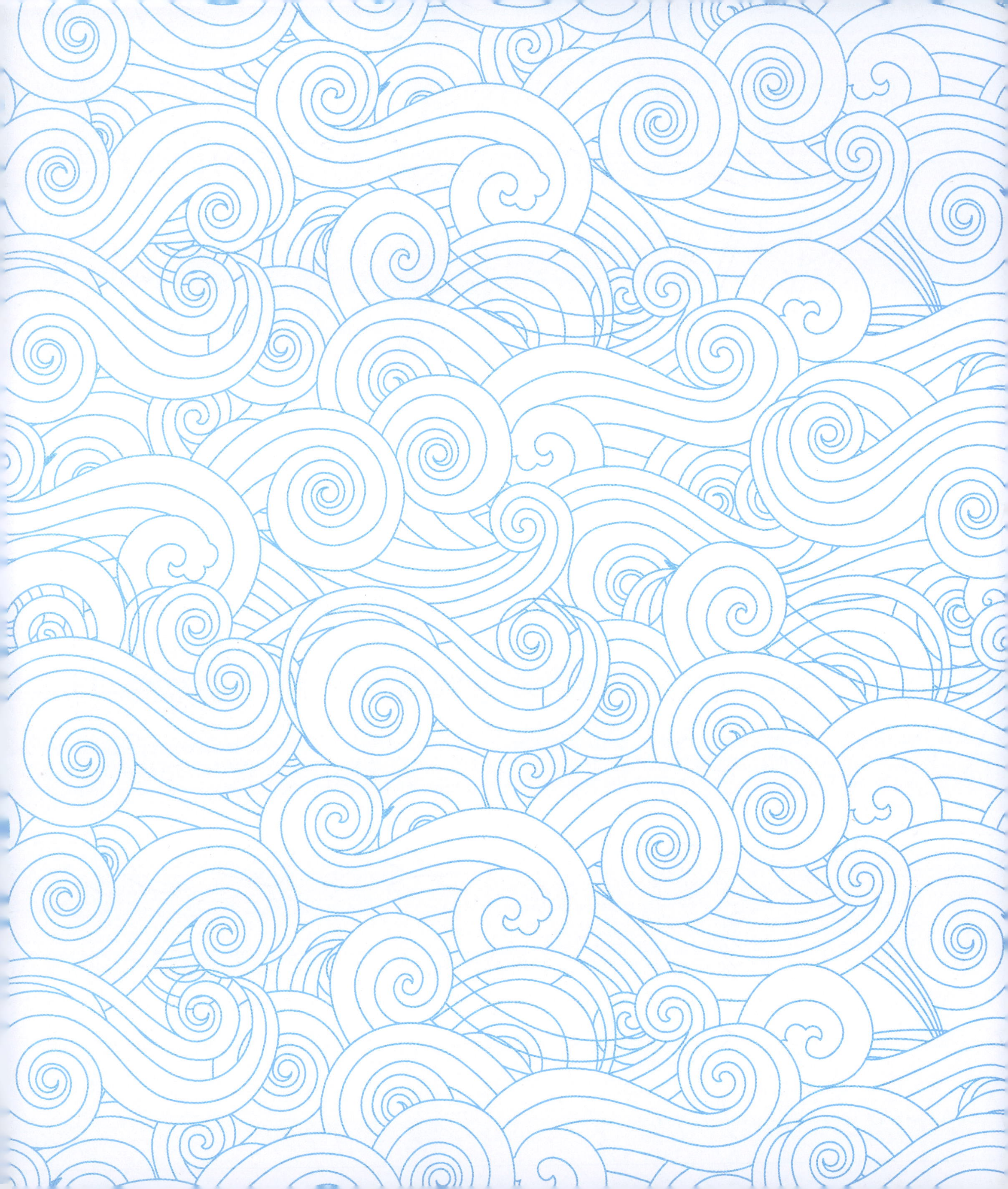

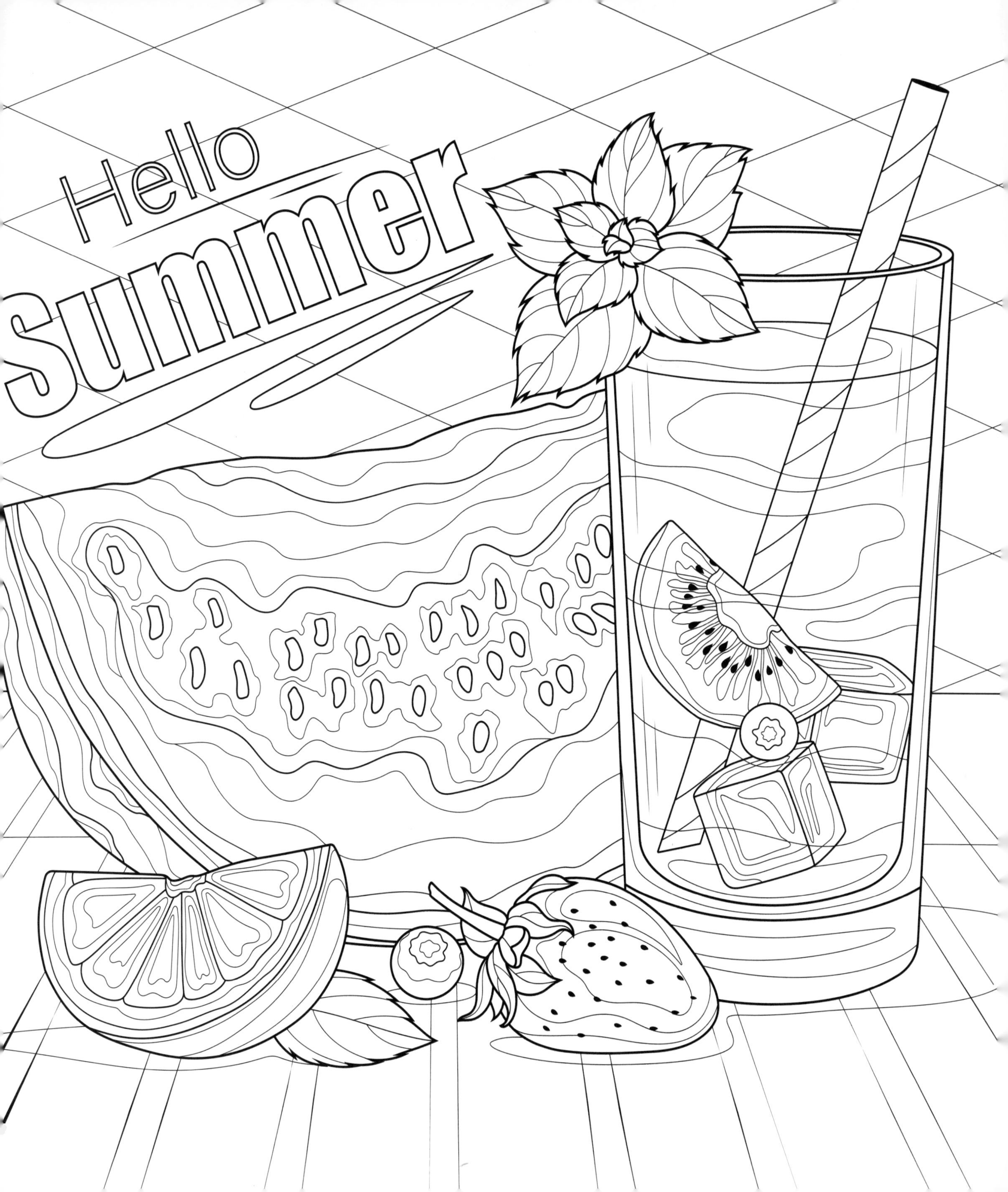
Hello
Summer

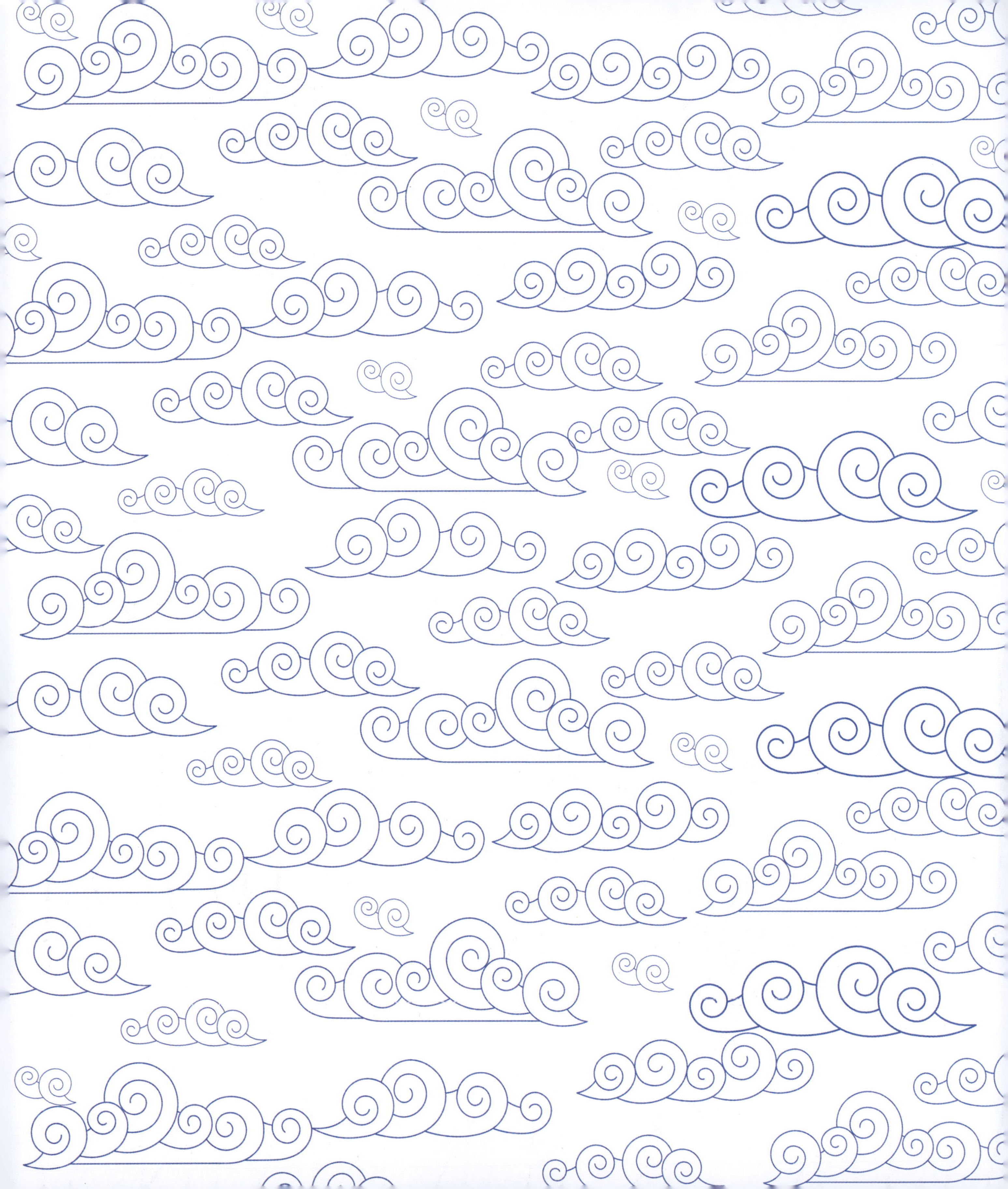

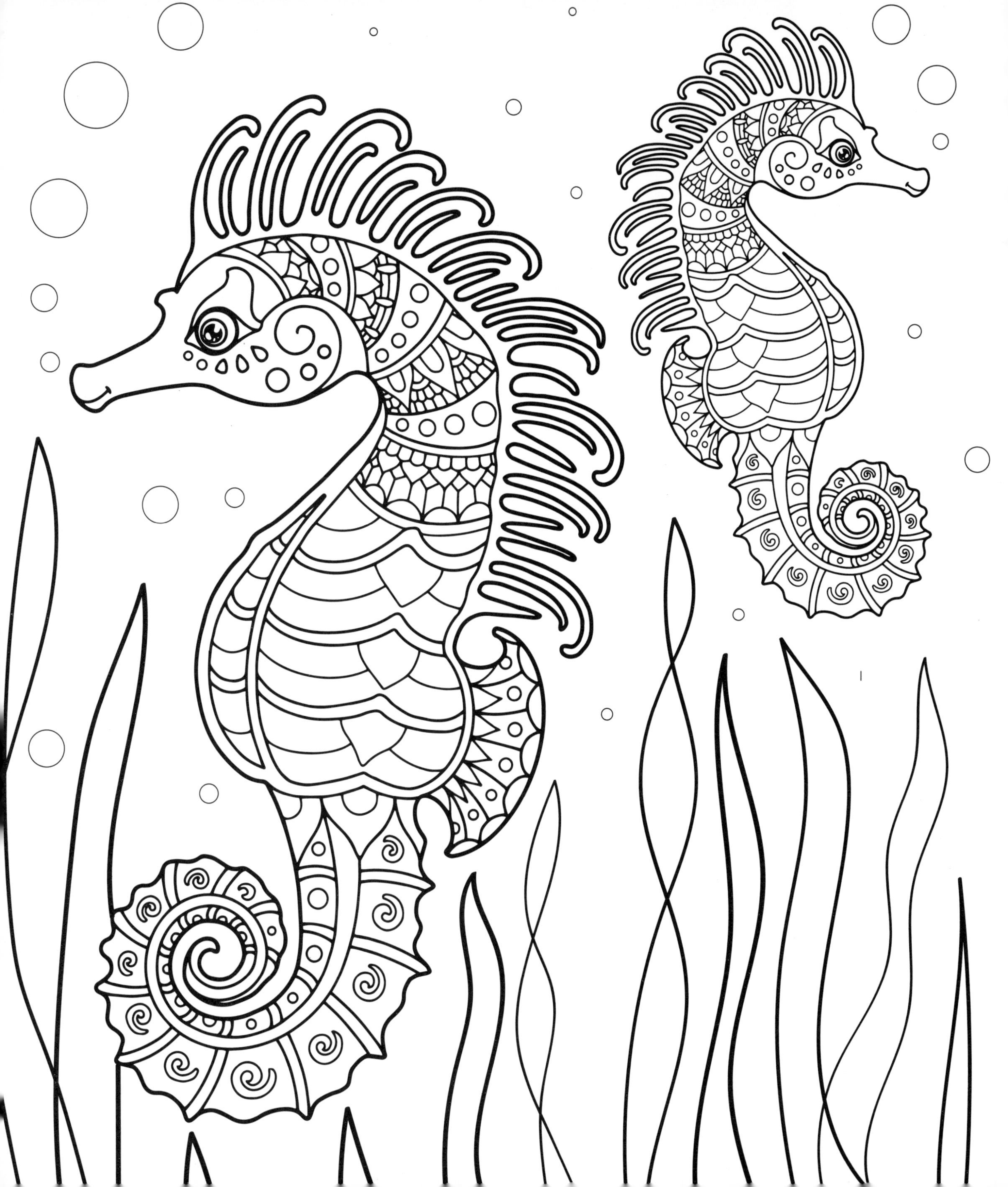

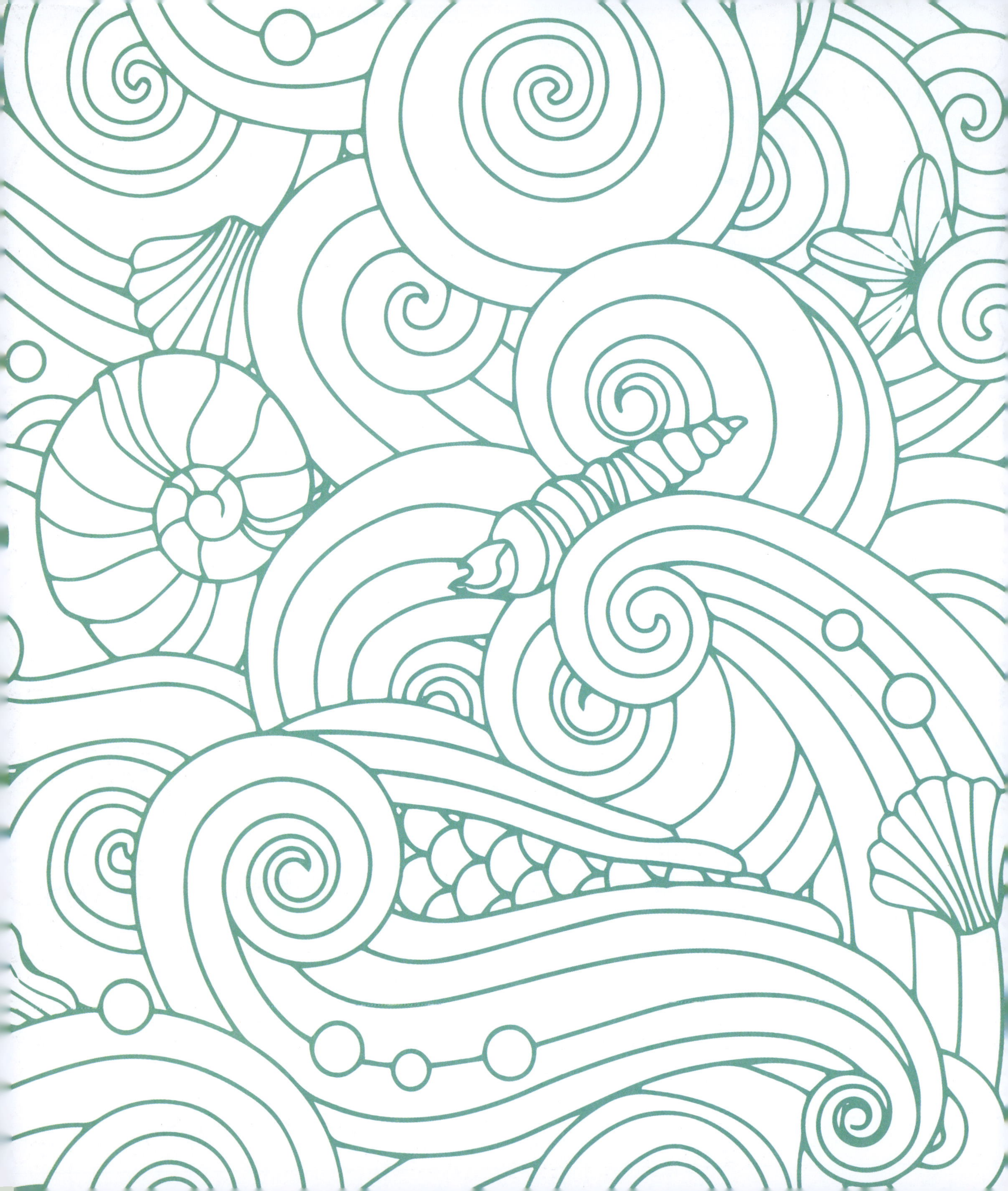

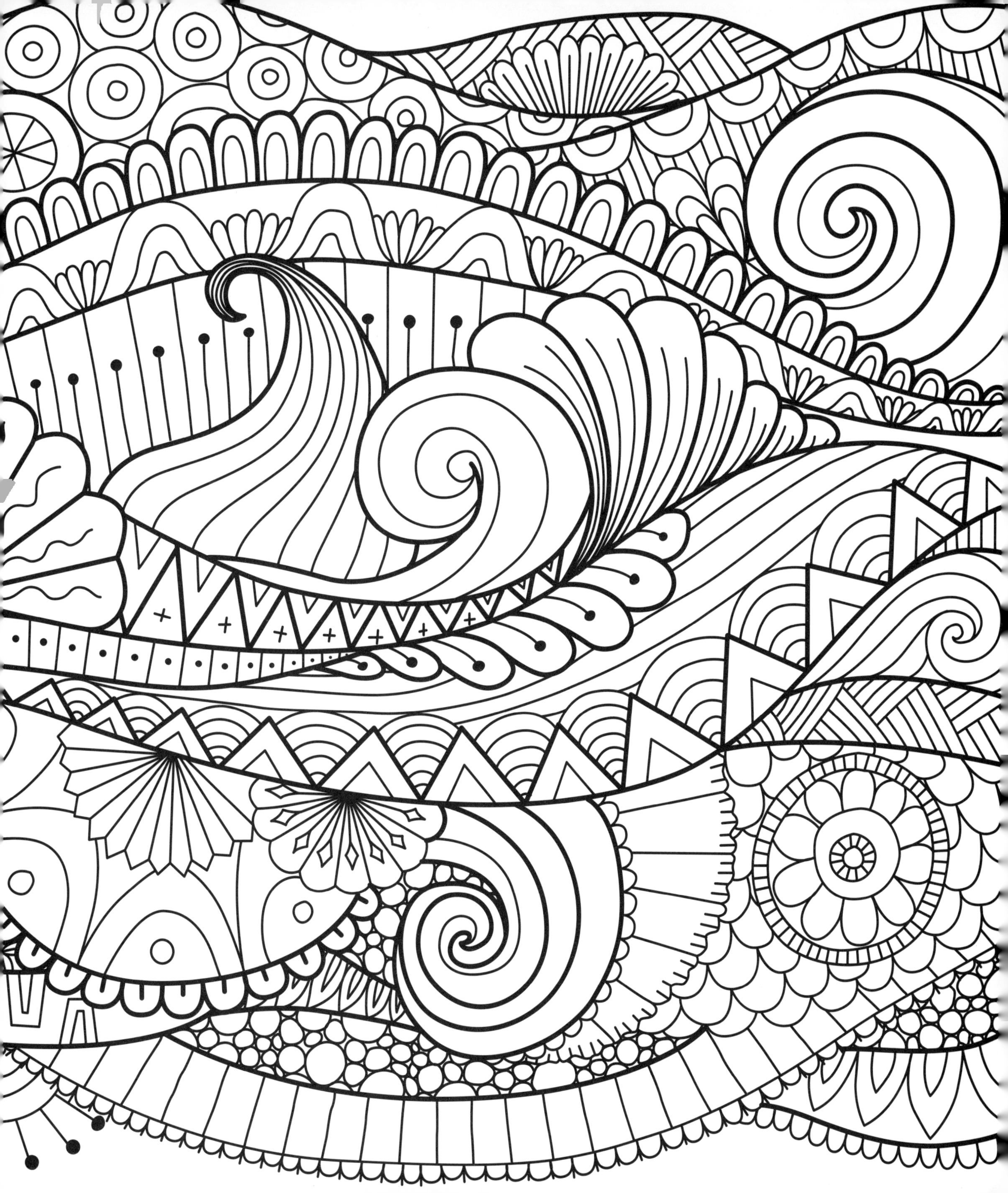

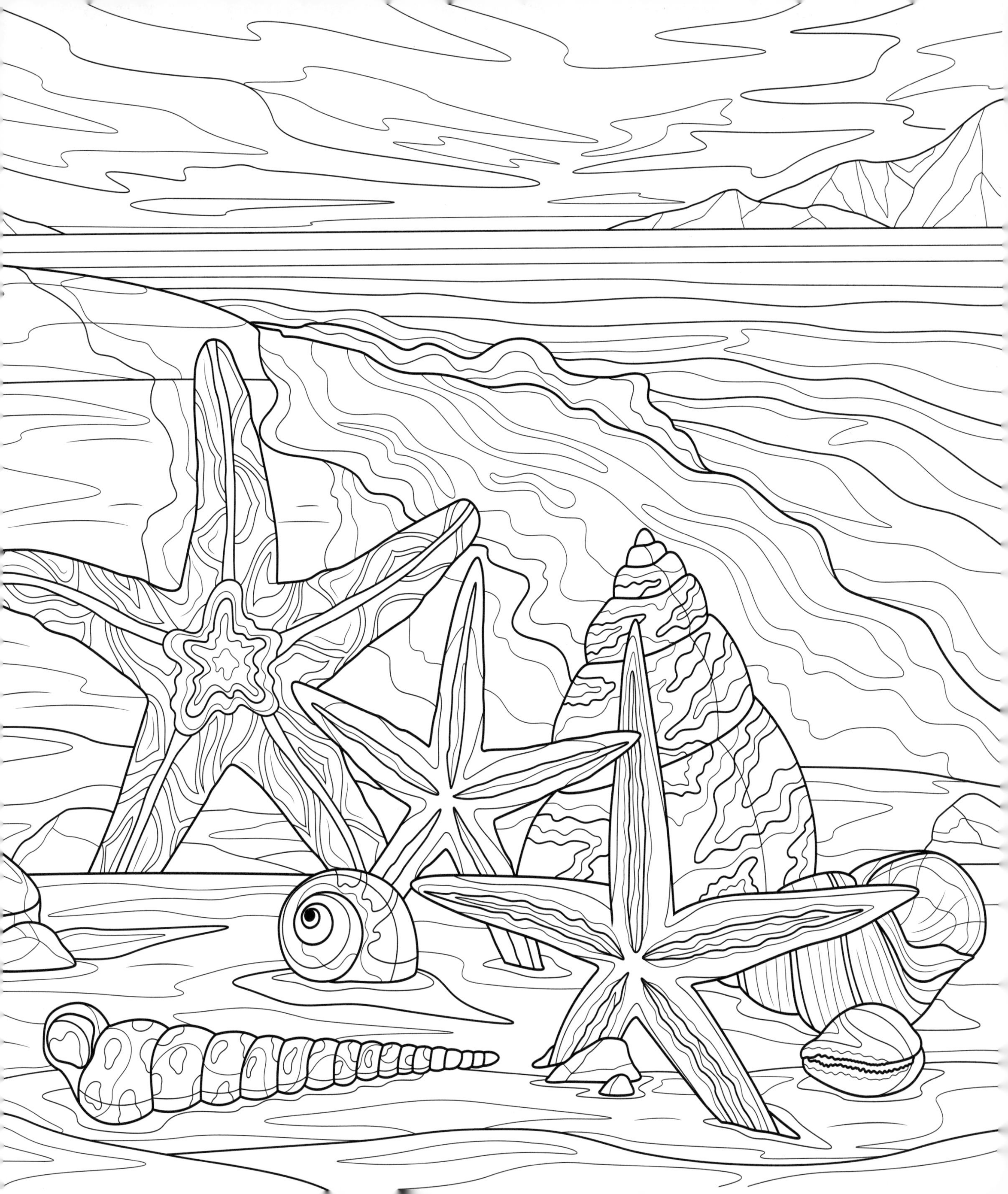

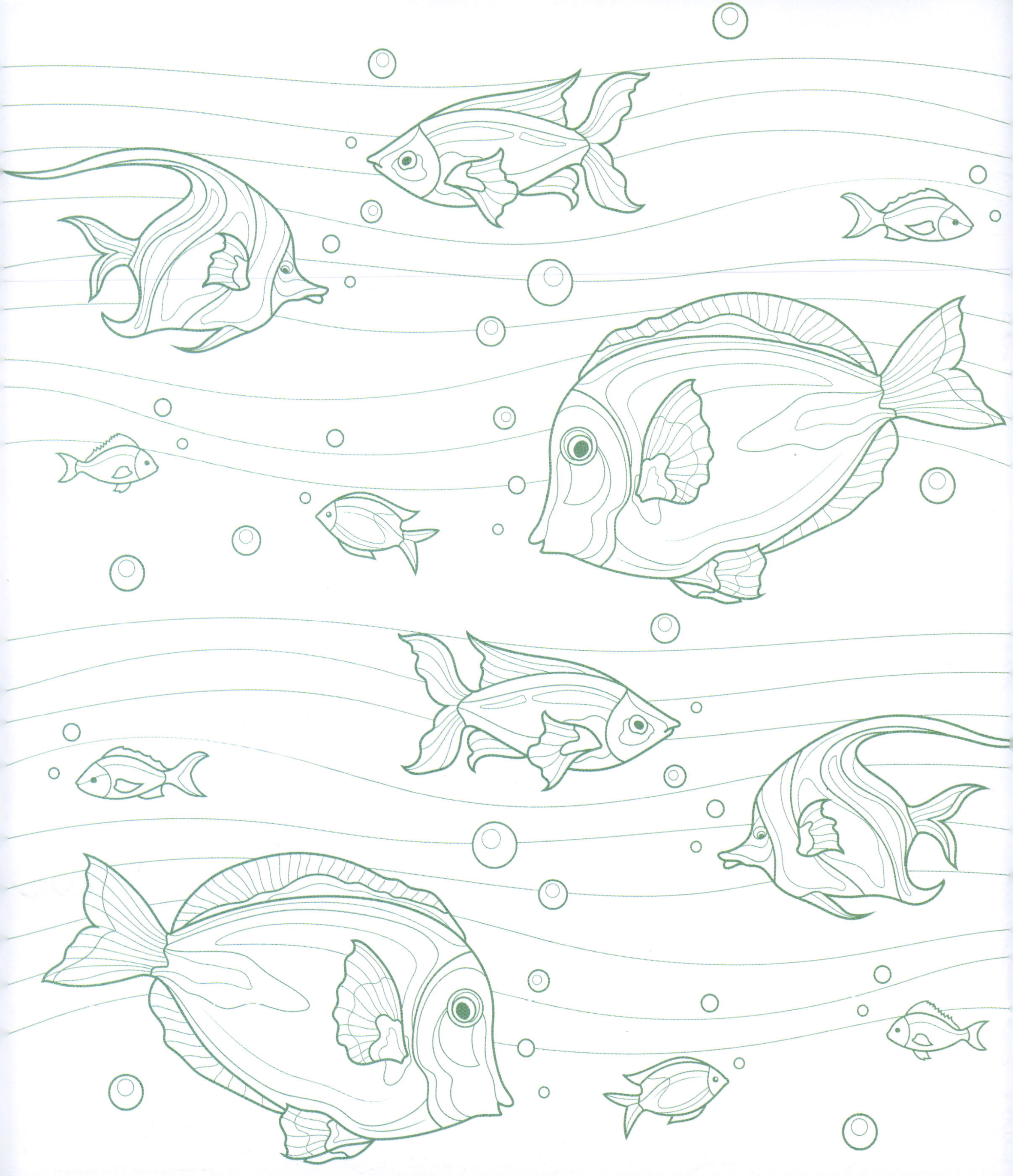

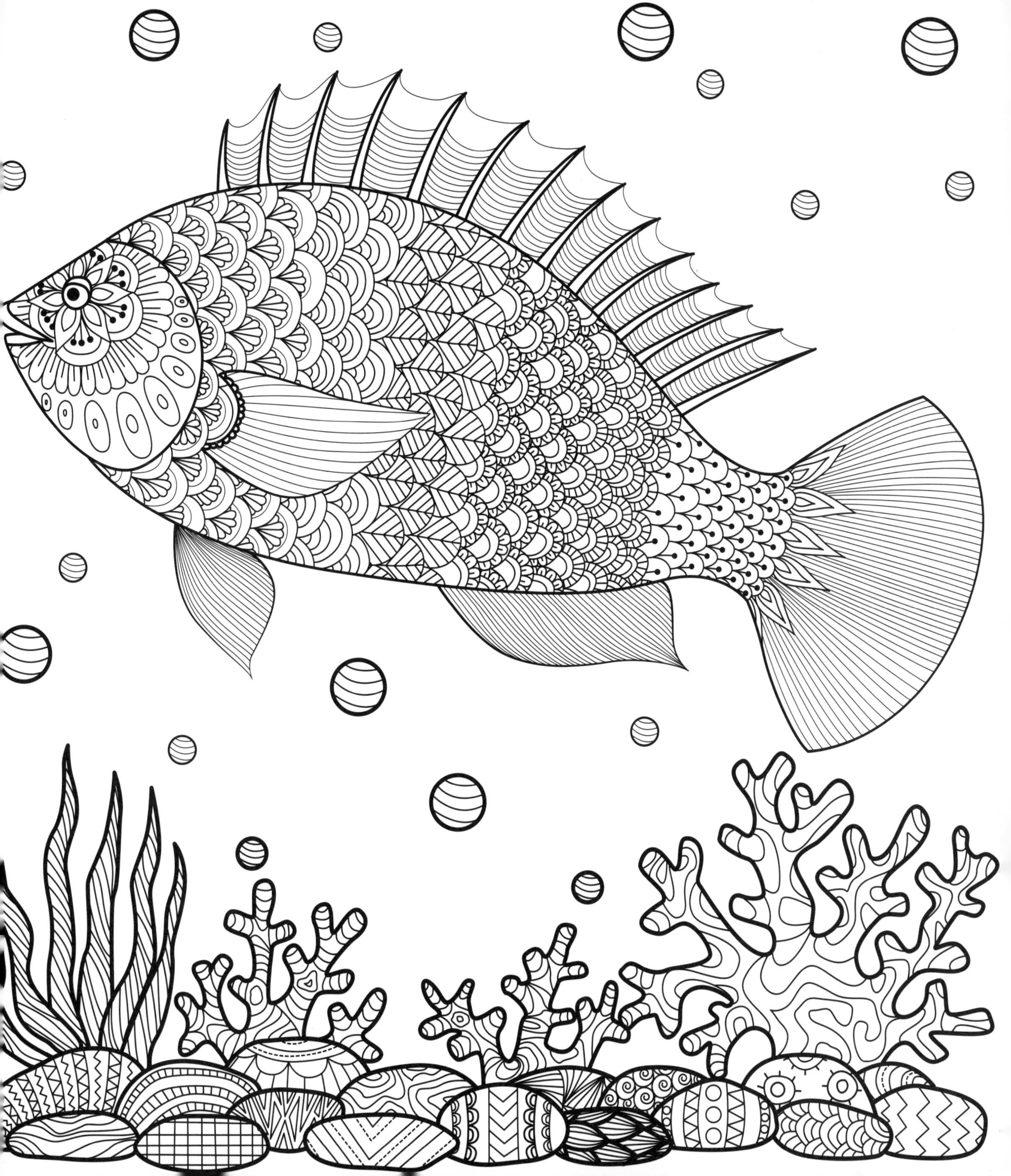

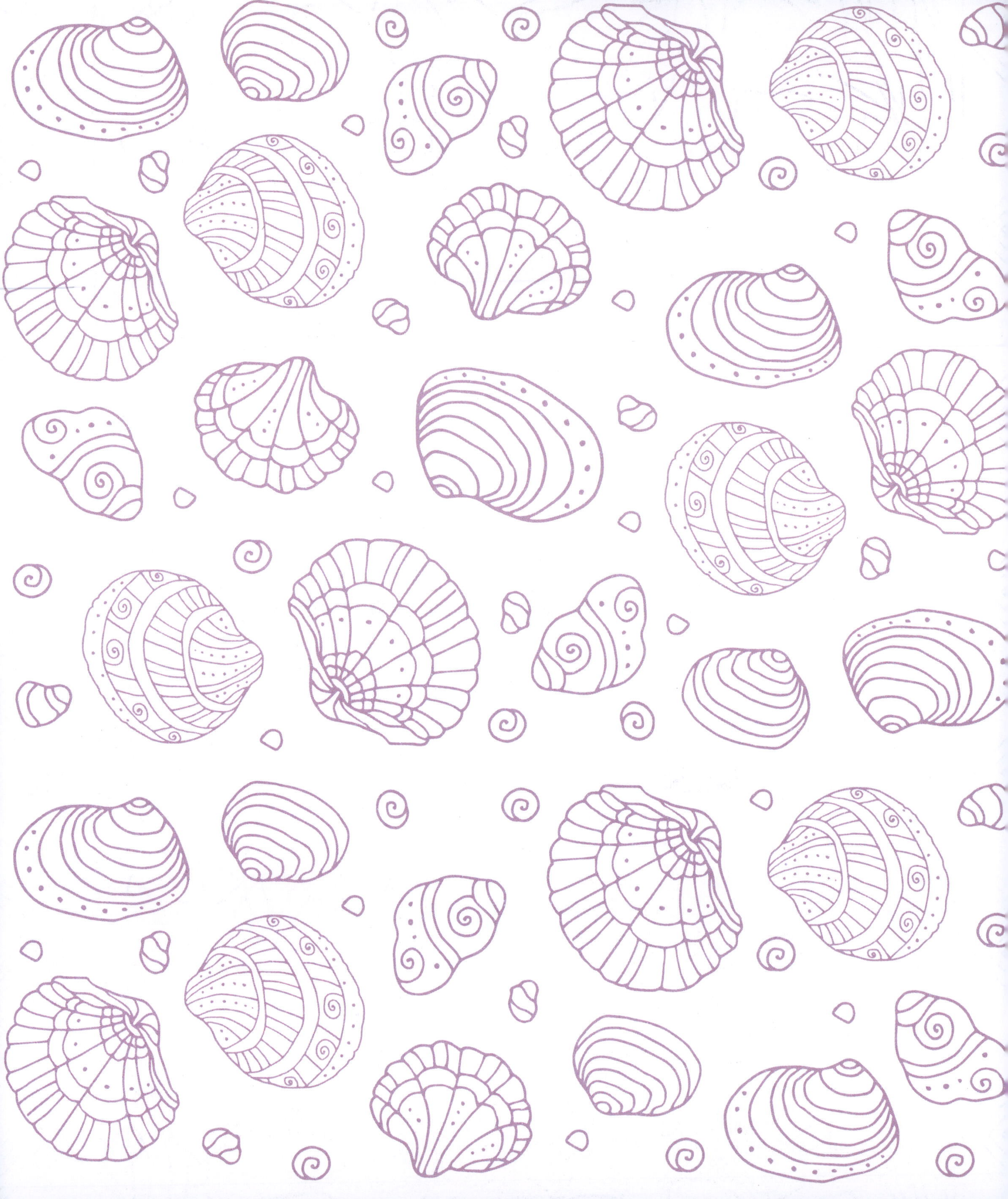

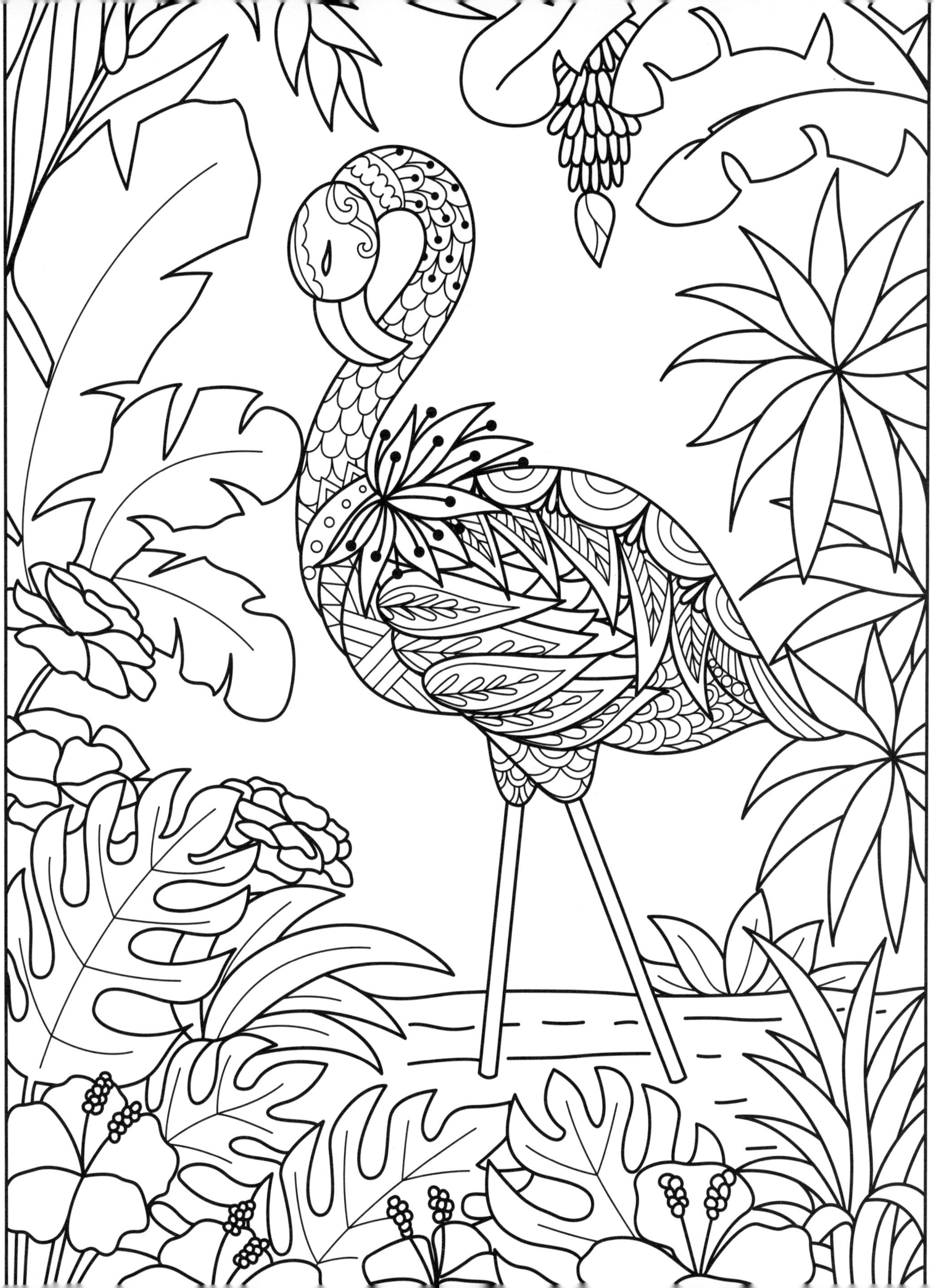

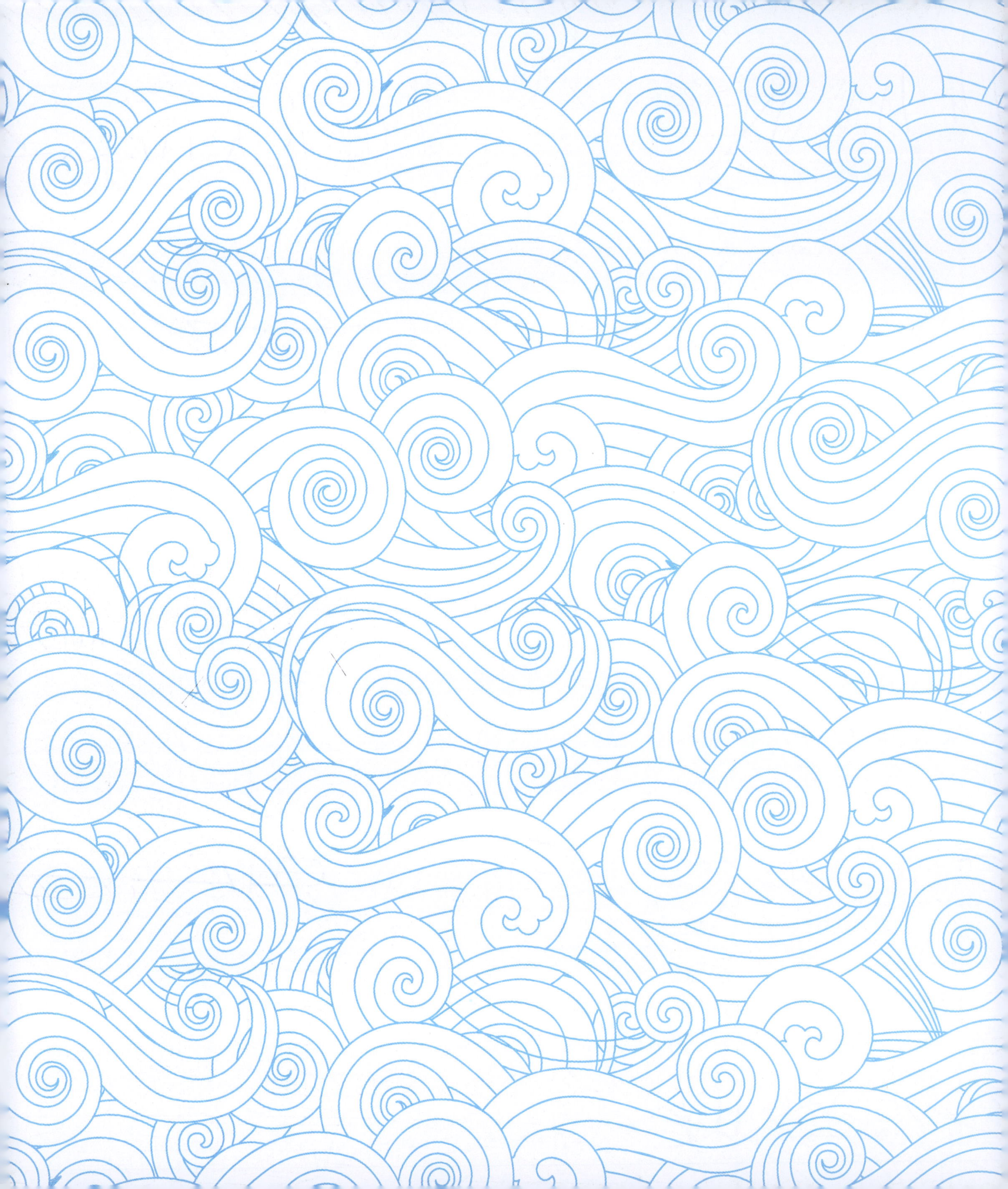

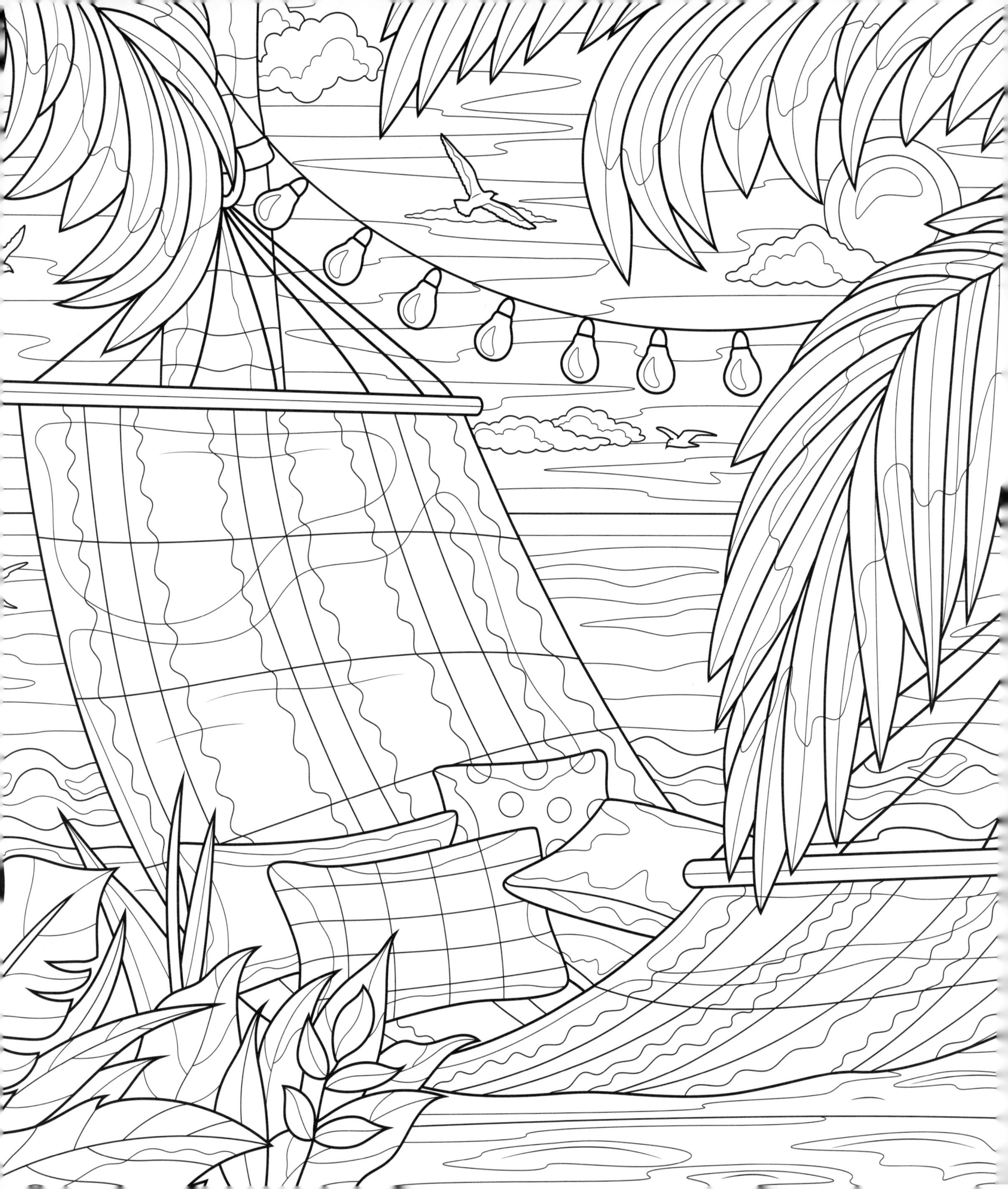

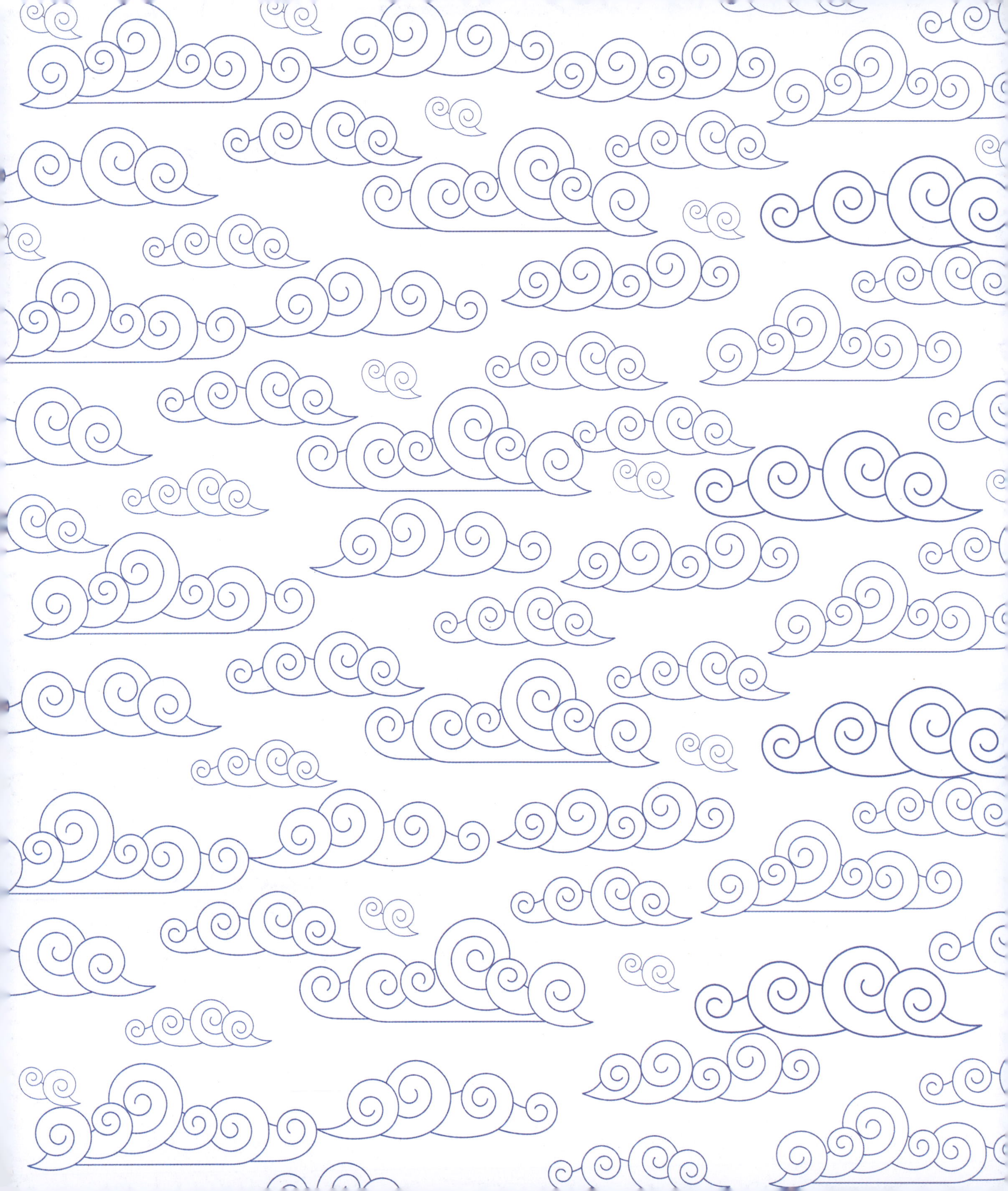

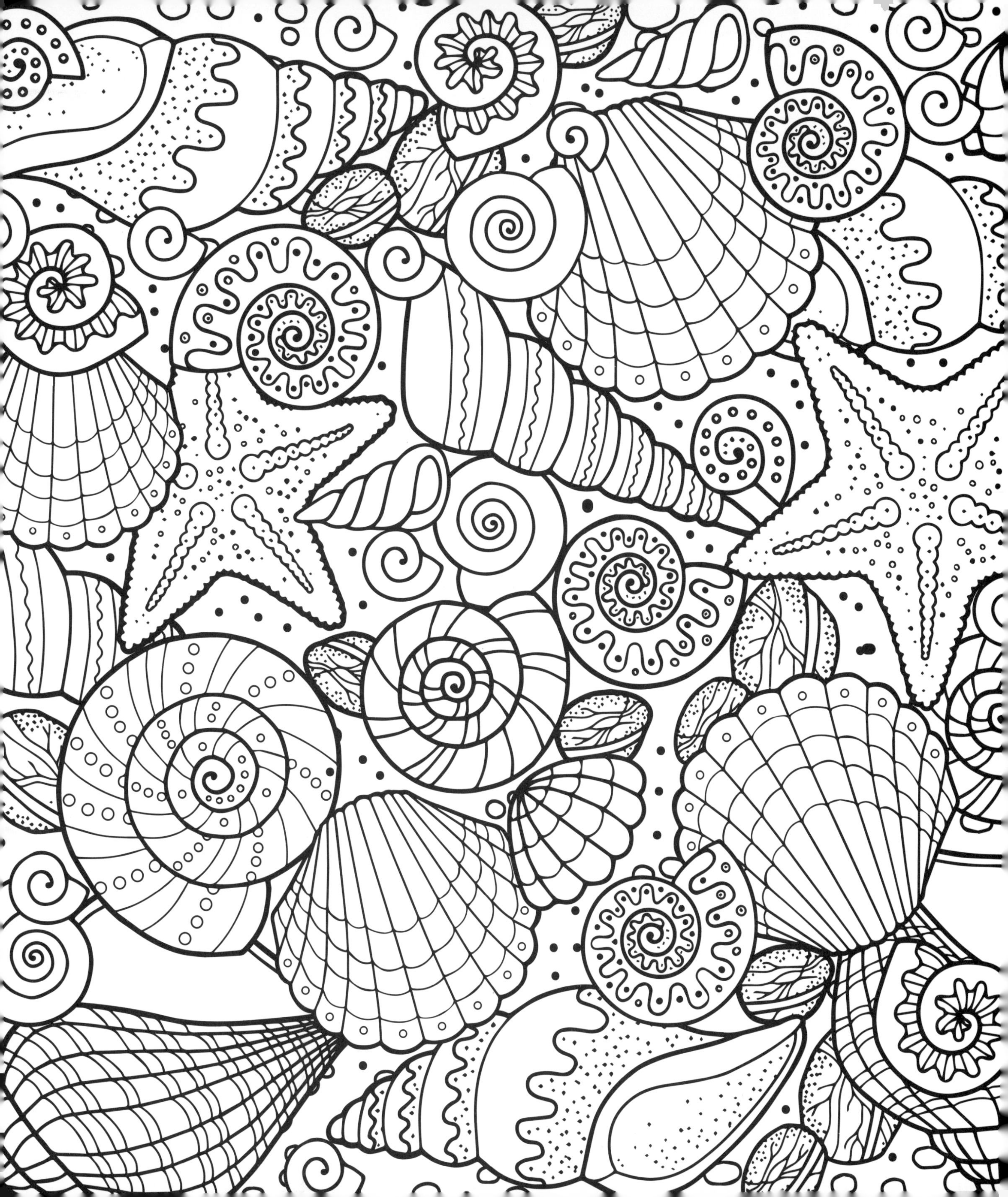

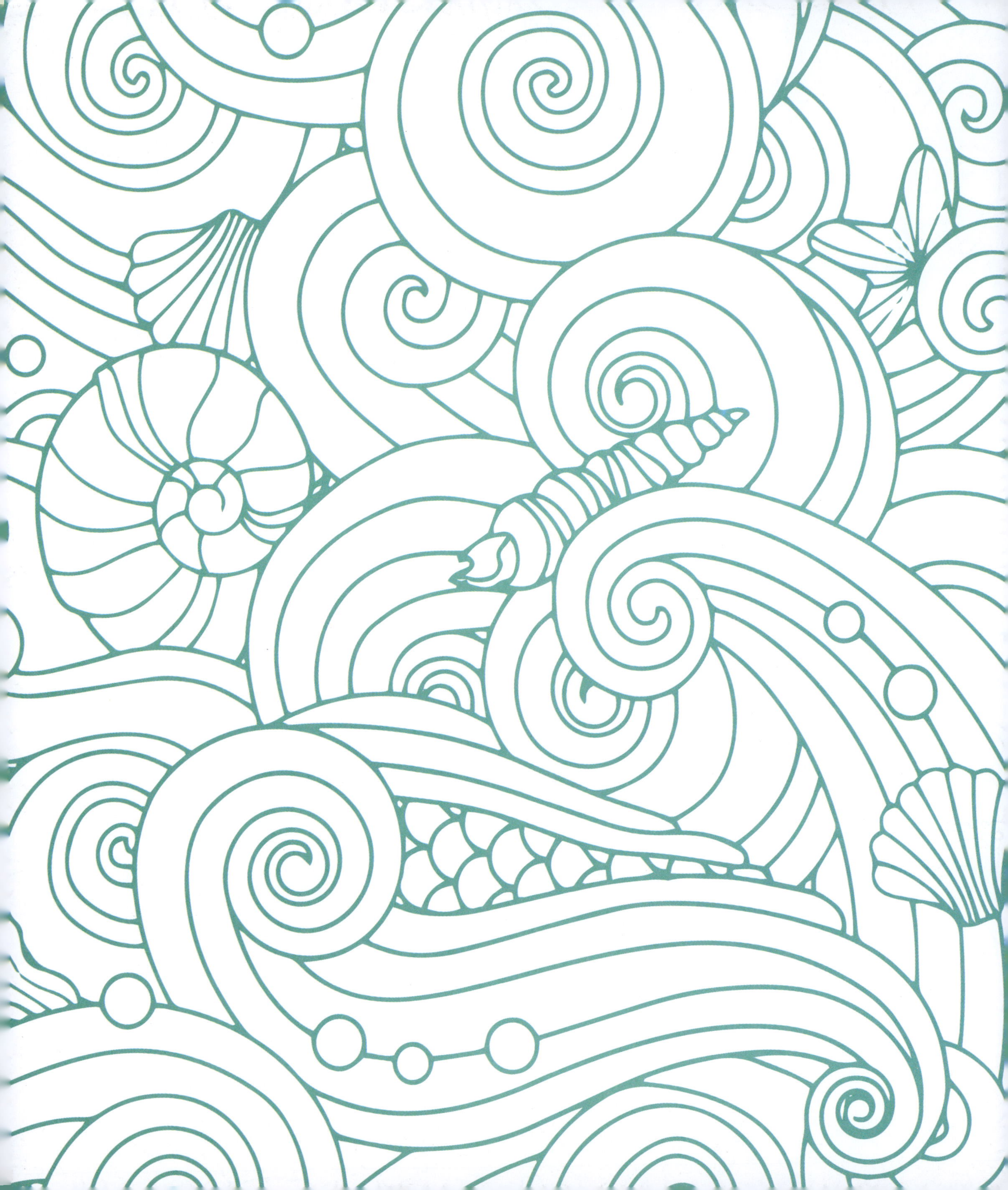

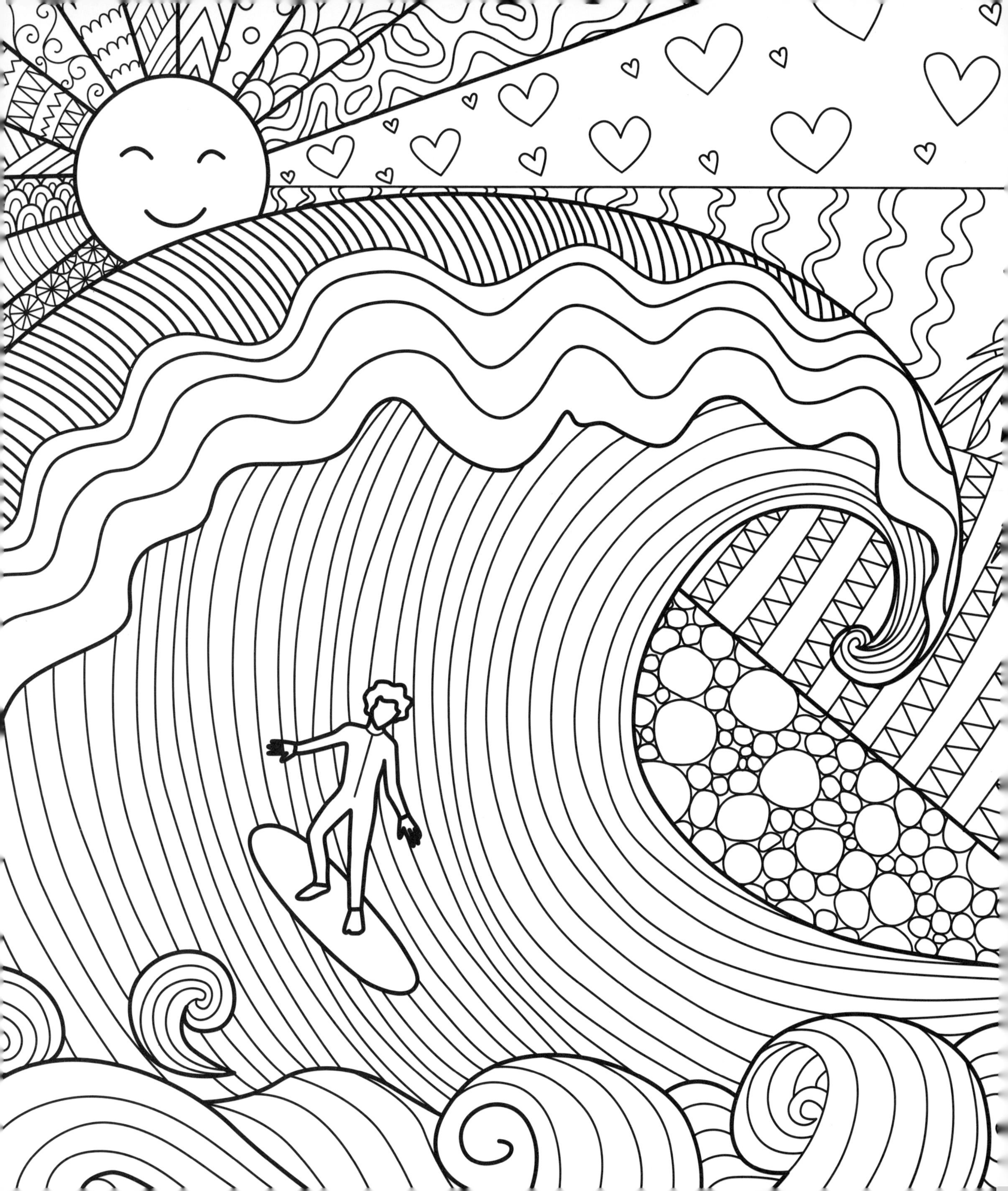

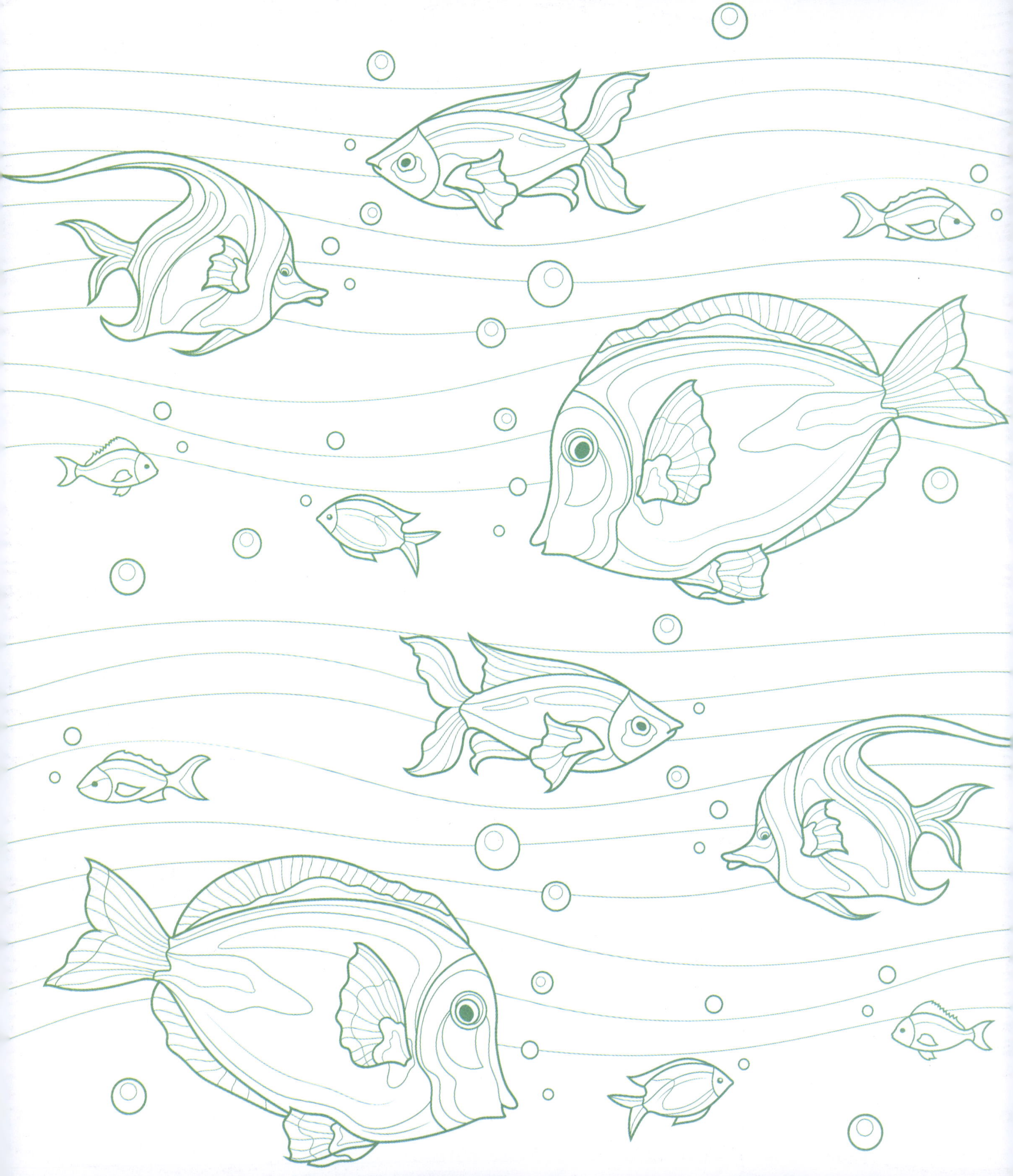

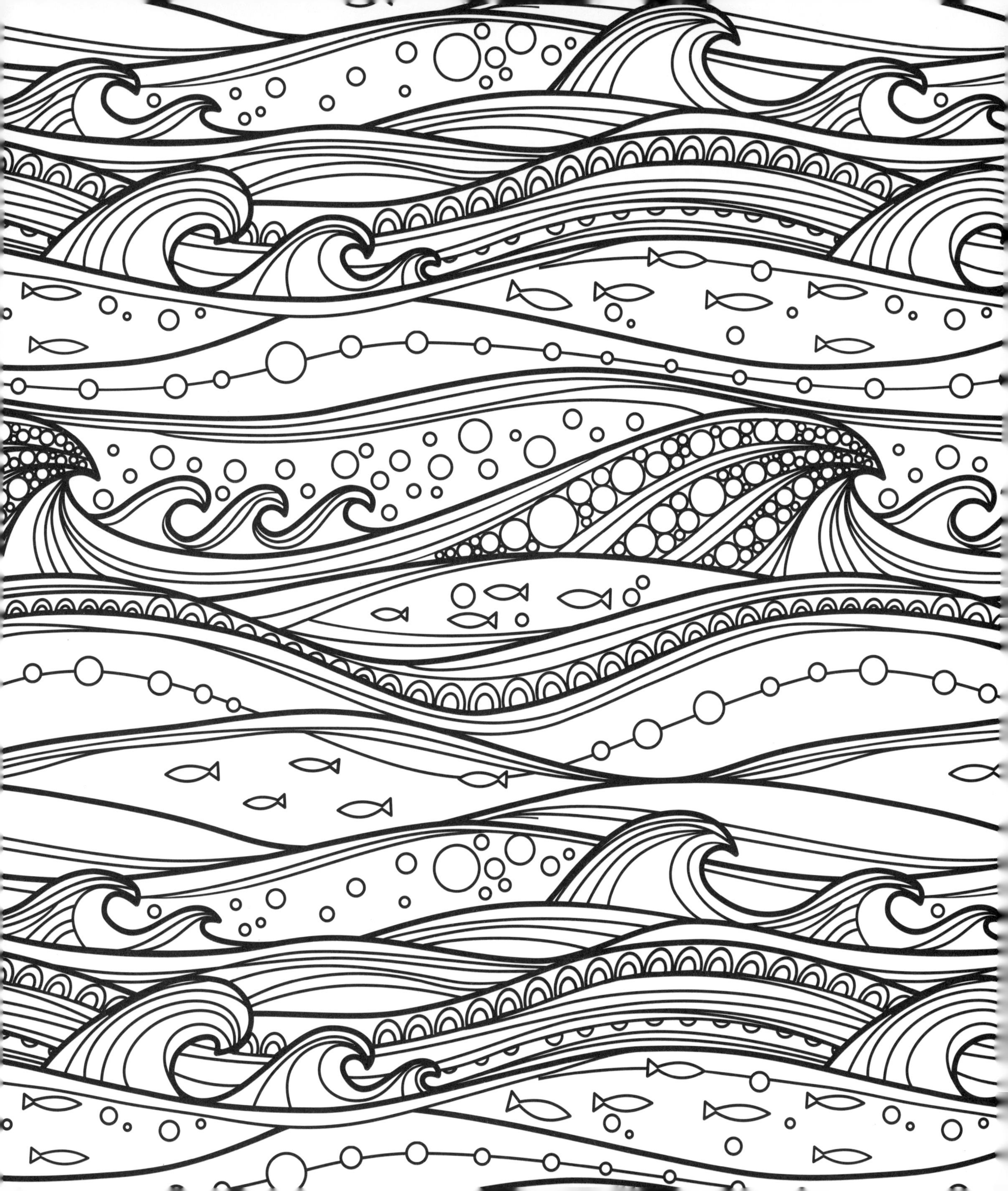

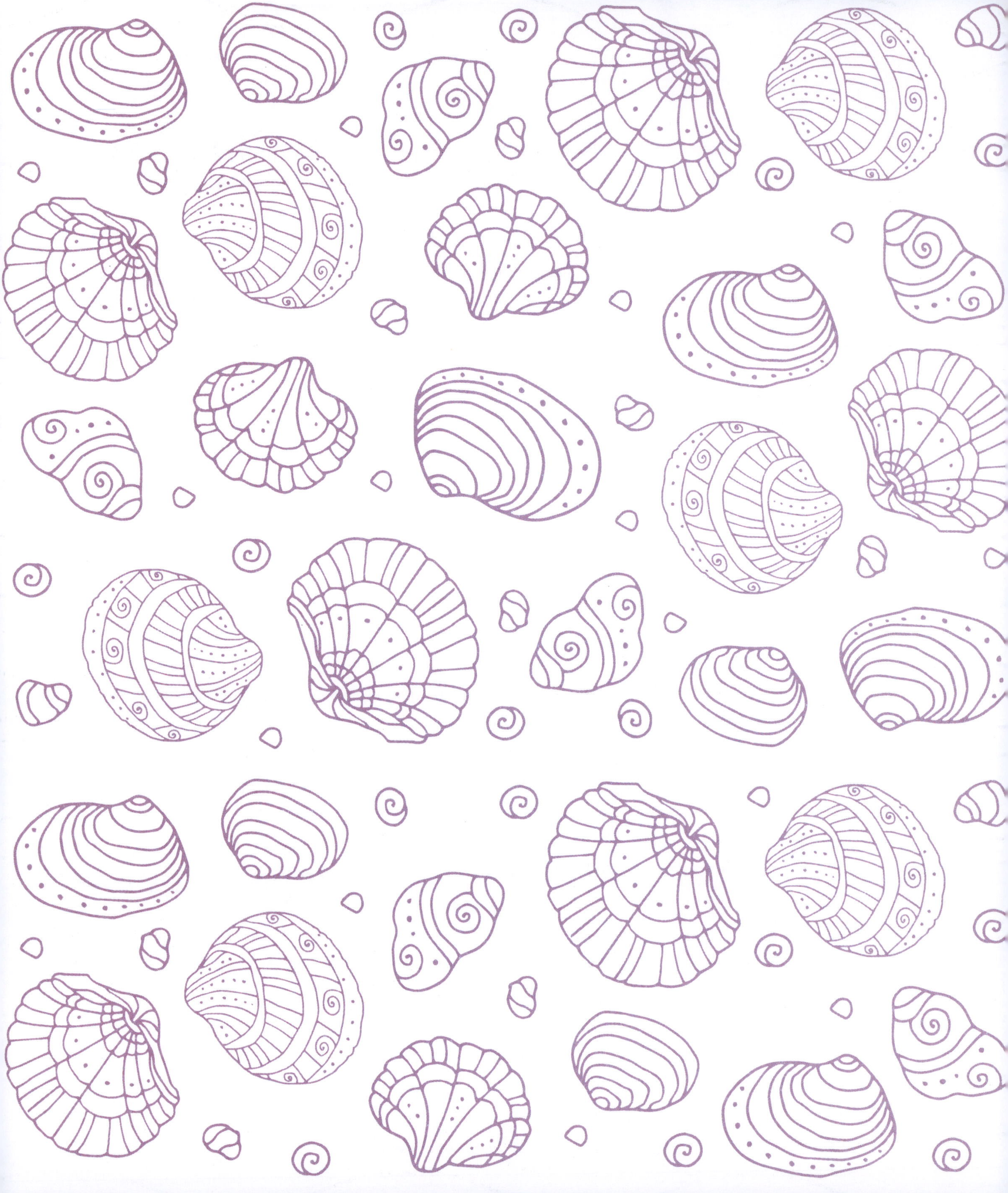

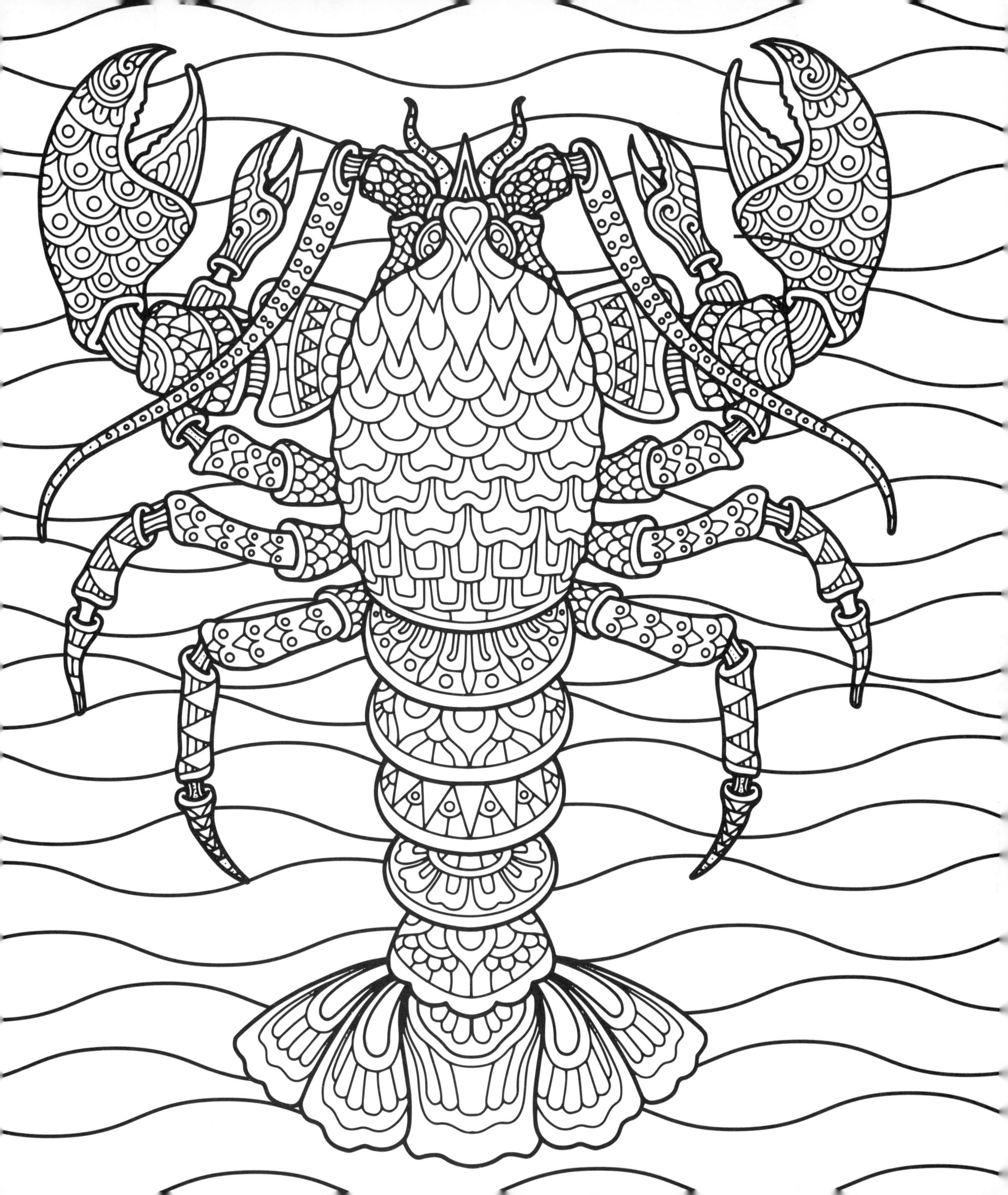

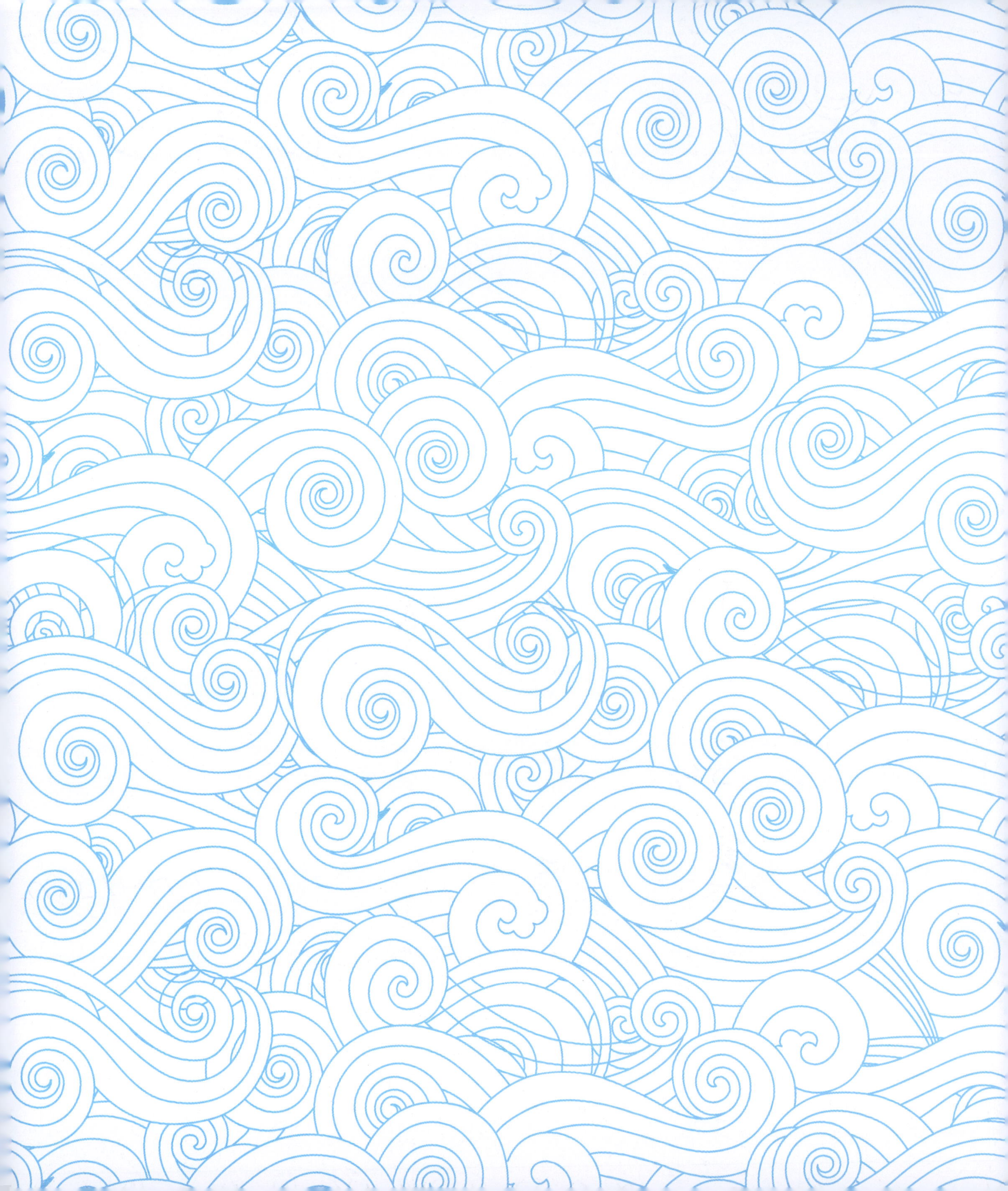

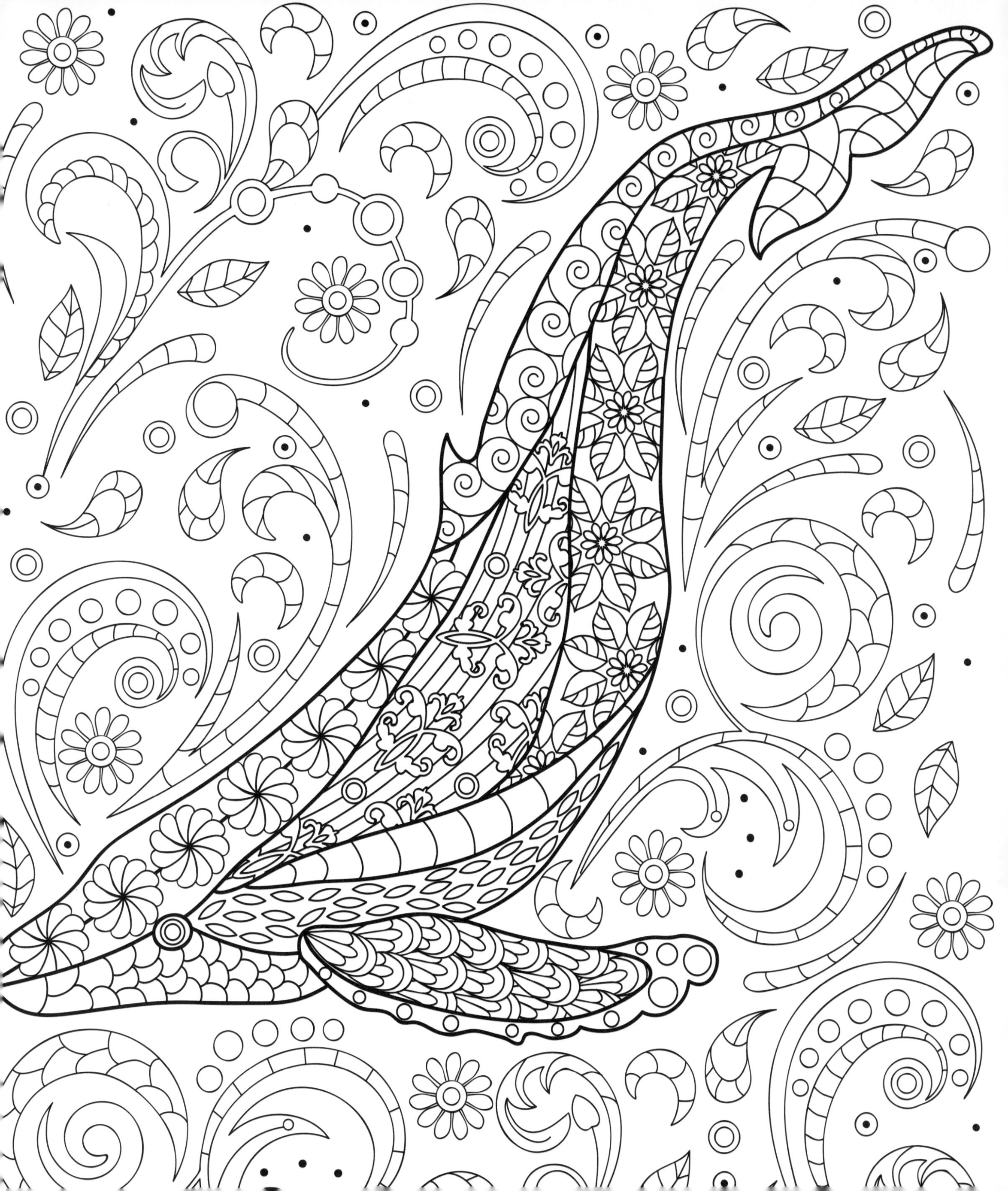

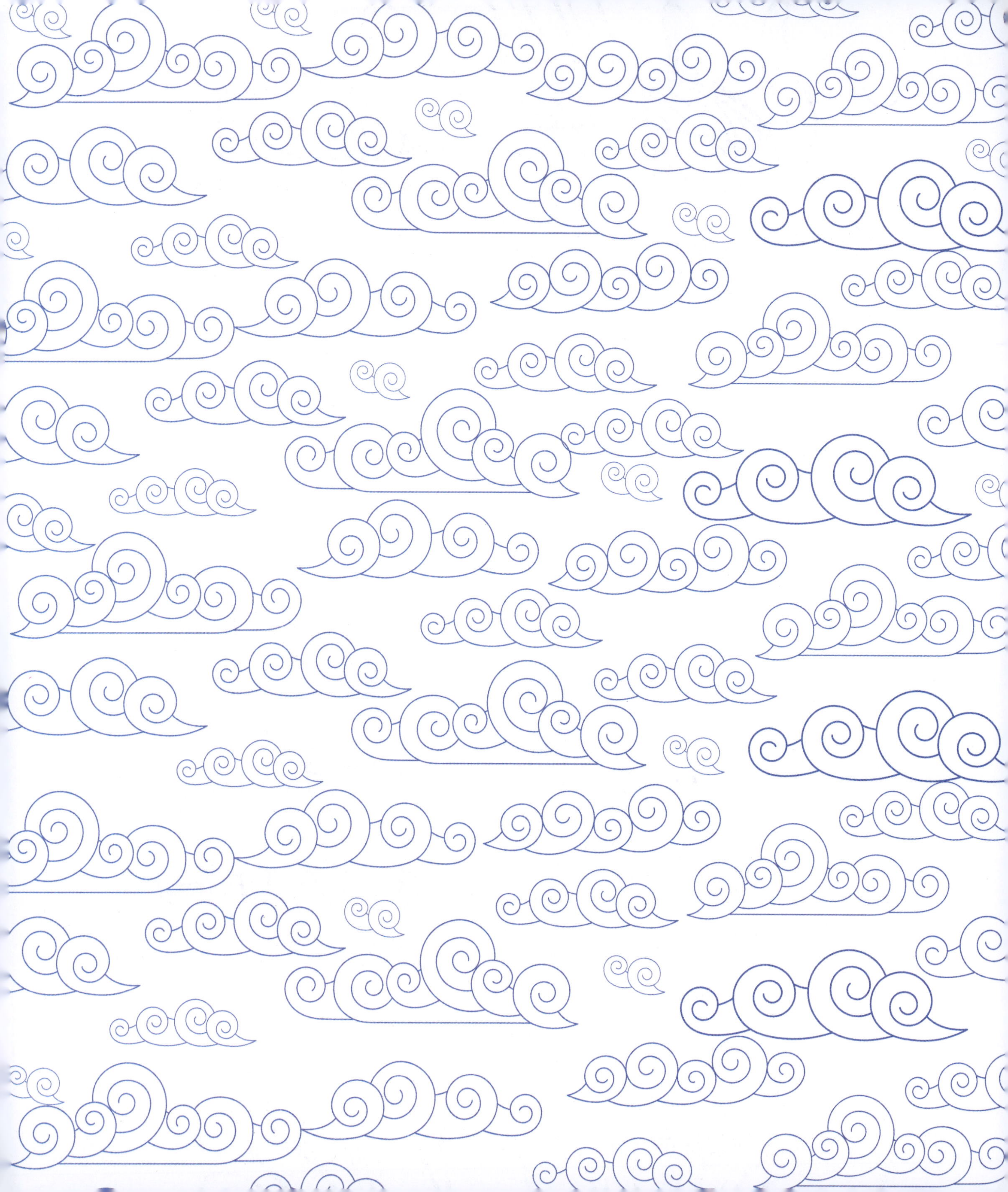

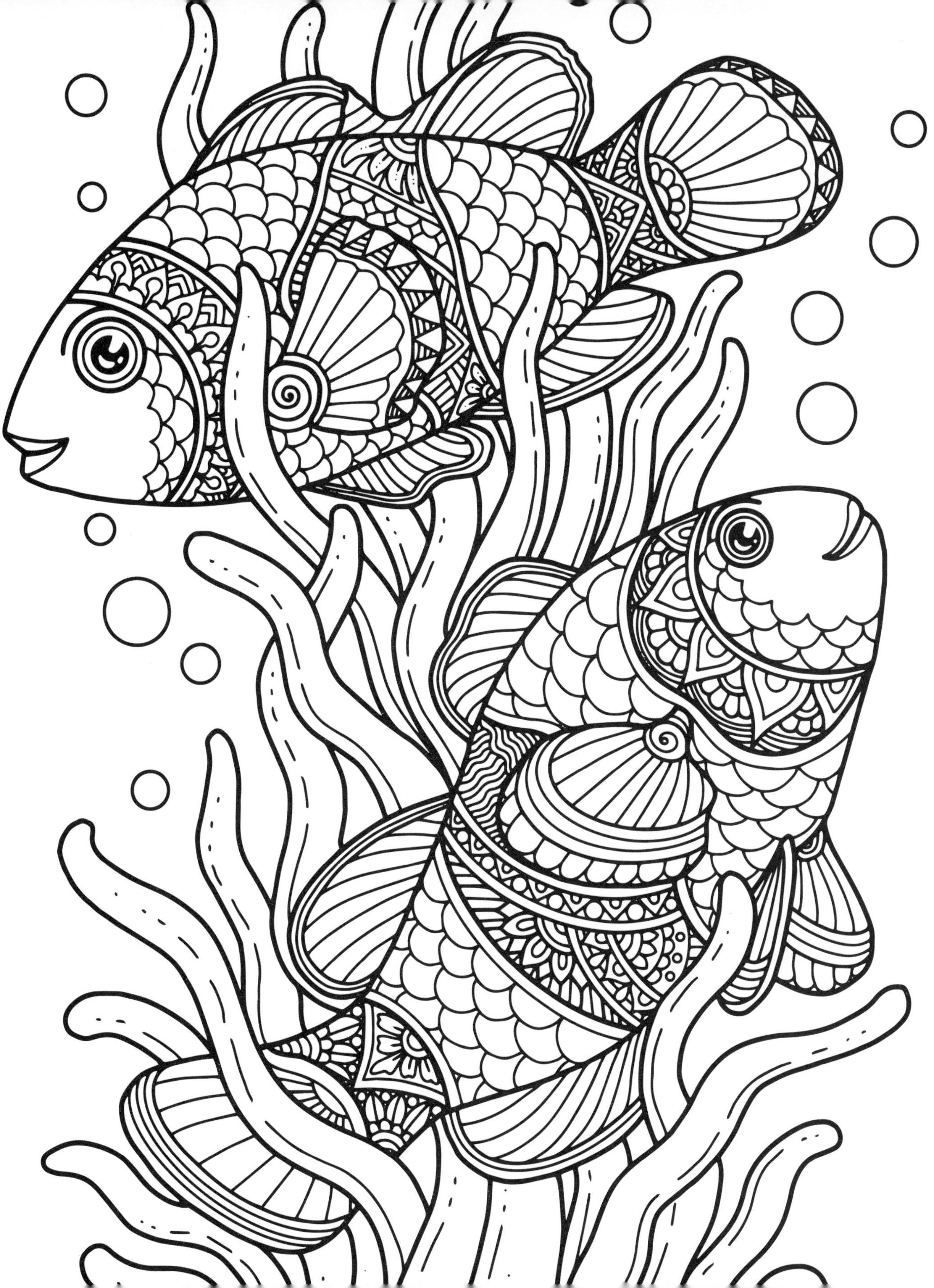

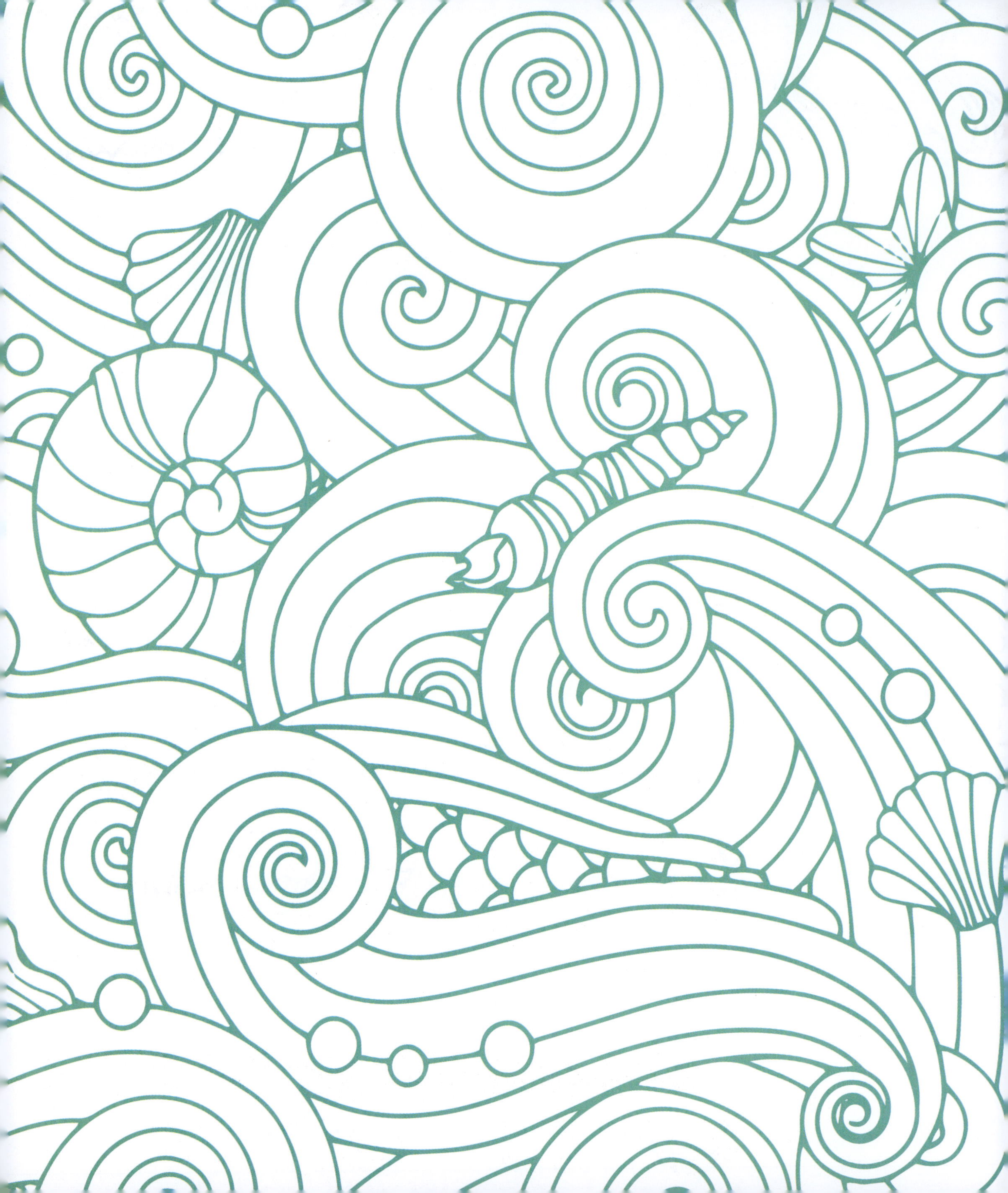

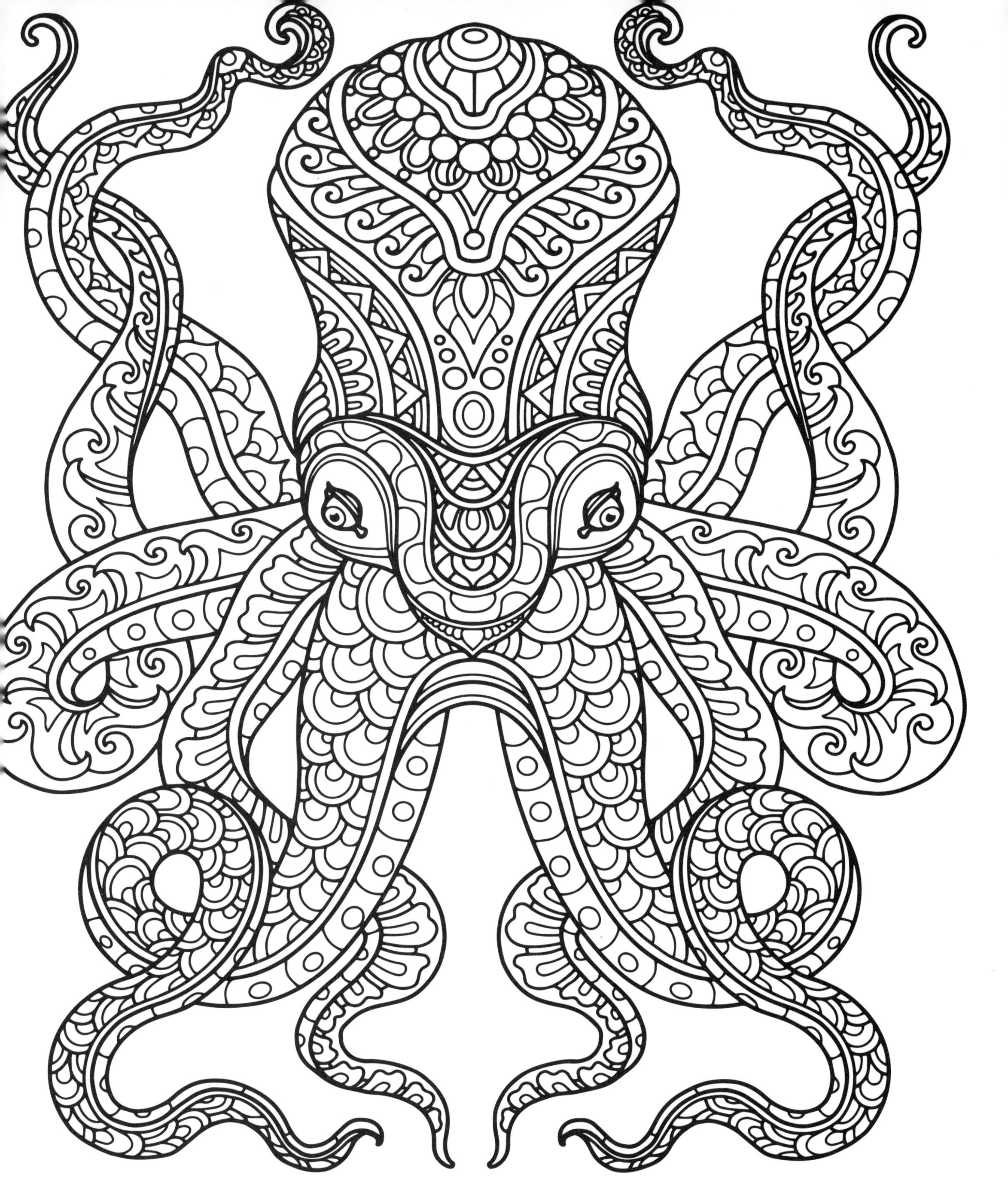

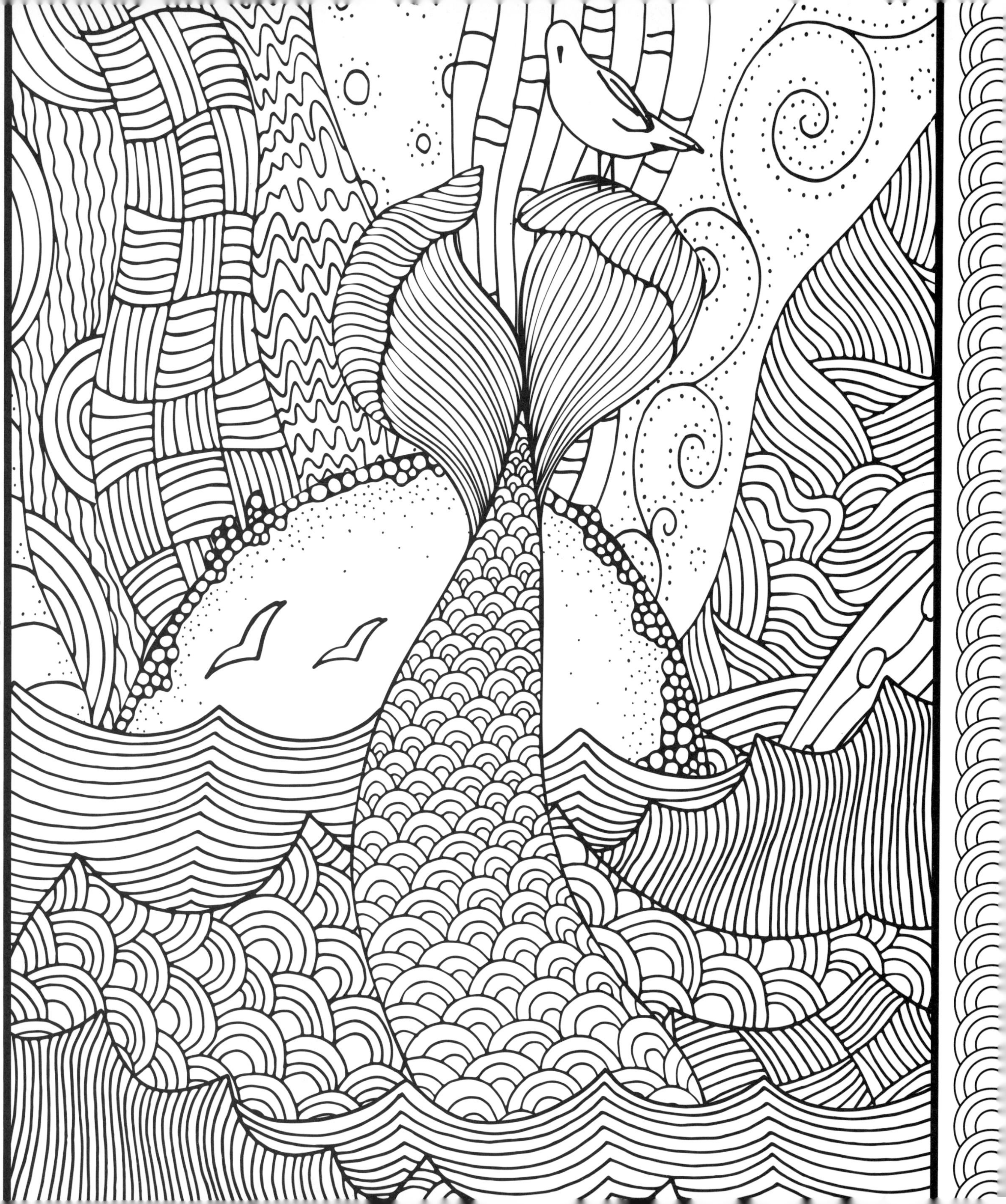

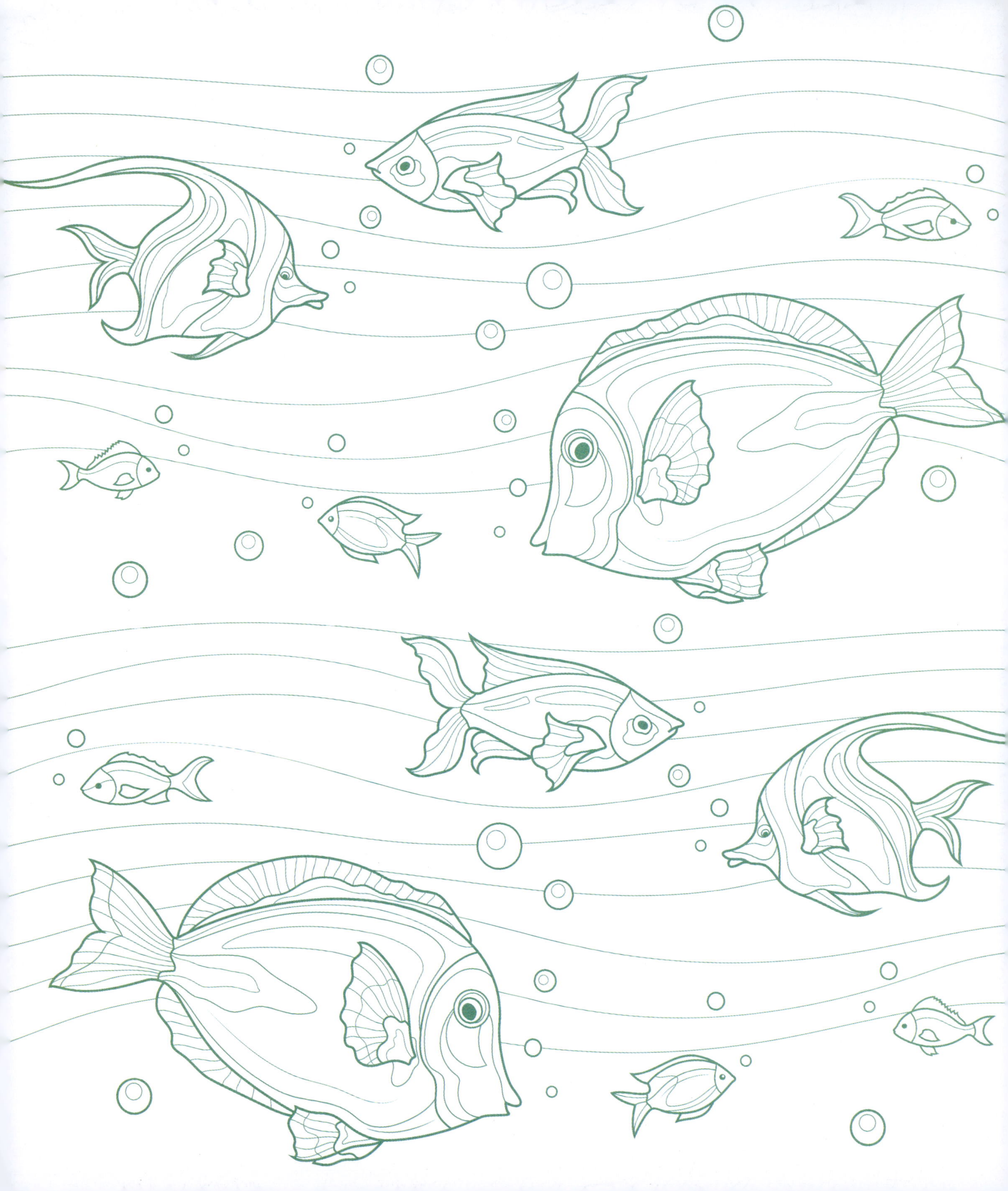

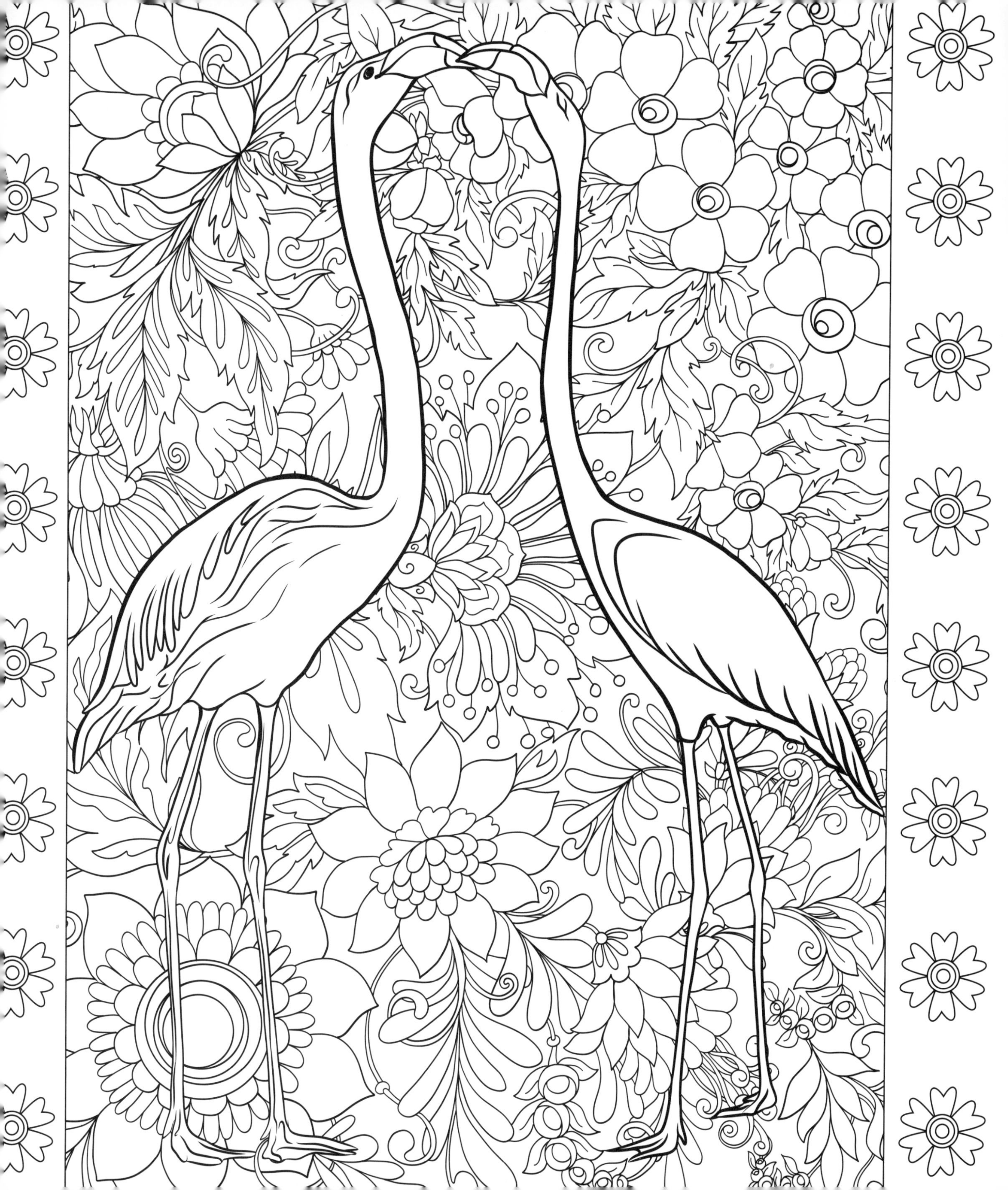

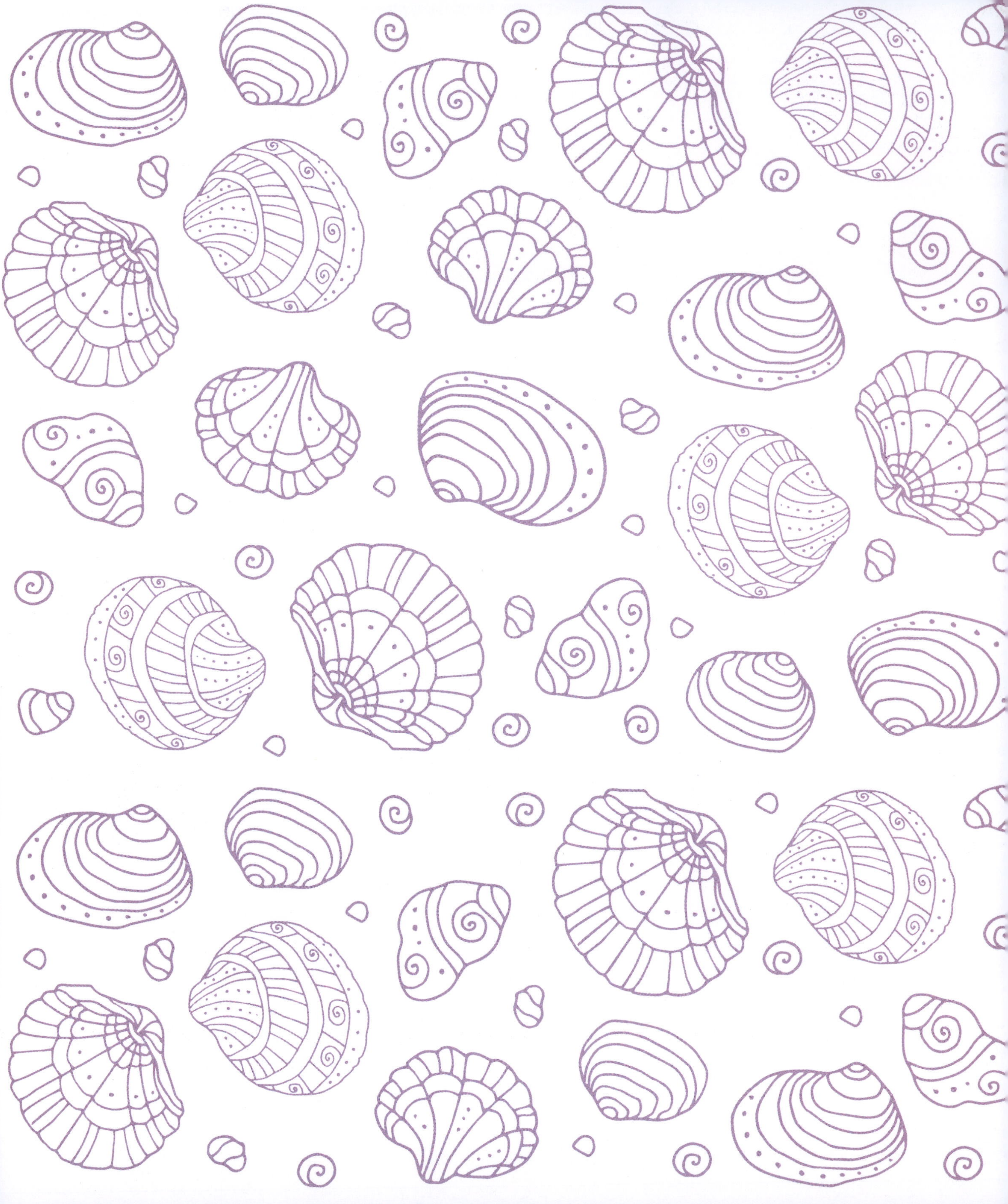

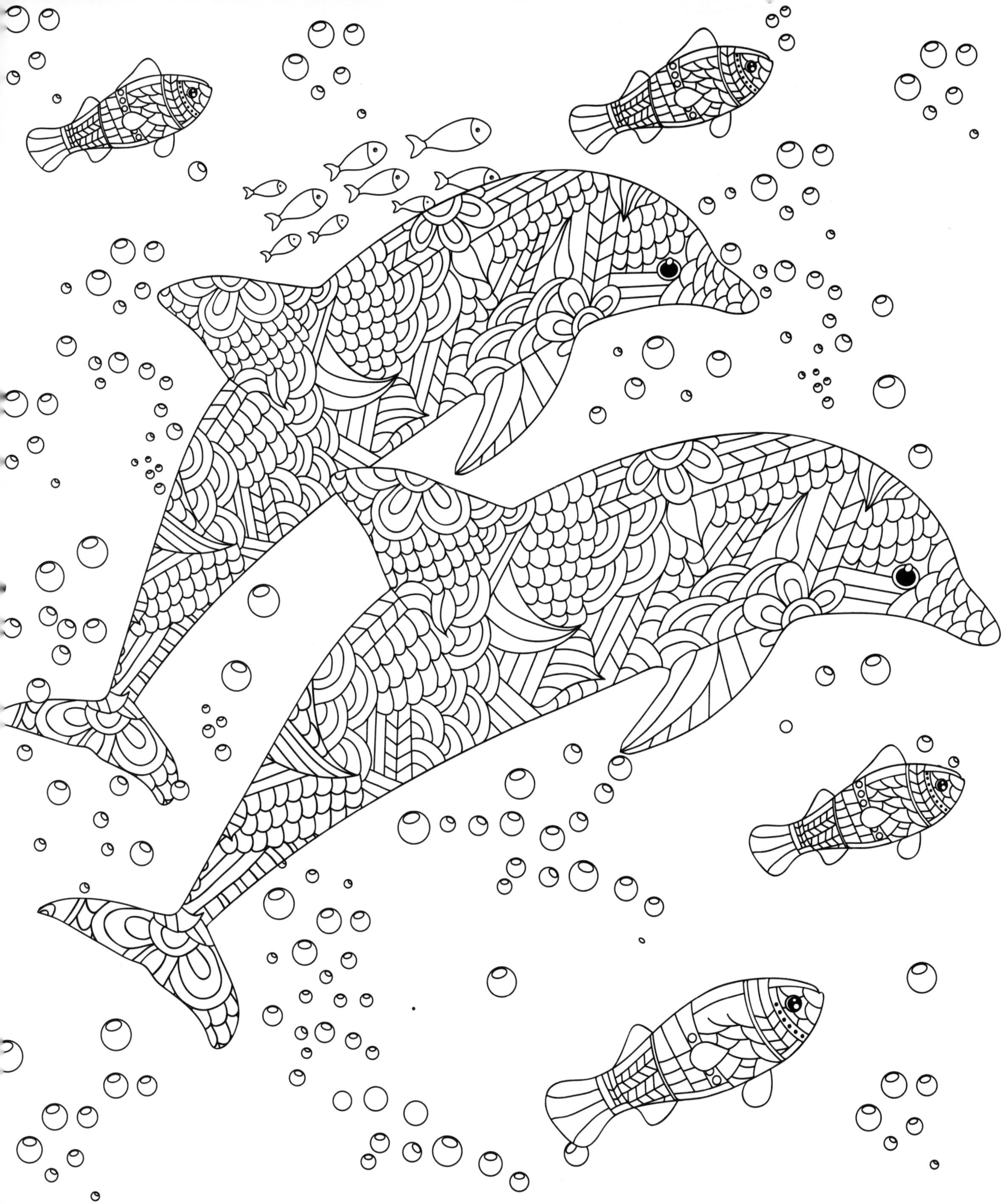

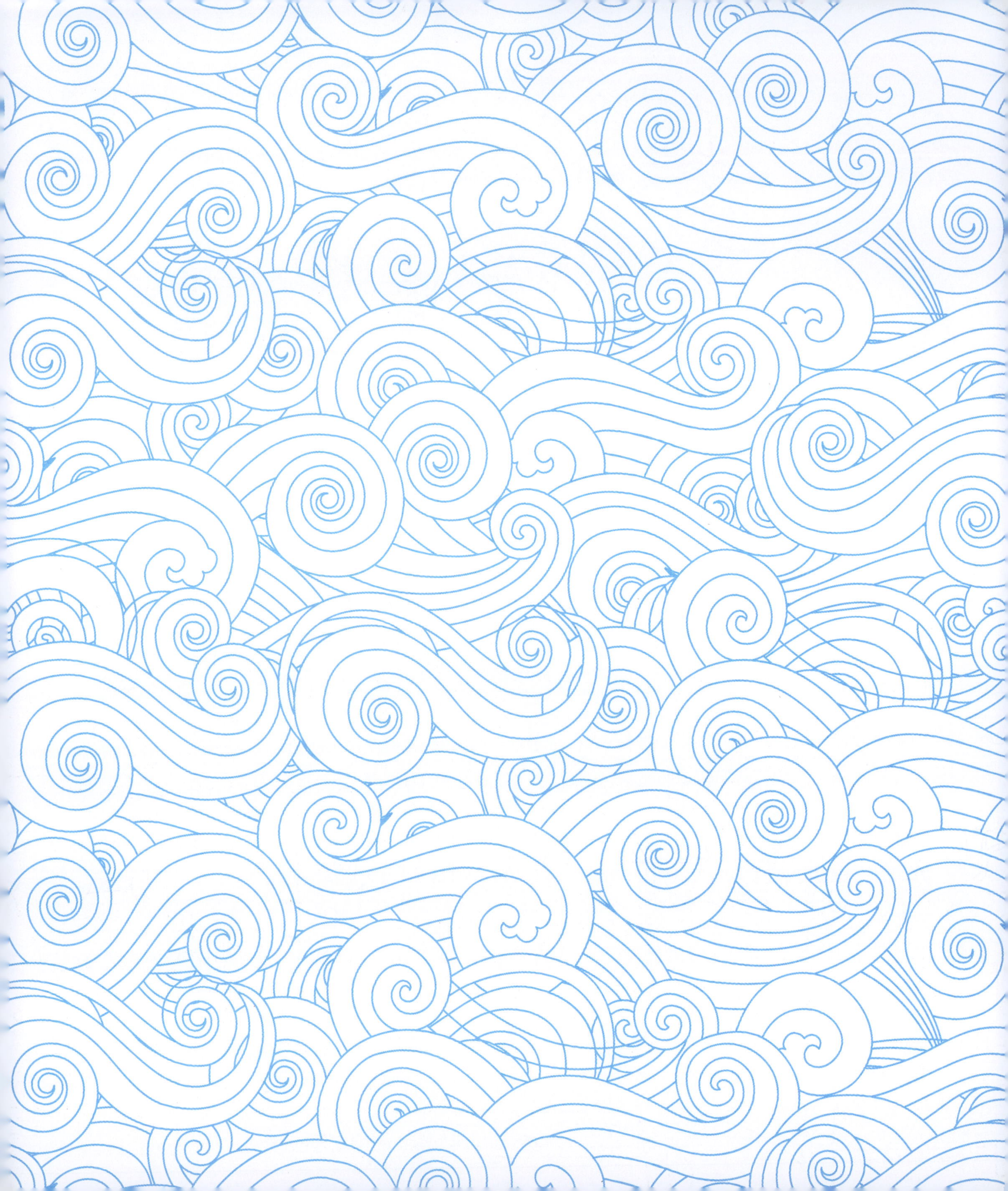

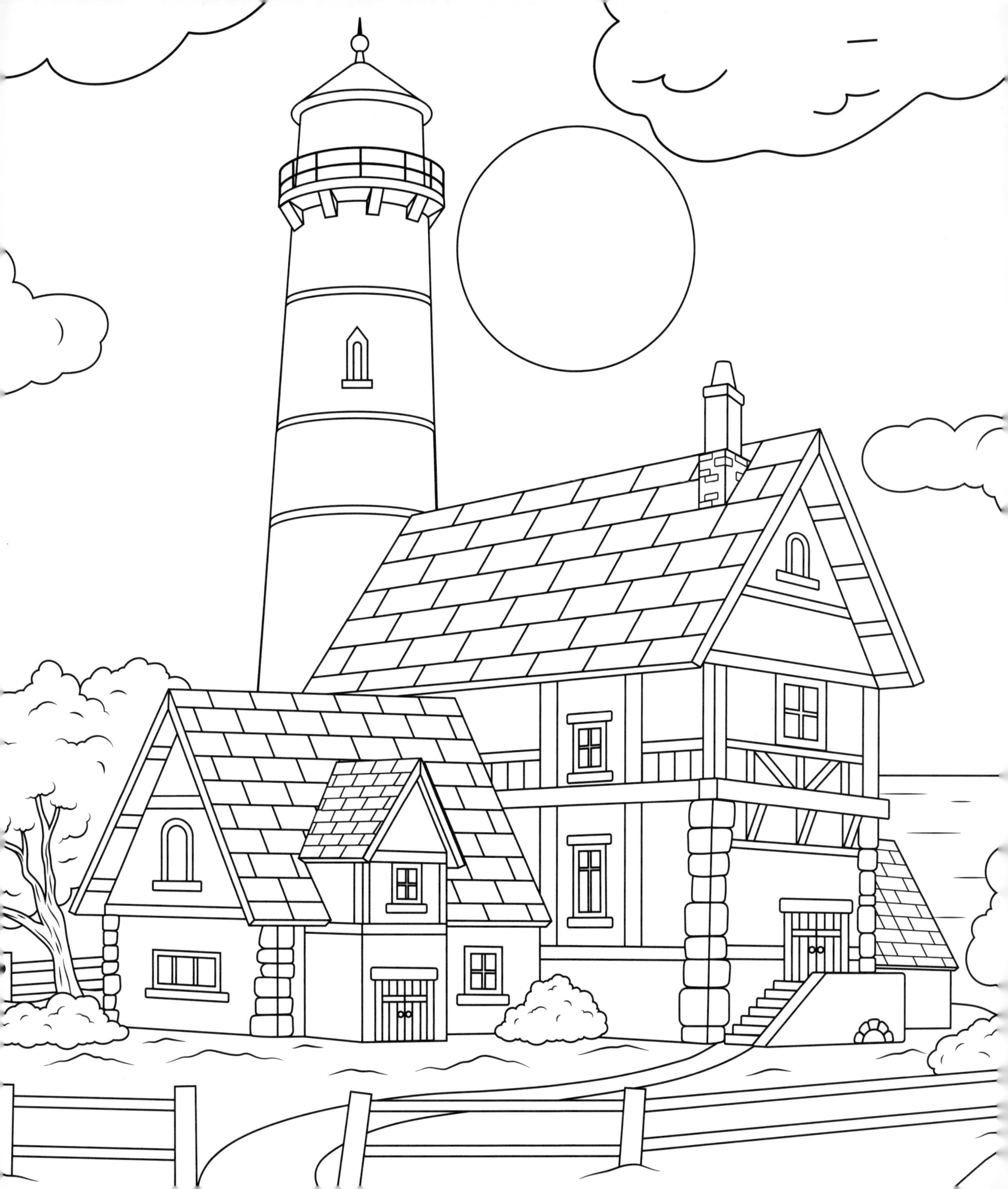

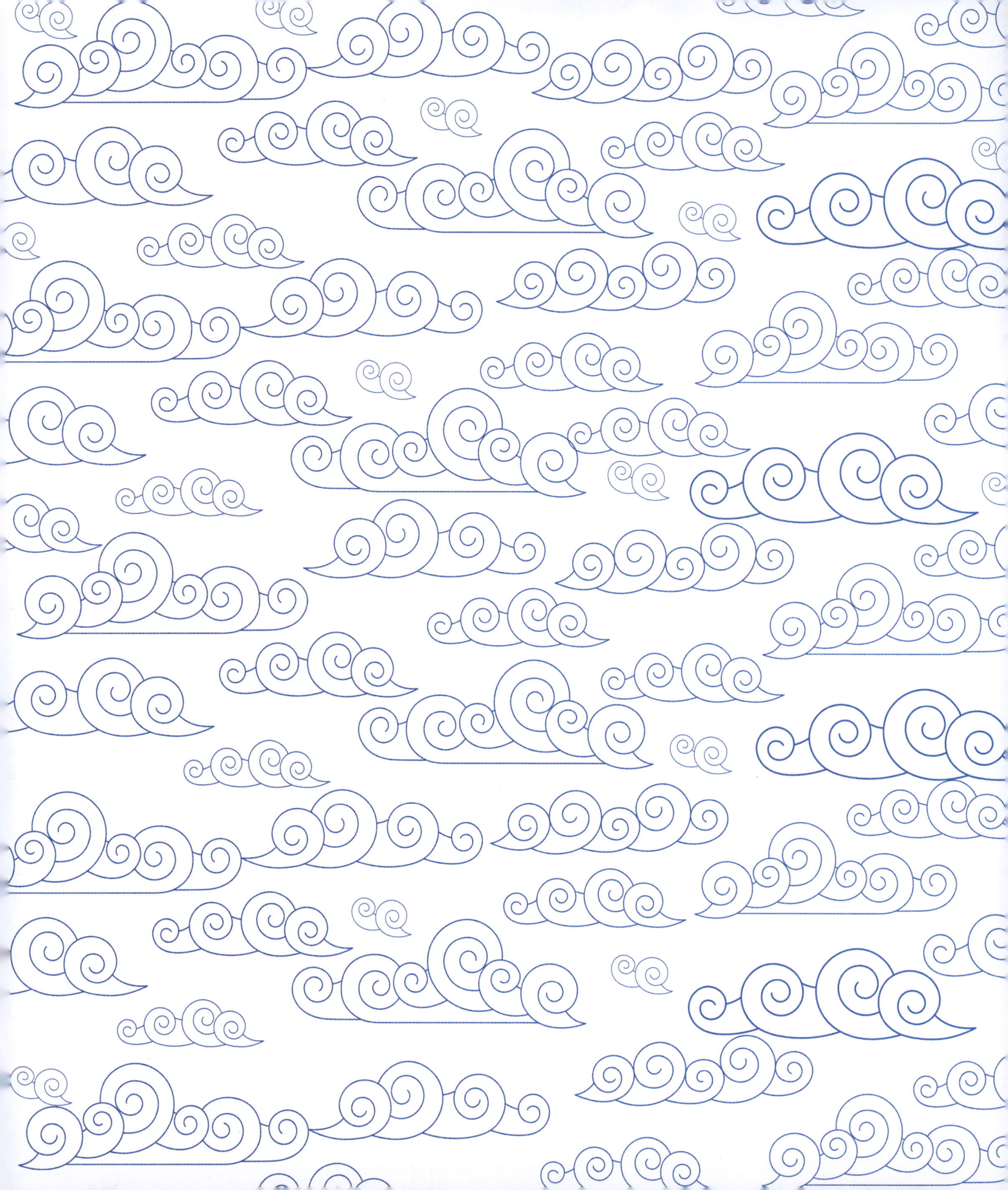

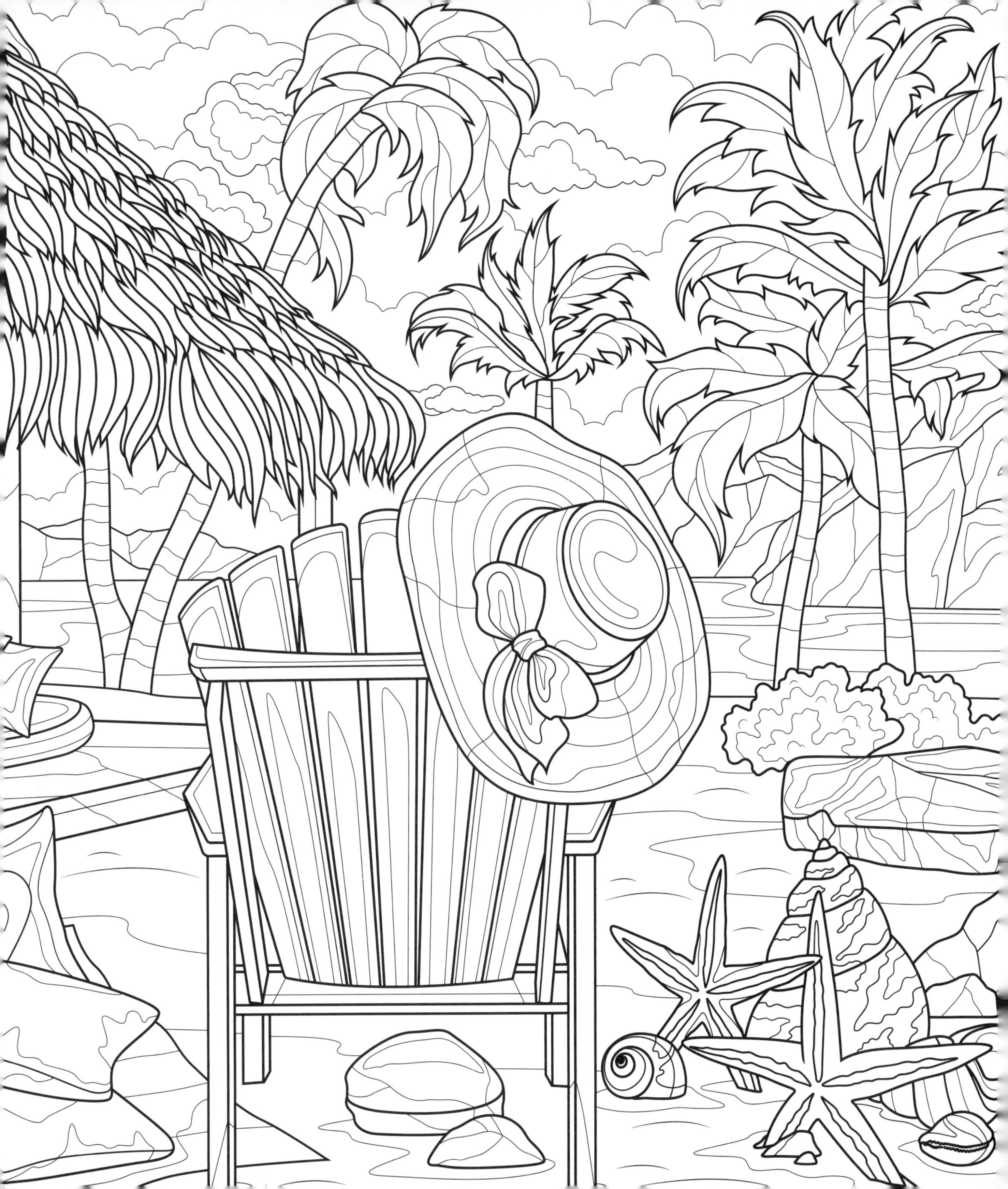

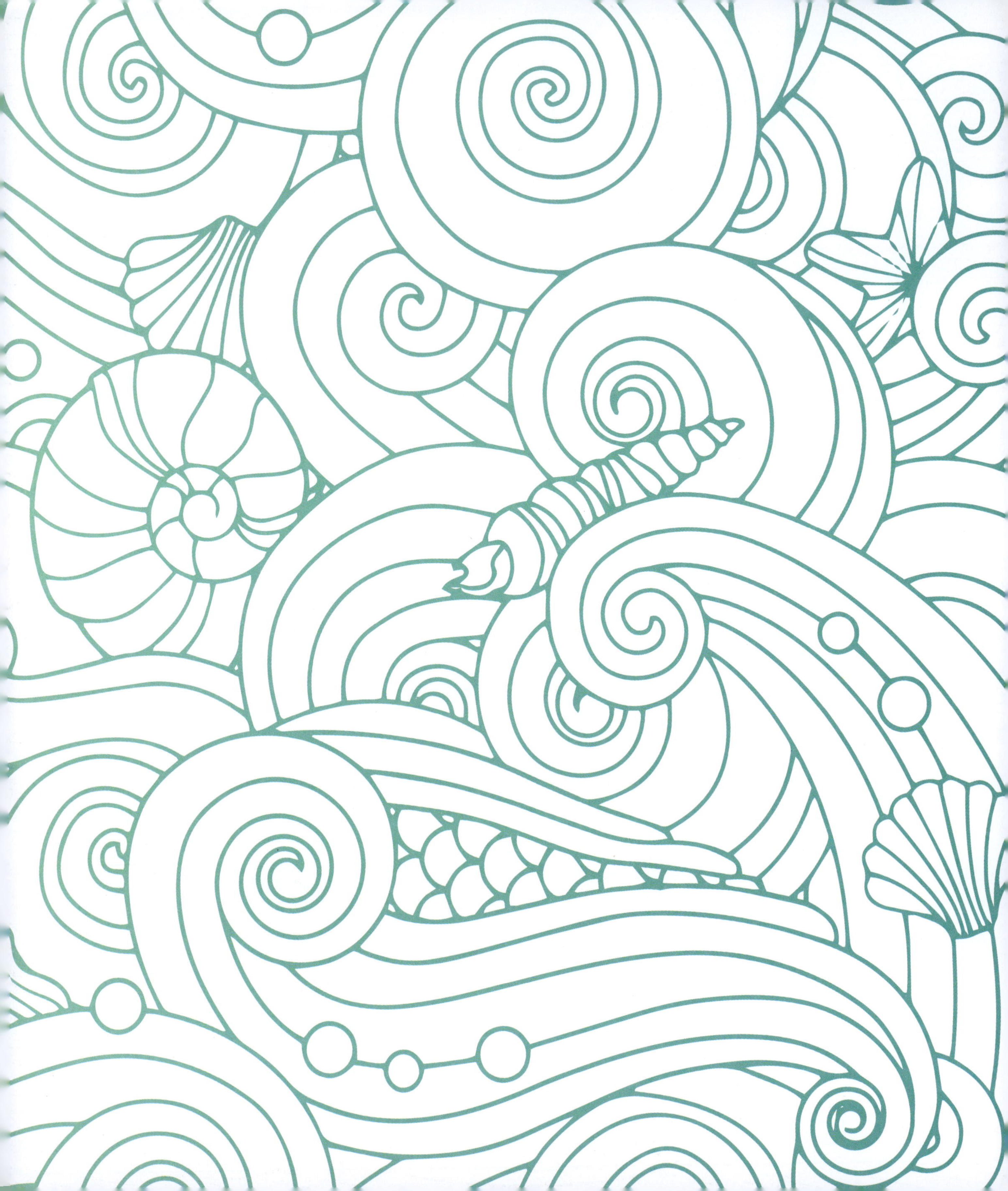

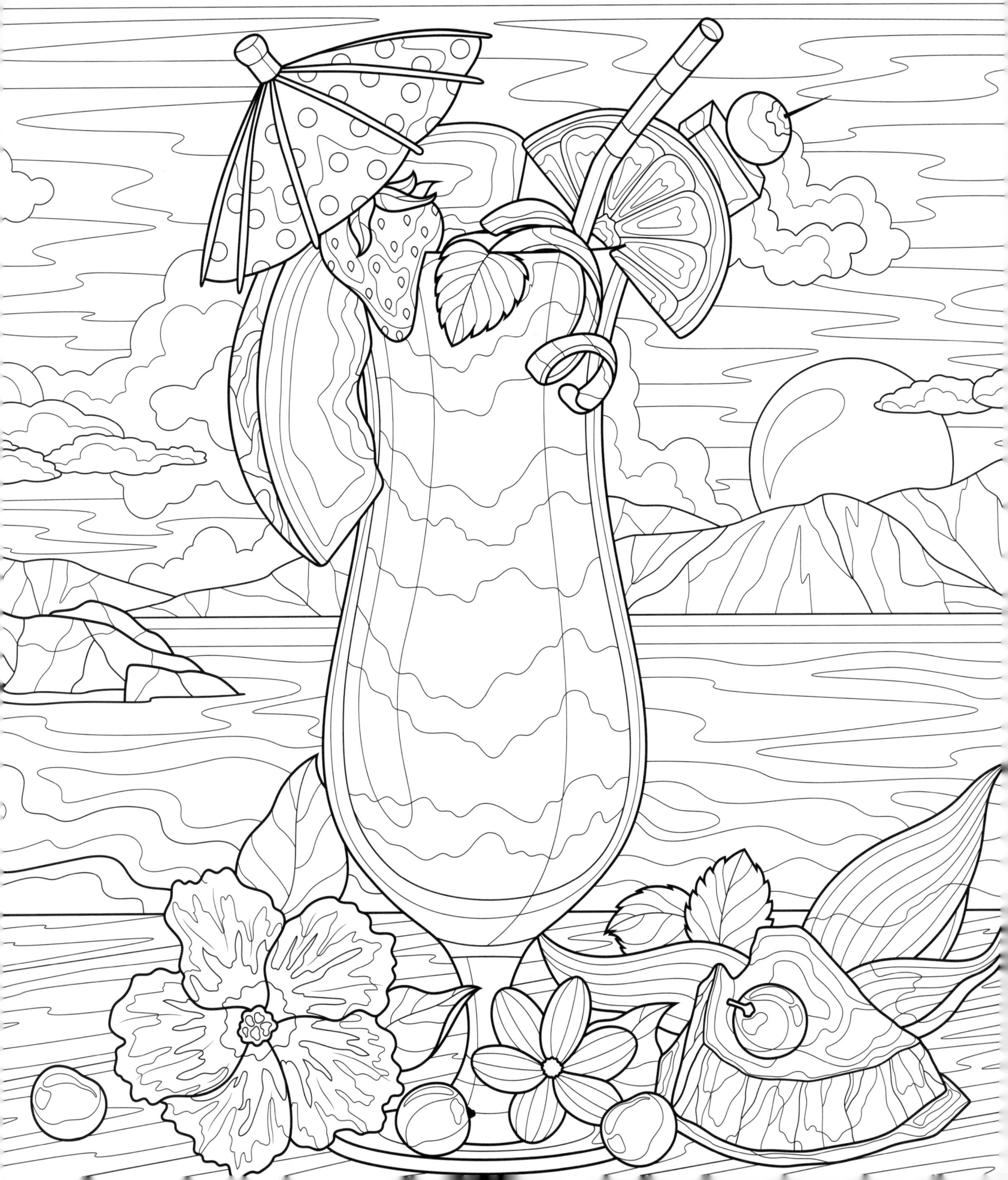

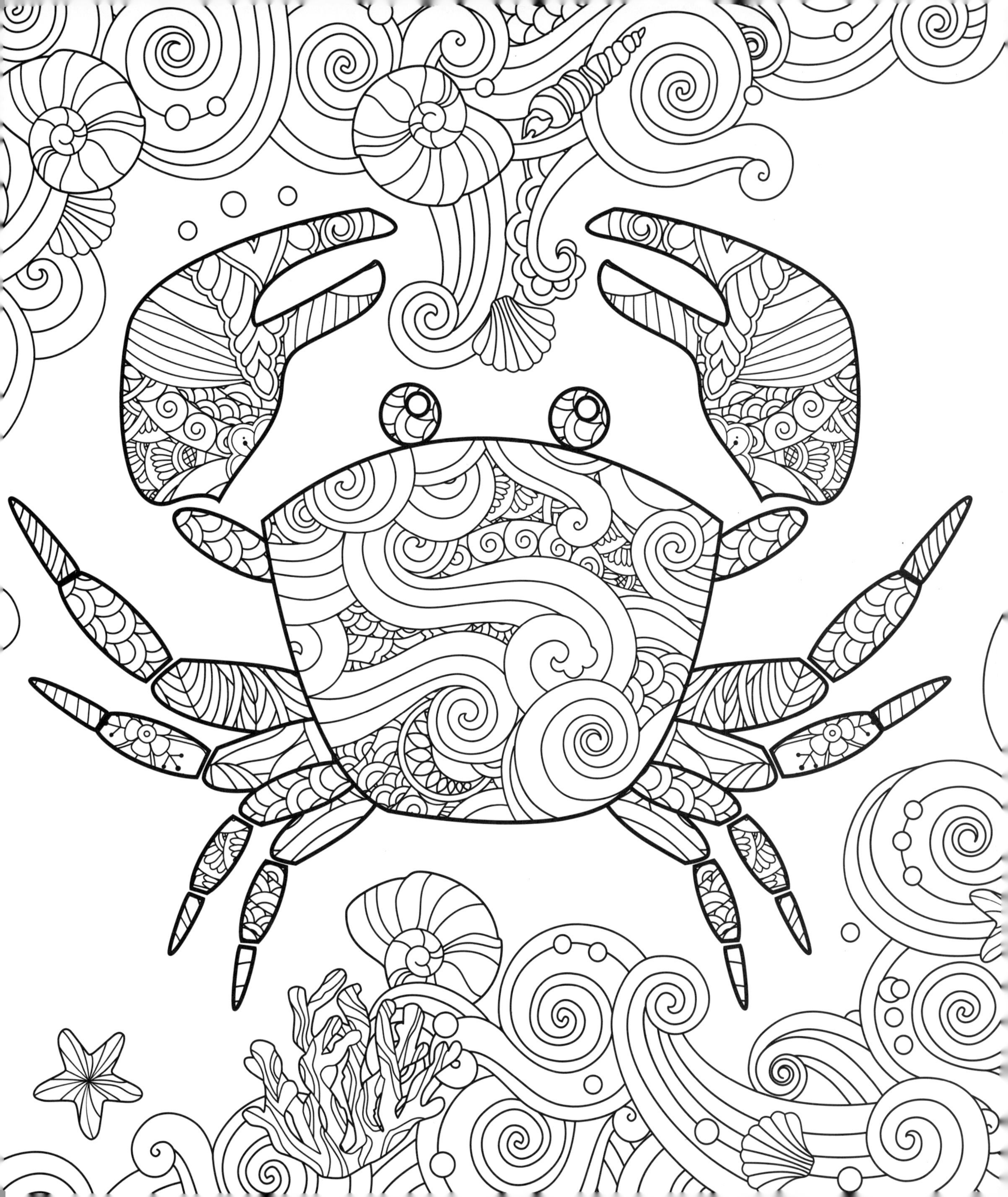

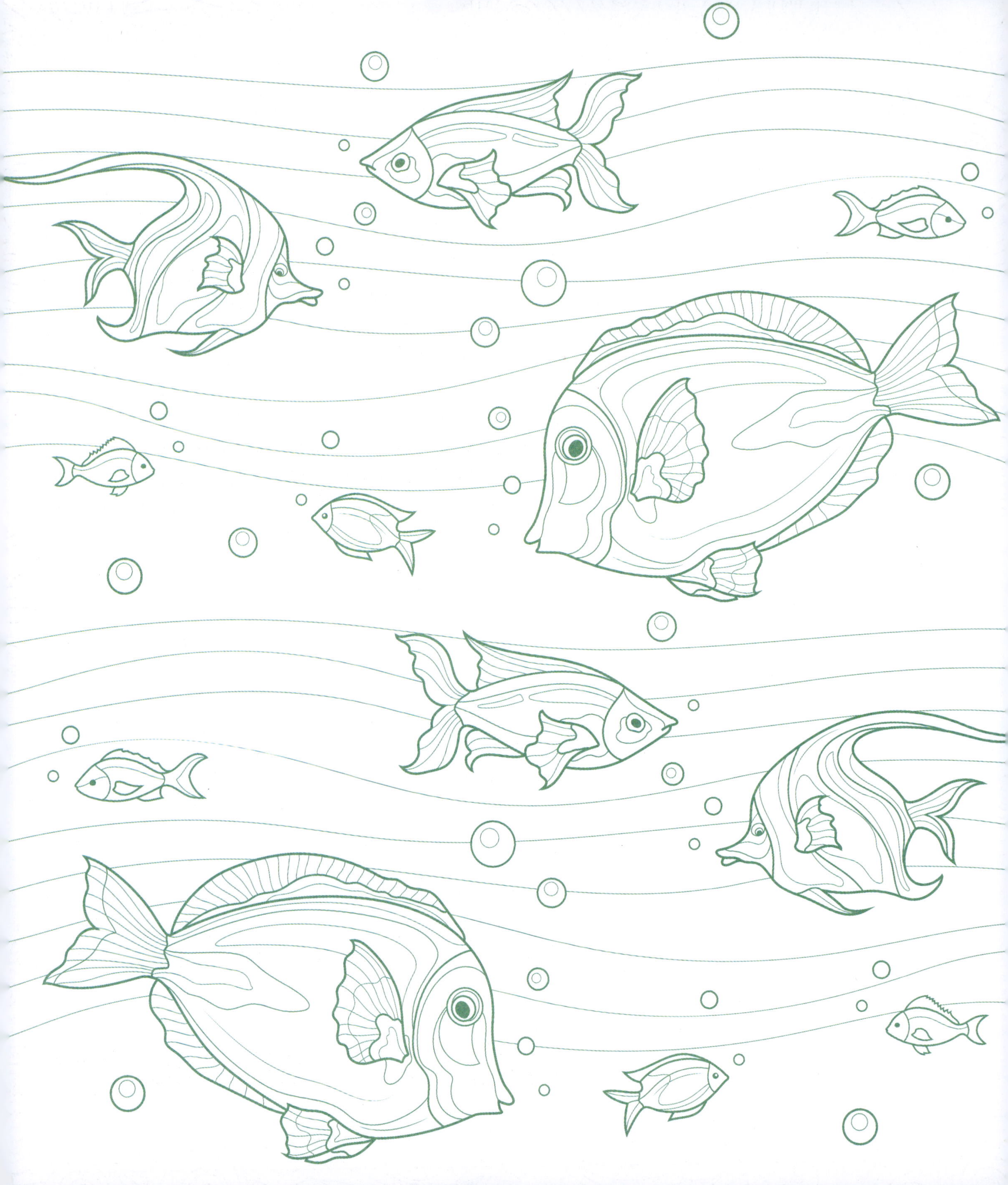

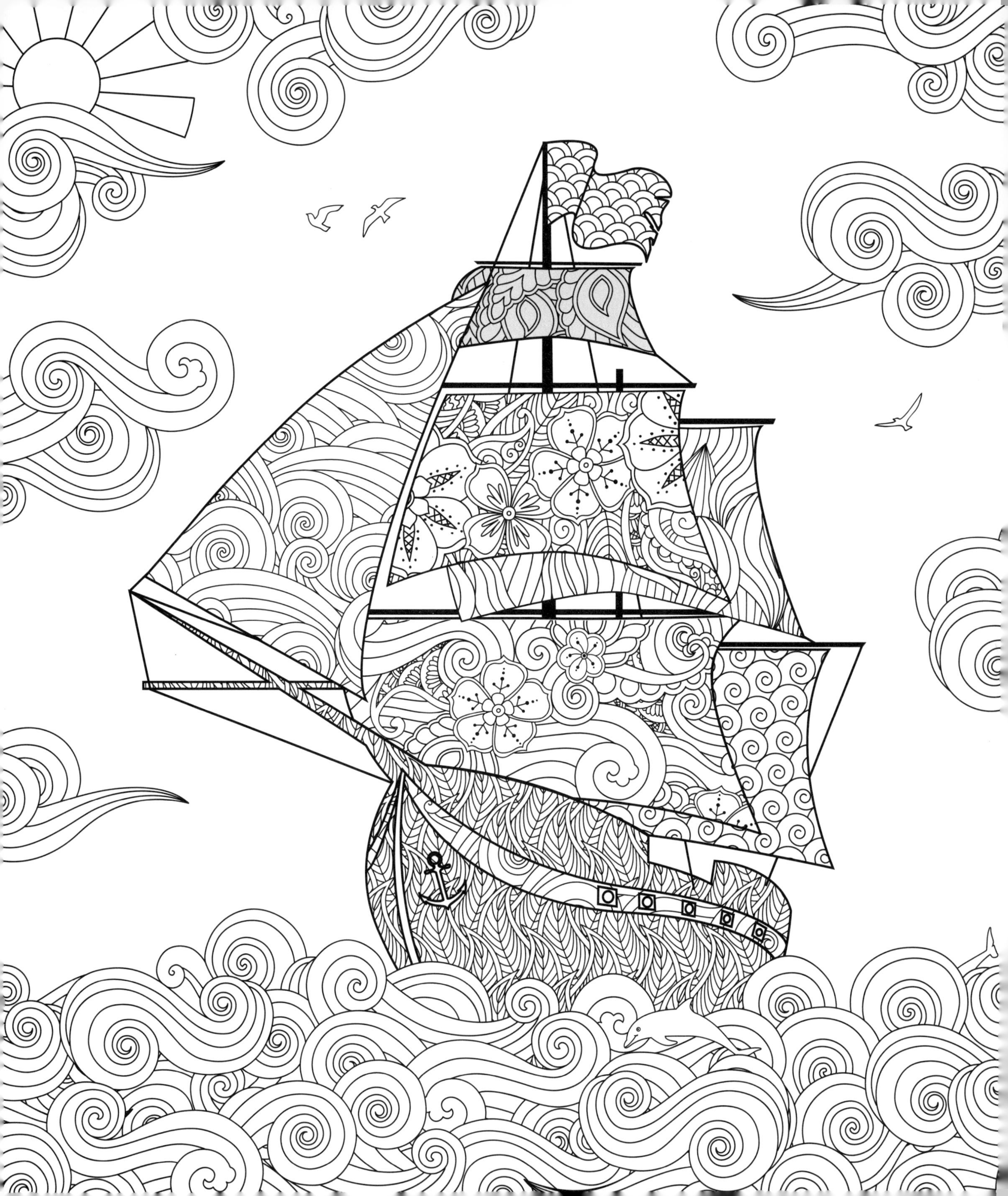

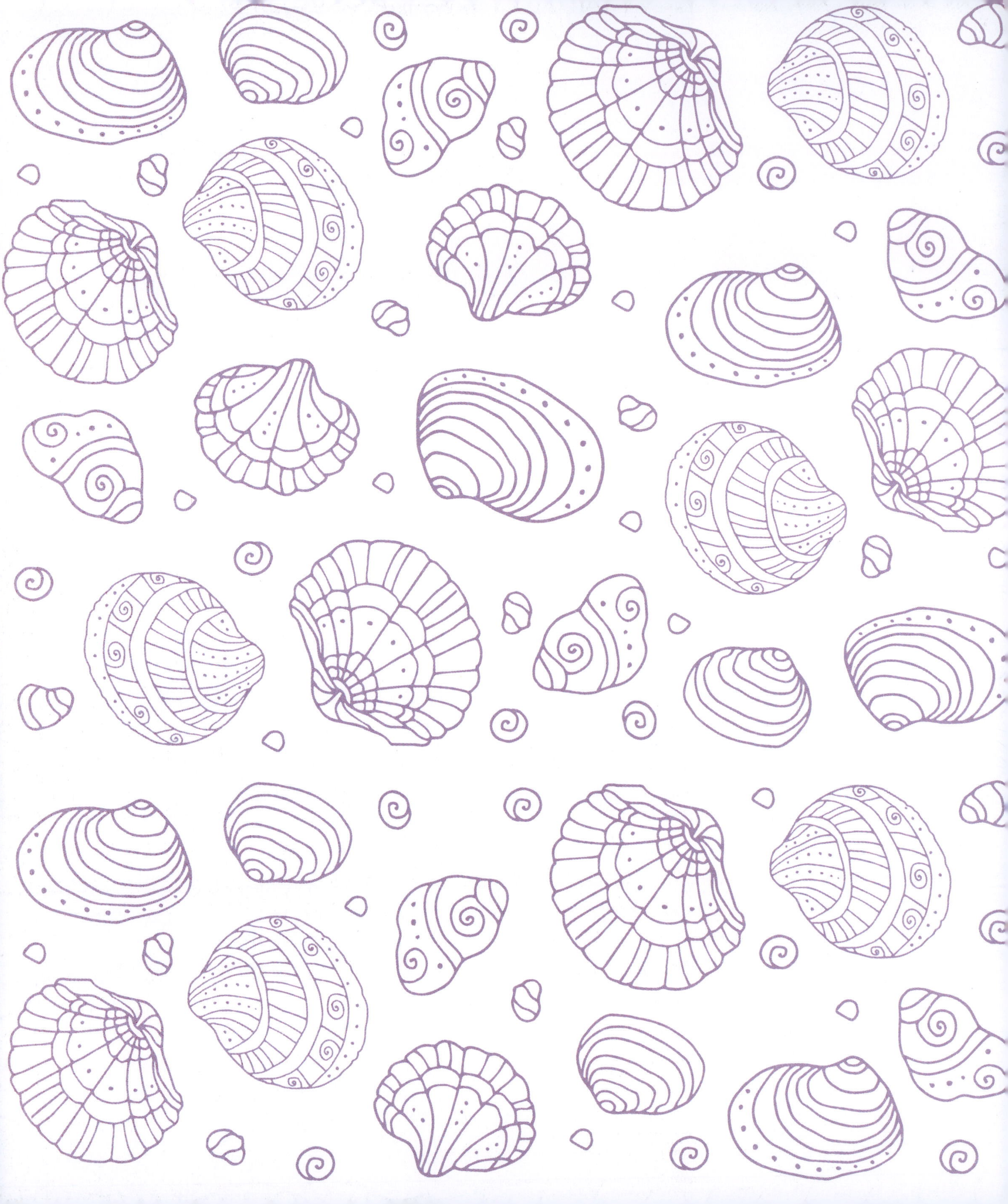

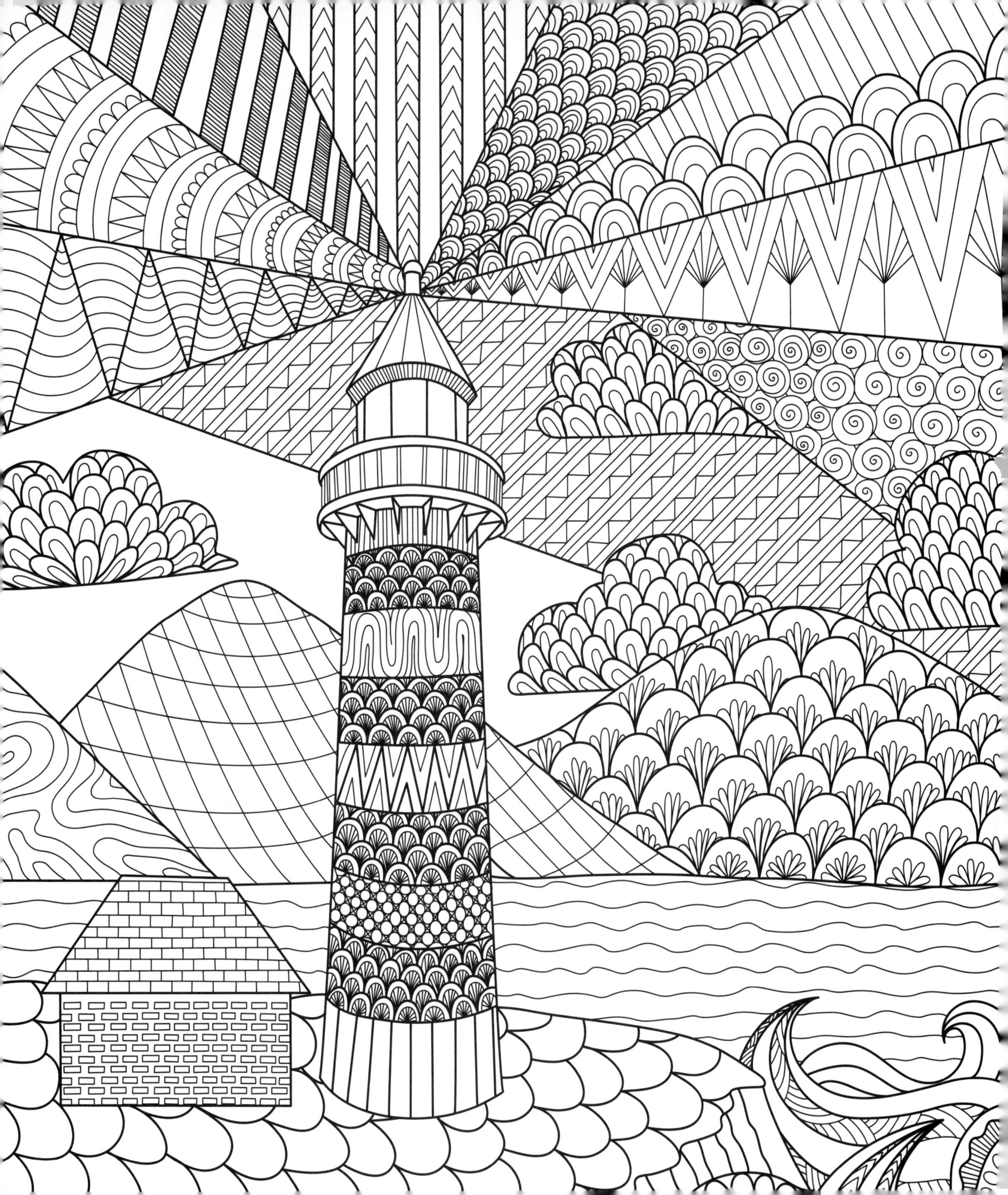

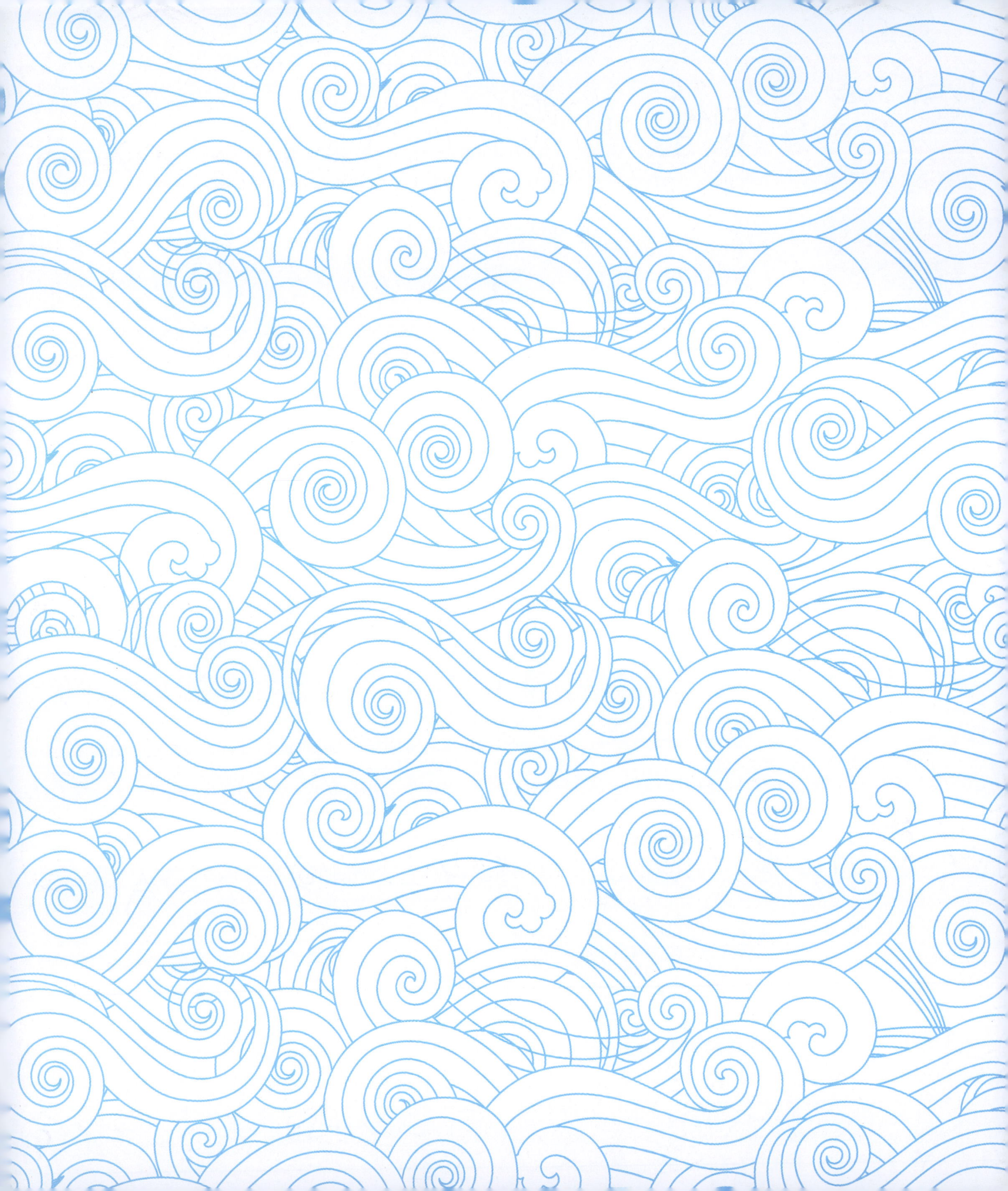

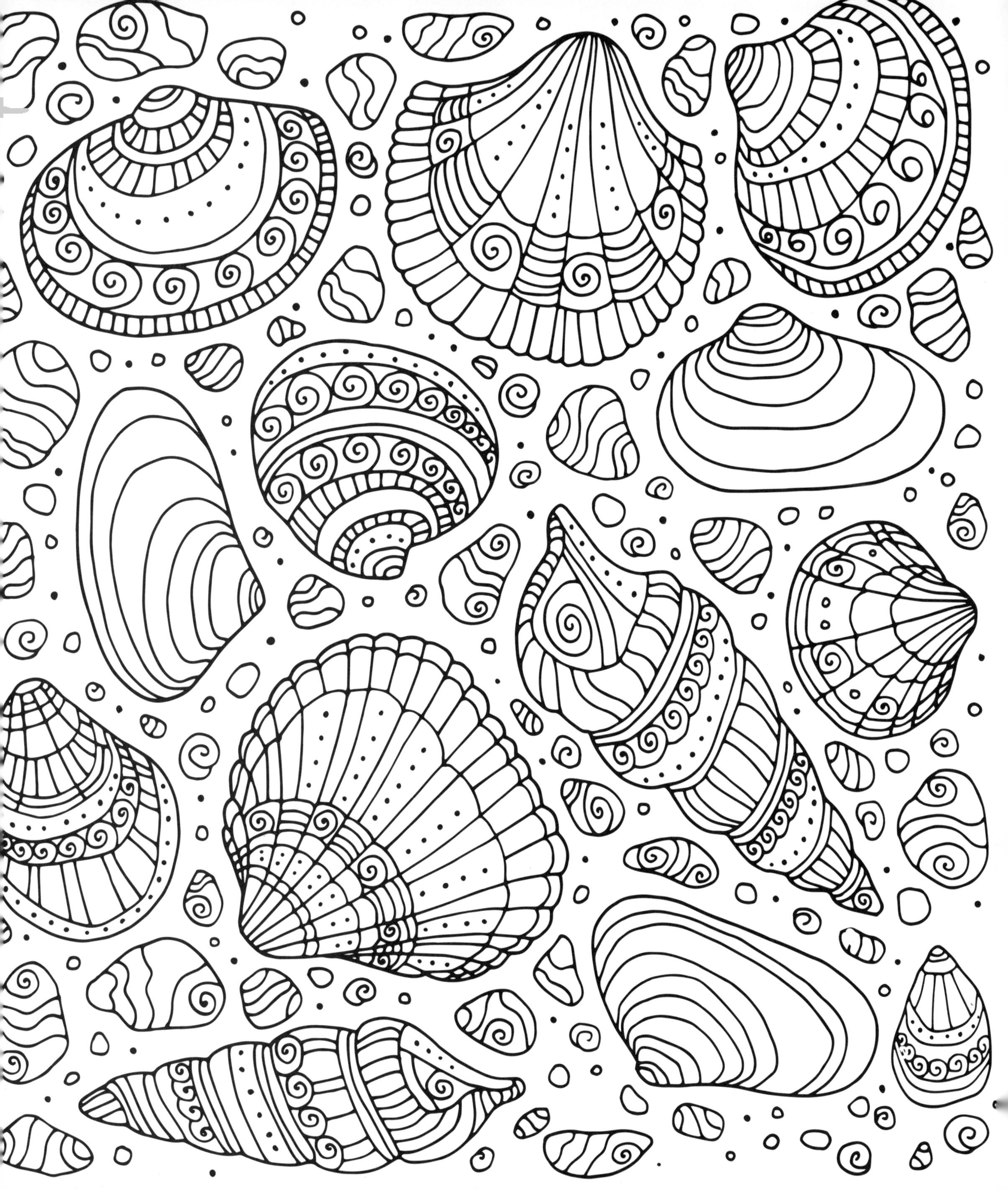

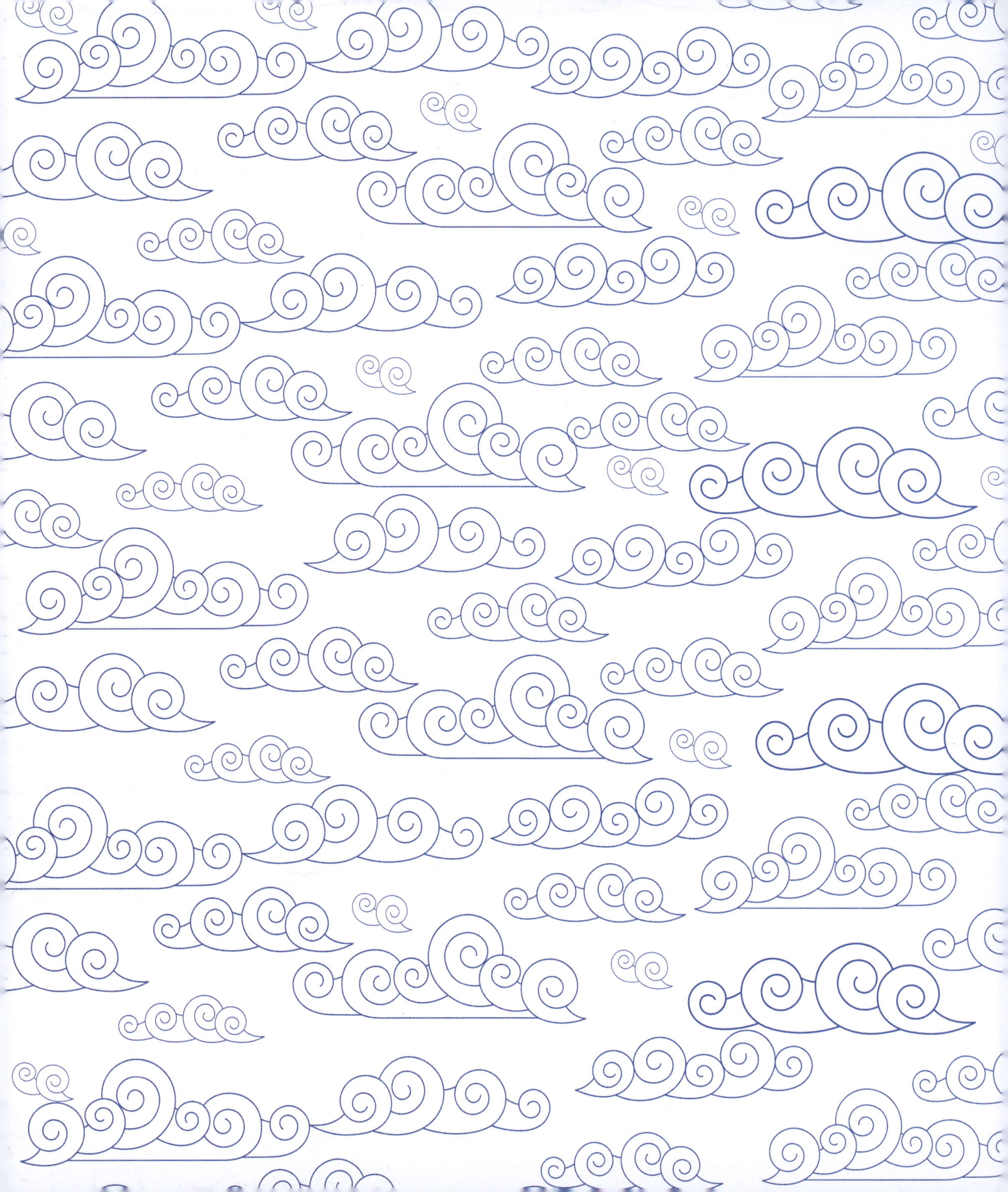

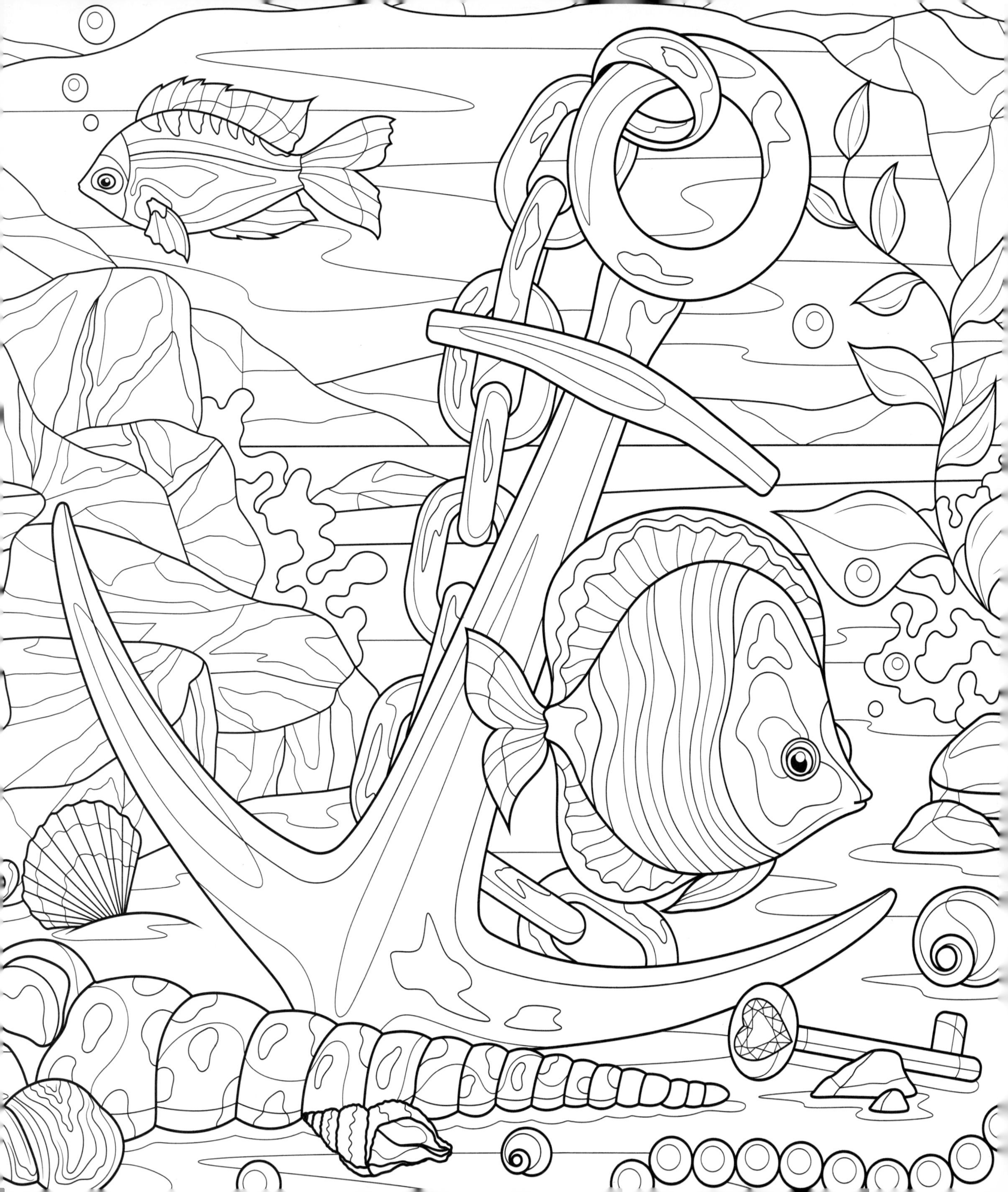

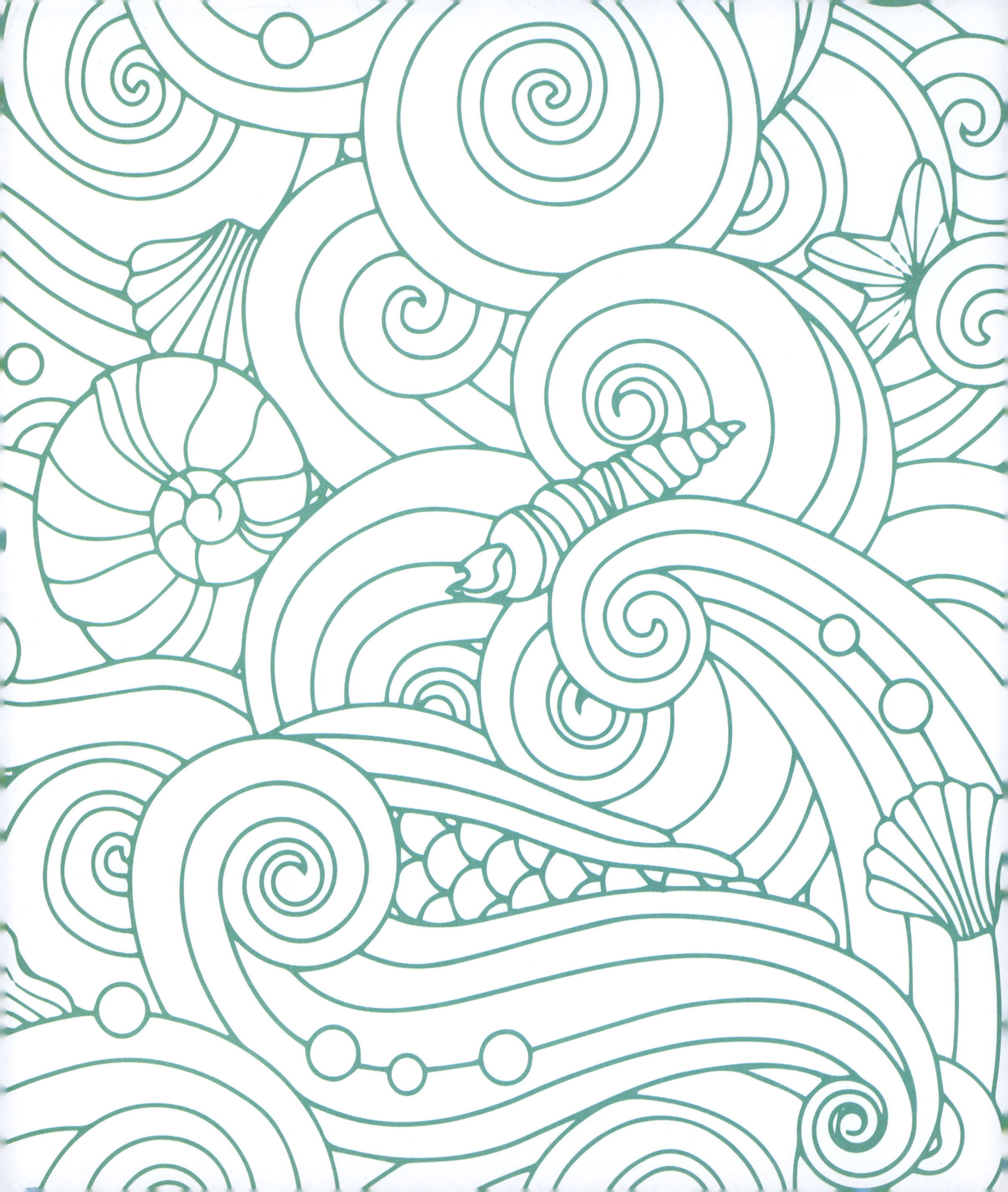

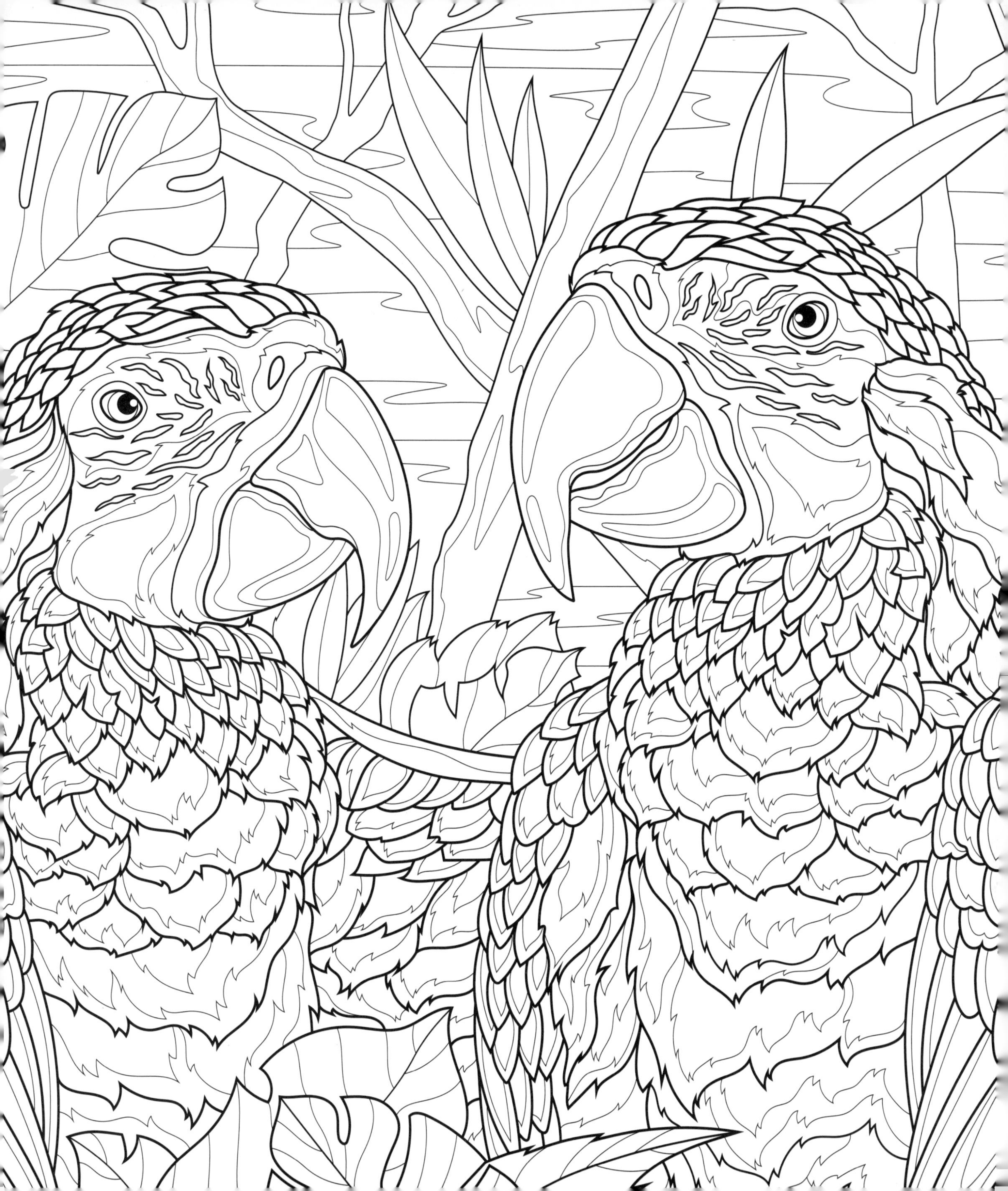

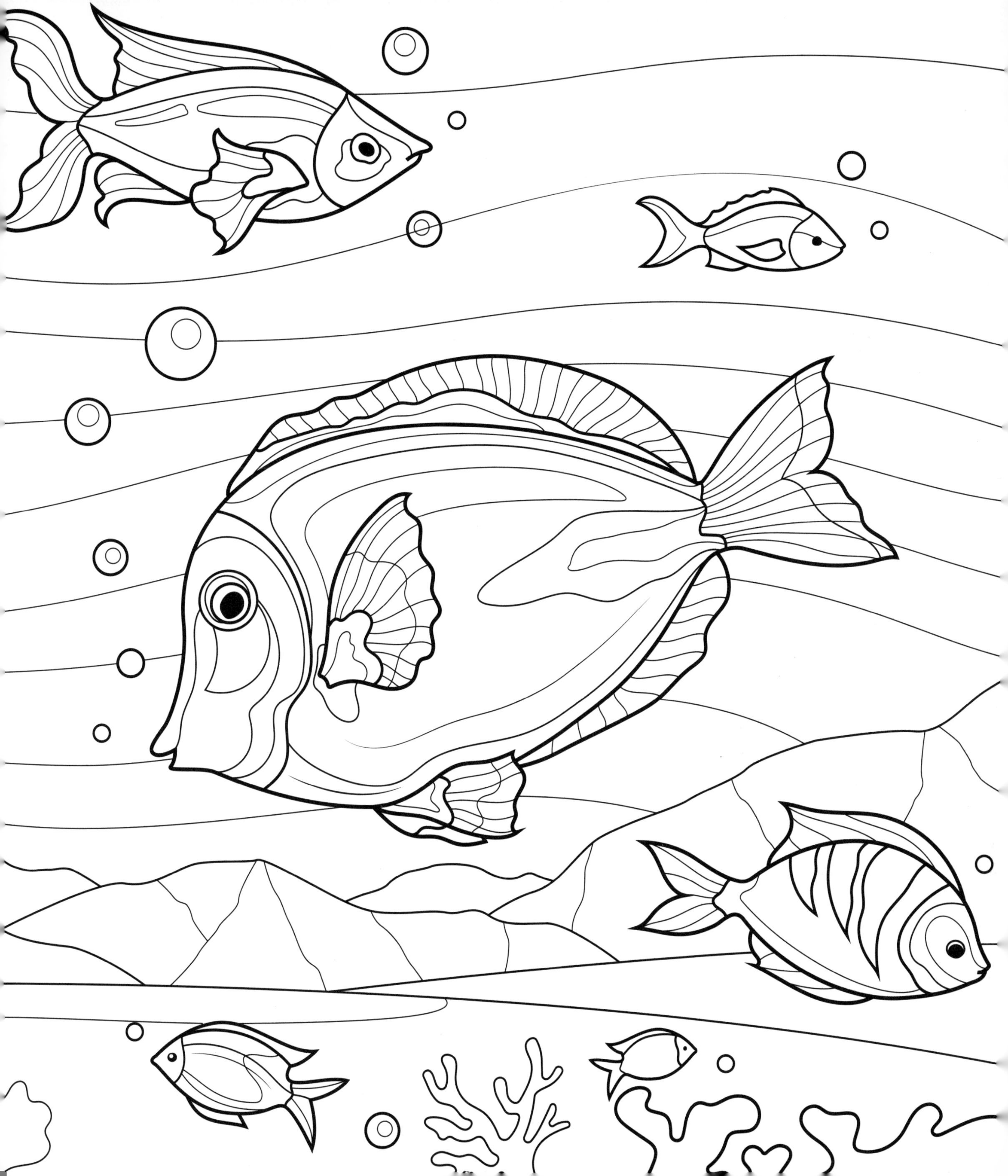

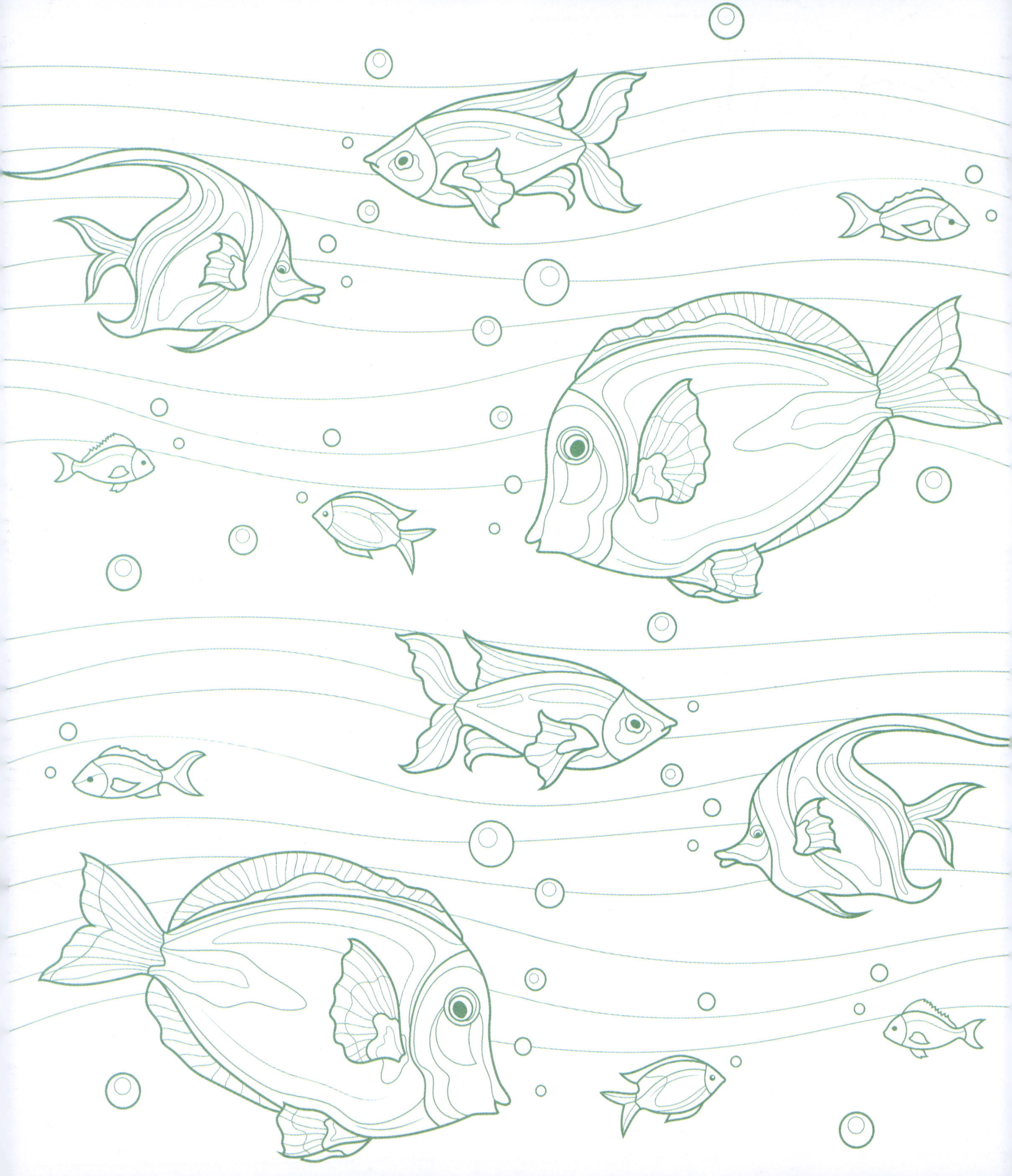

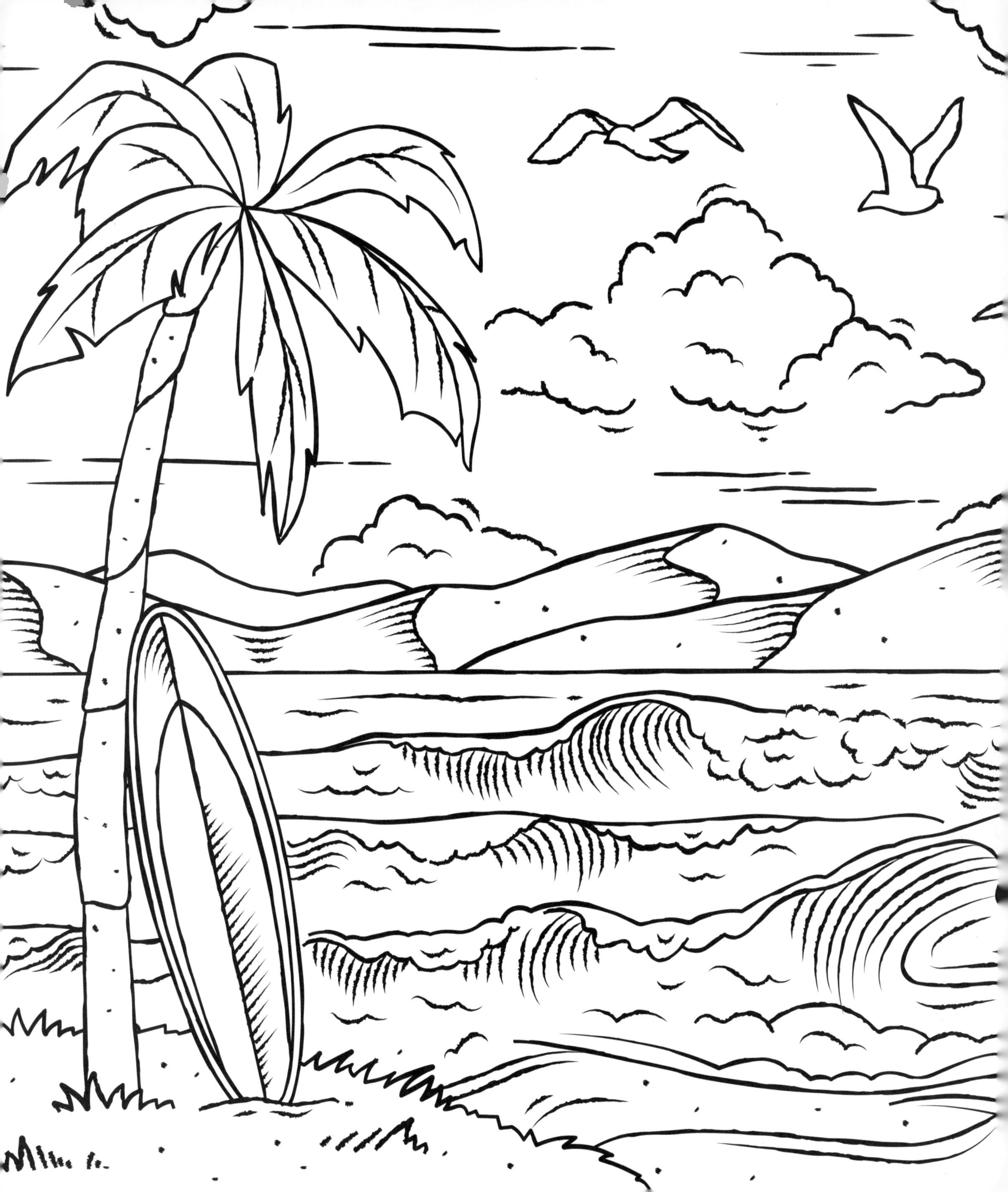

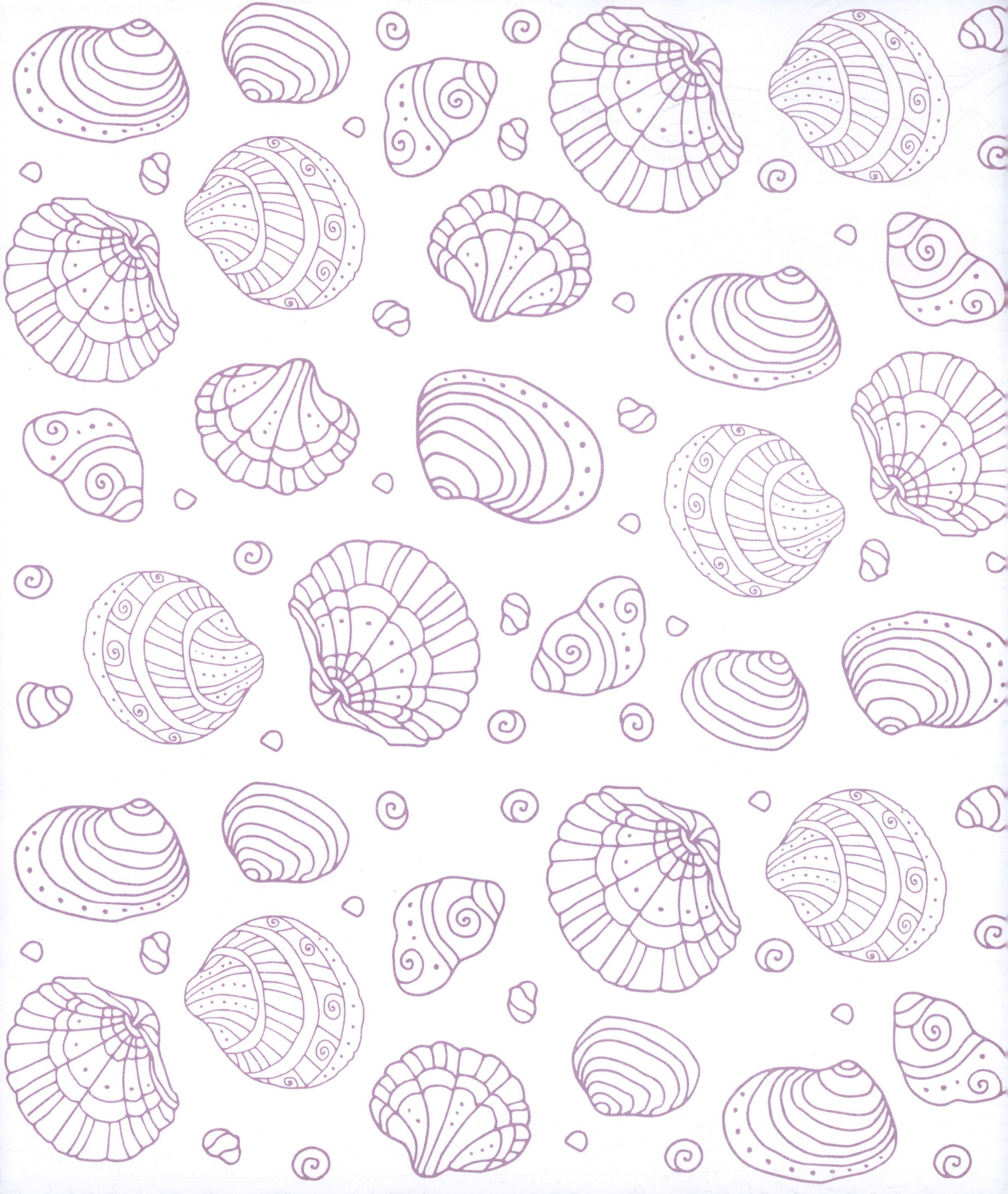

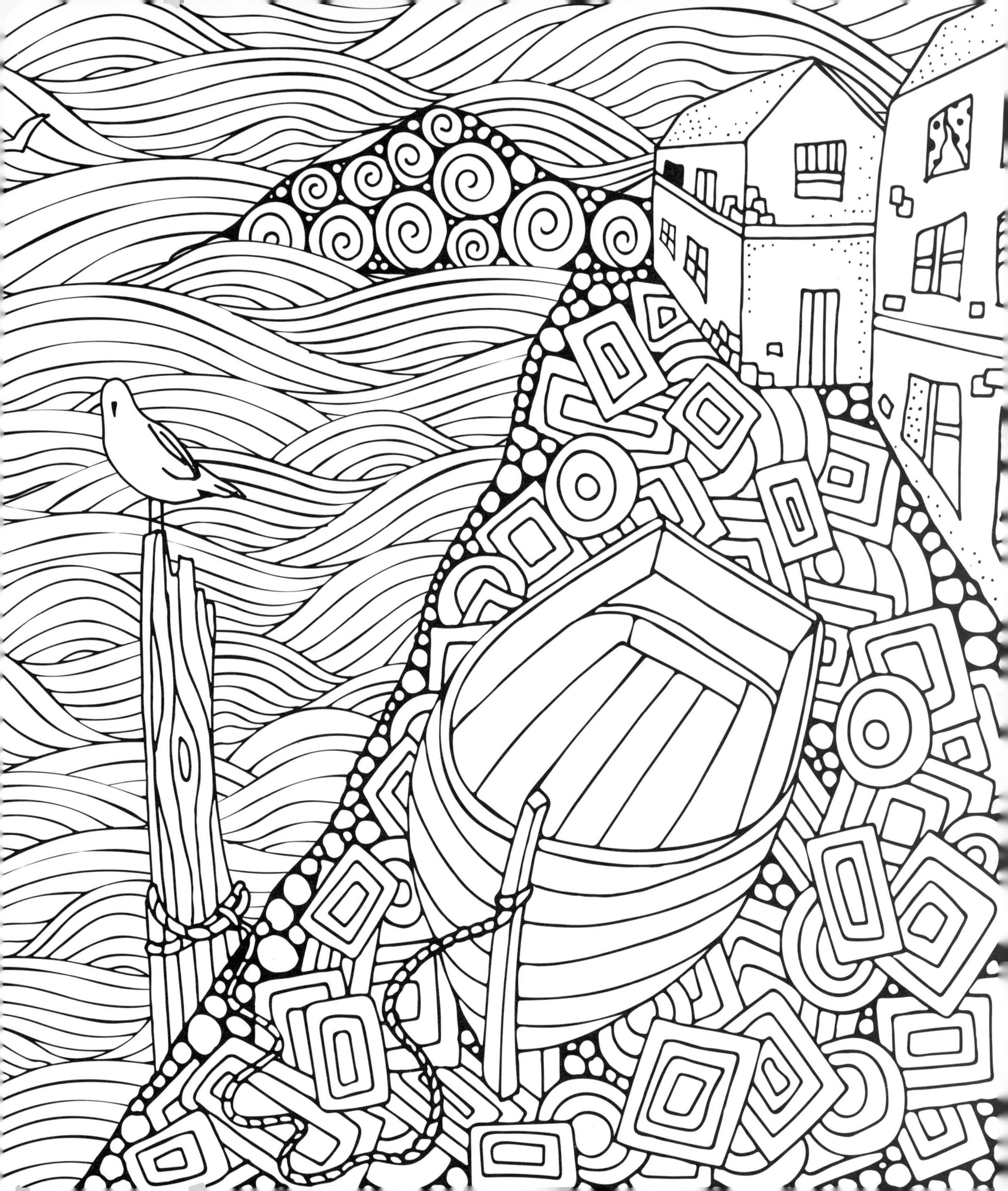

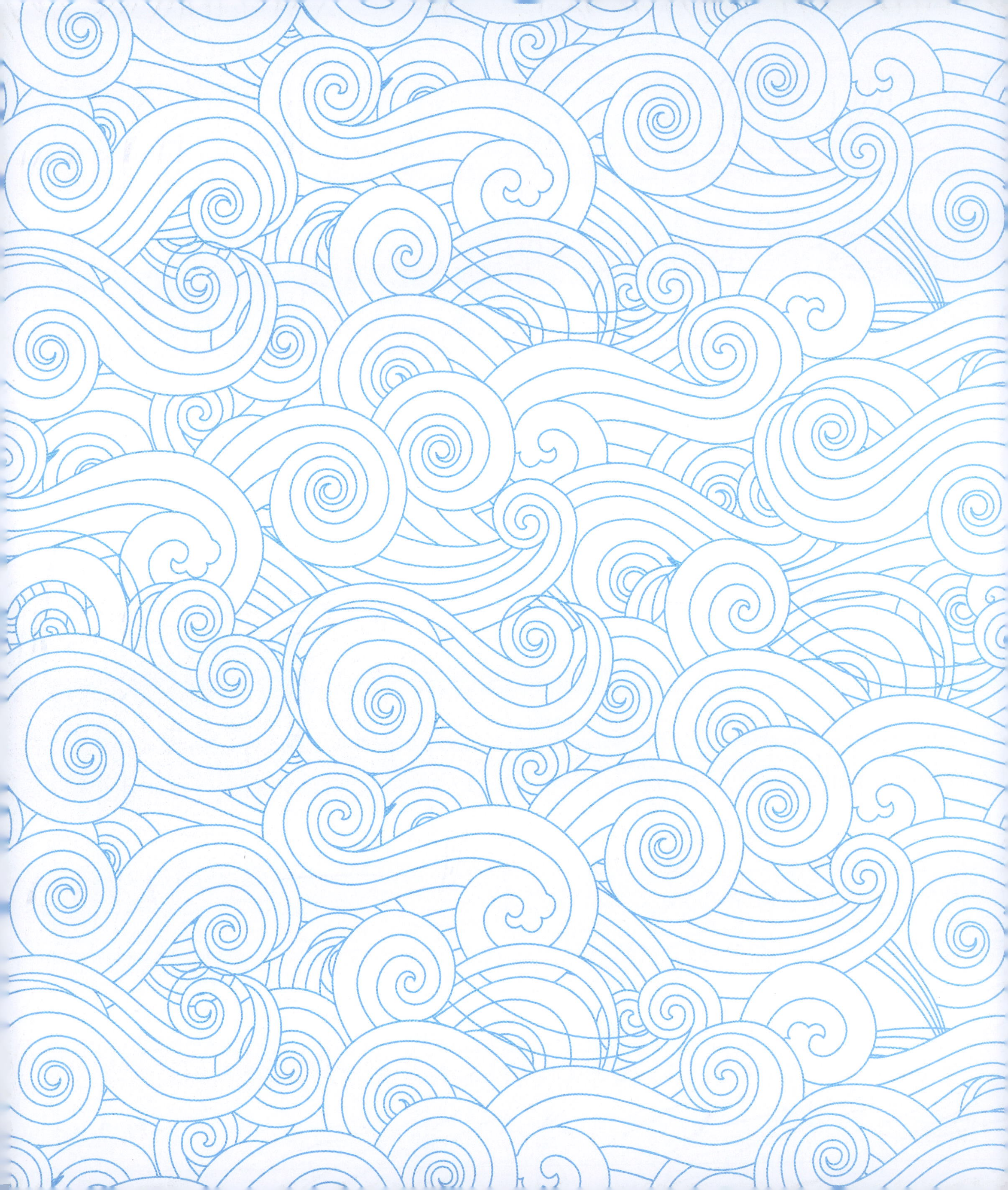

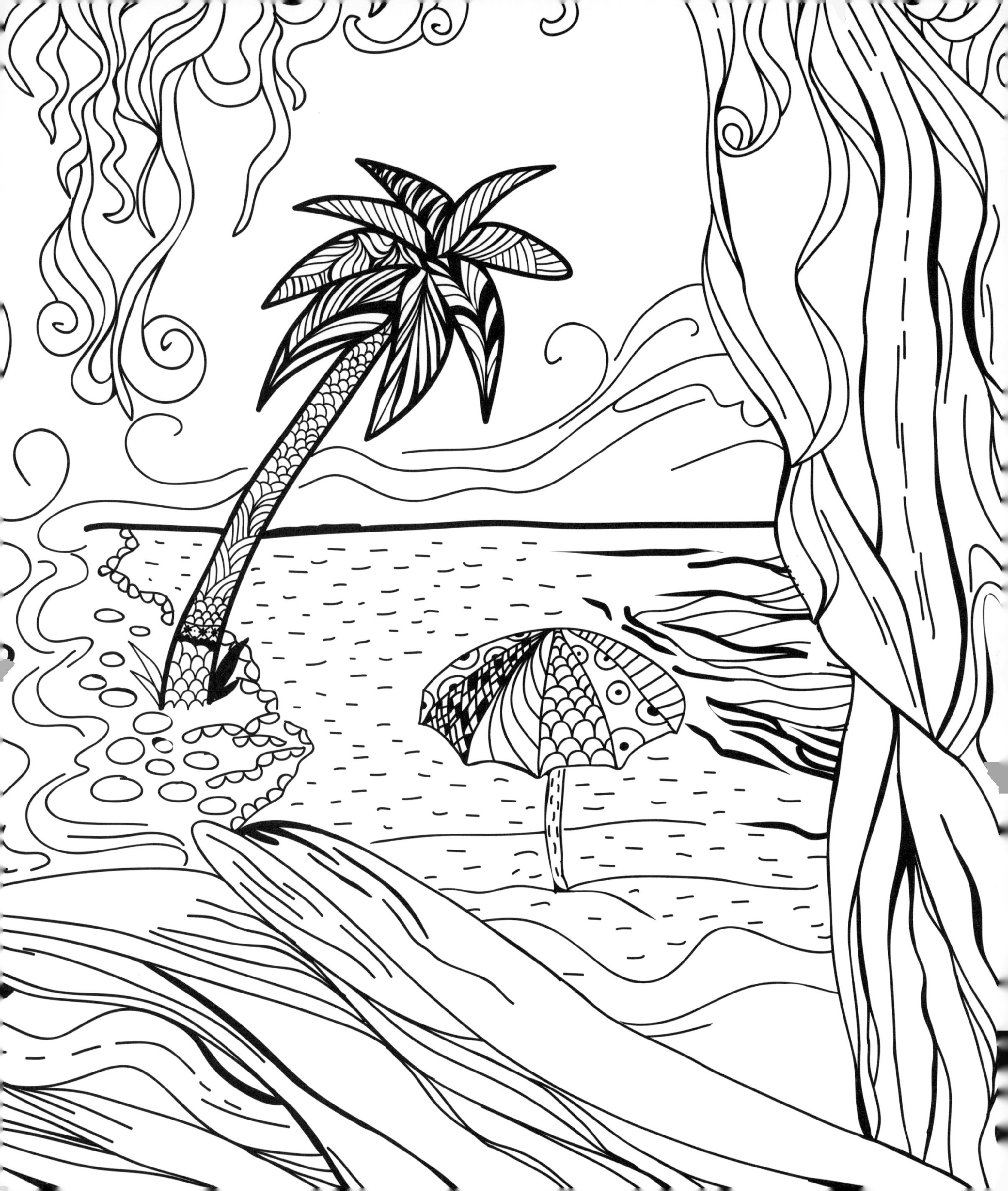

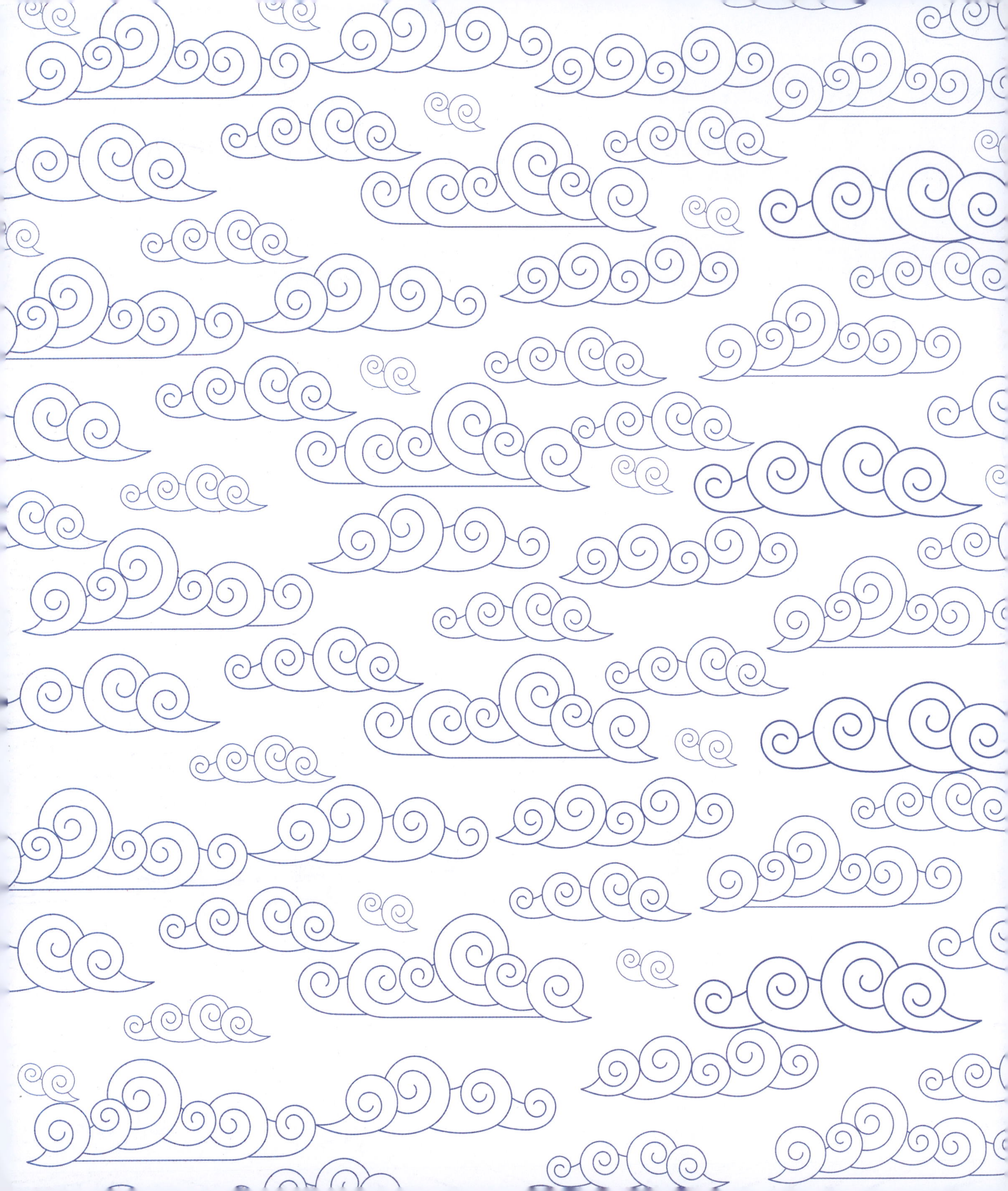

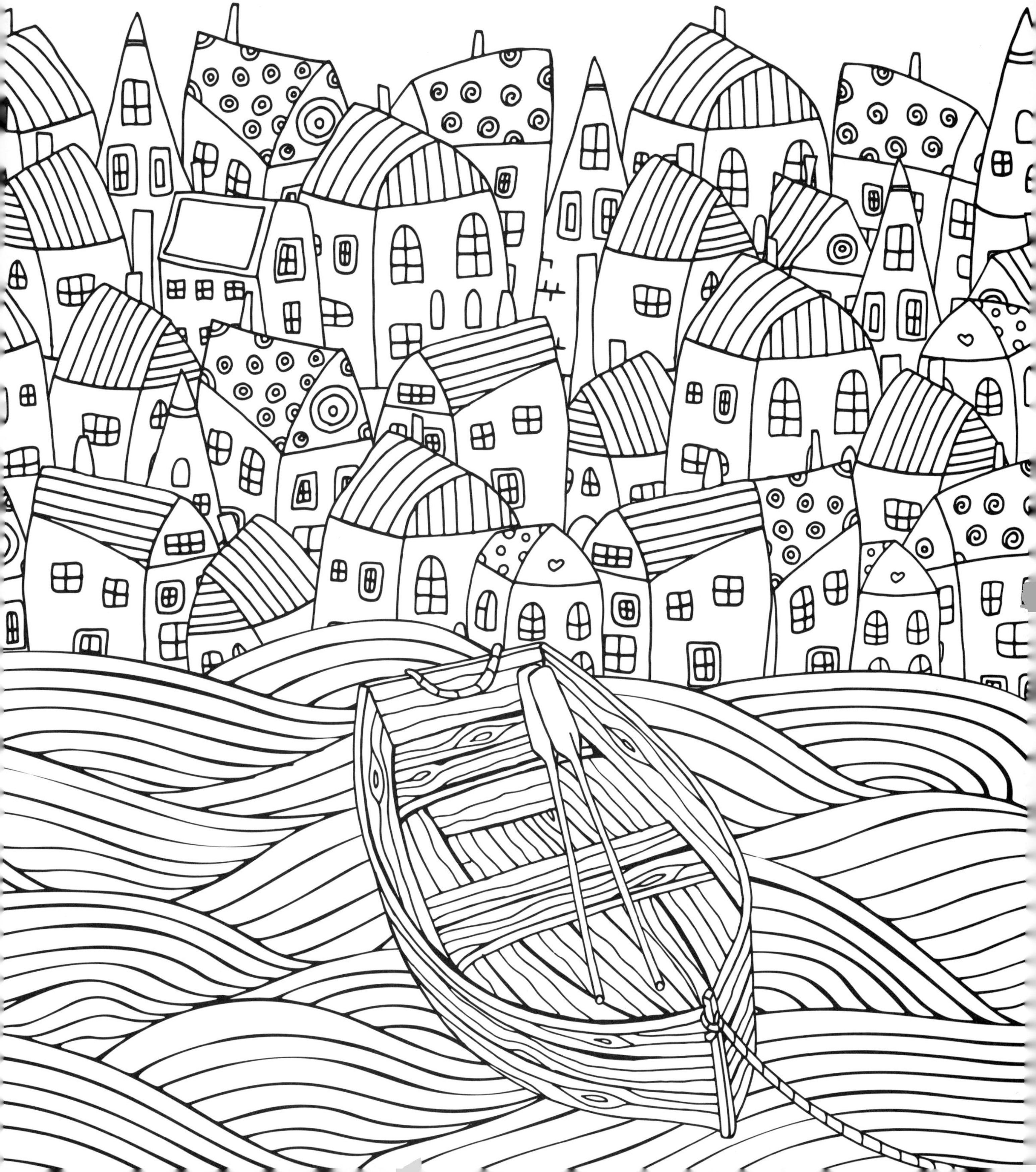

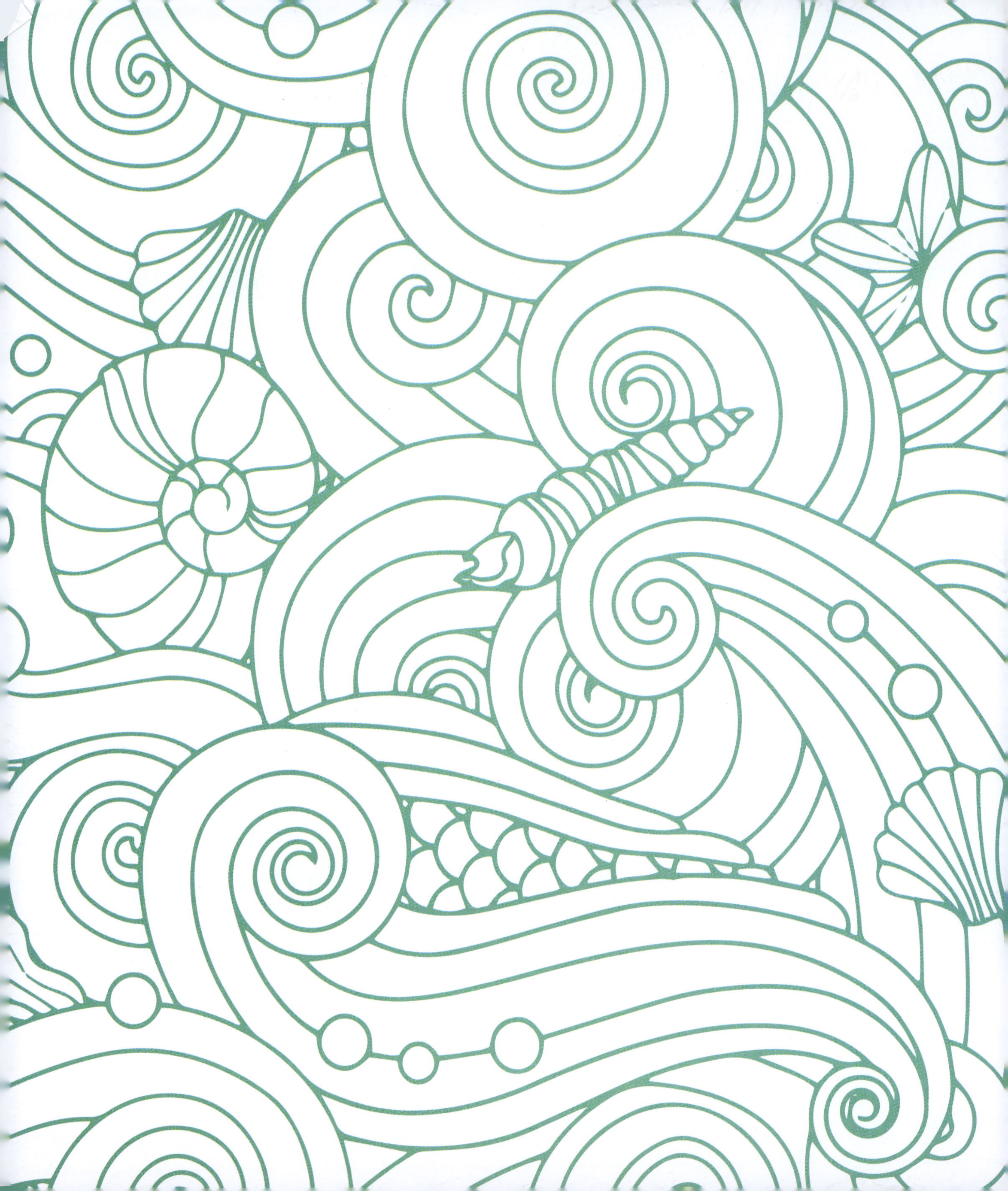

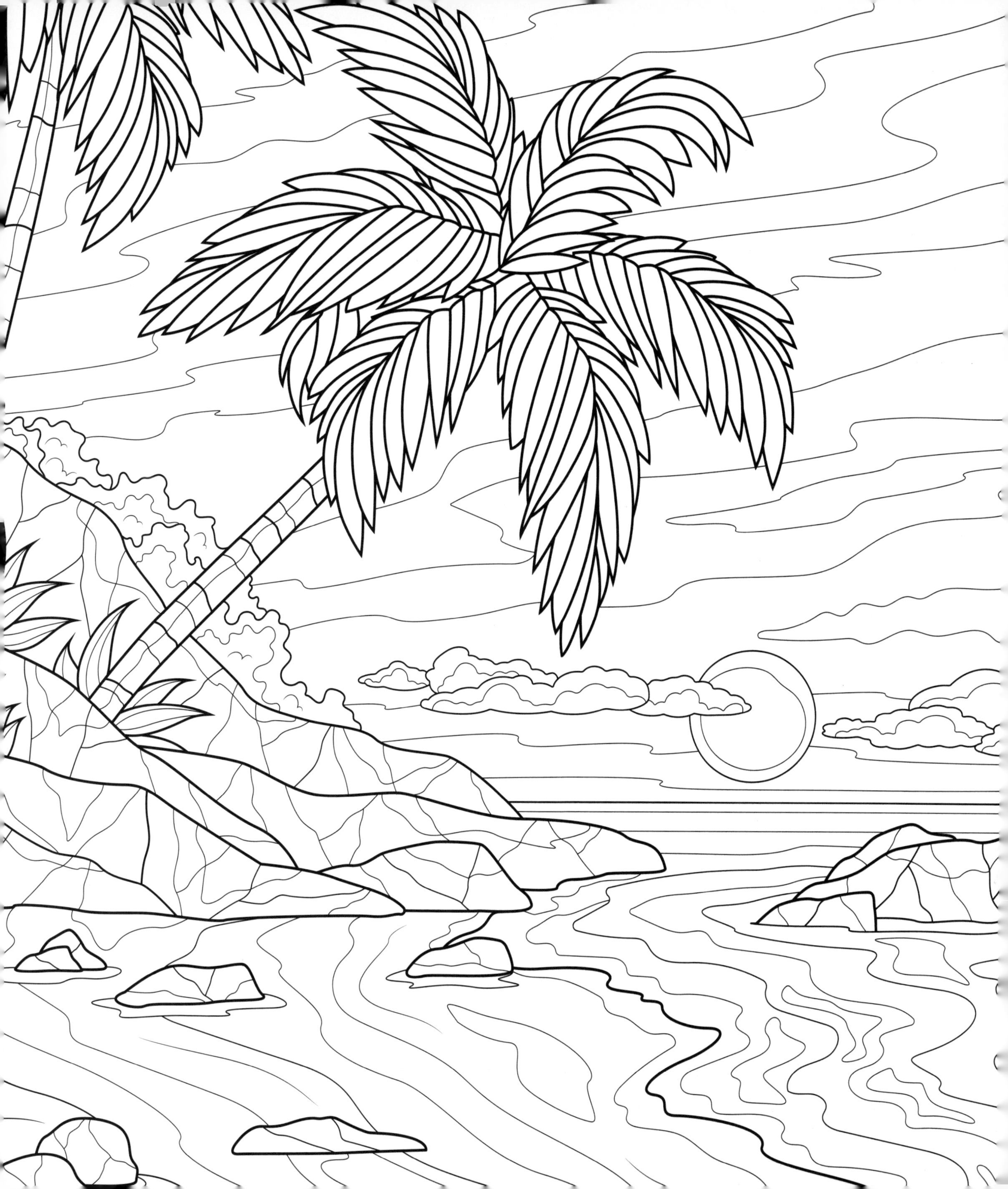

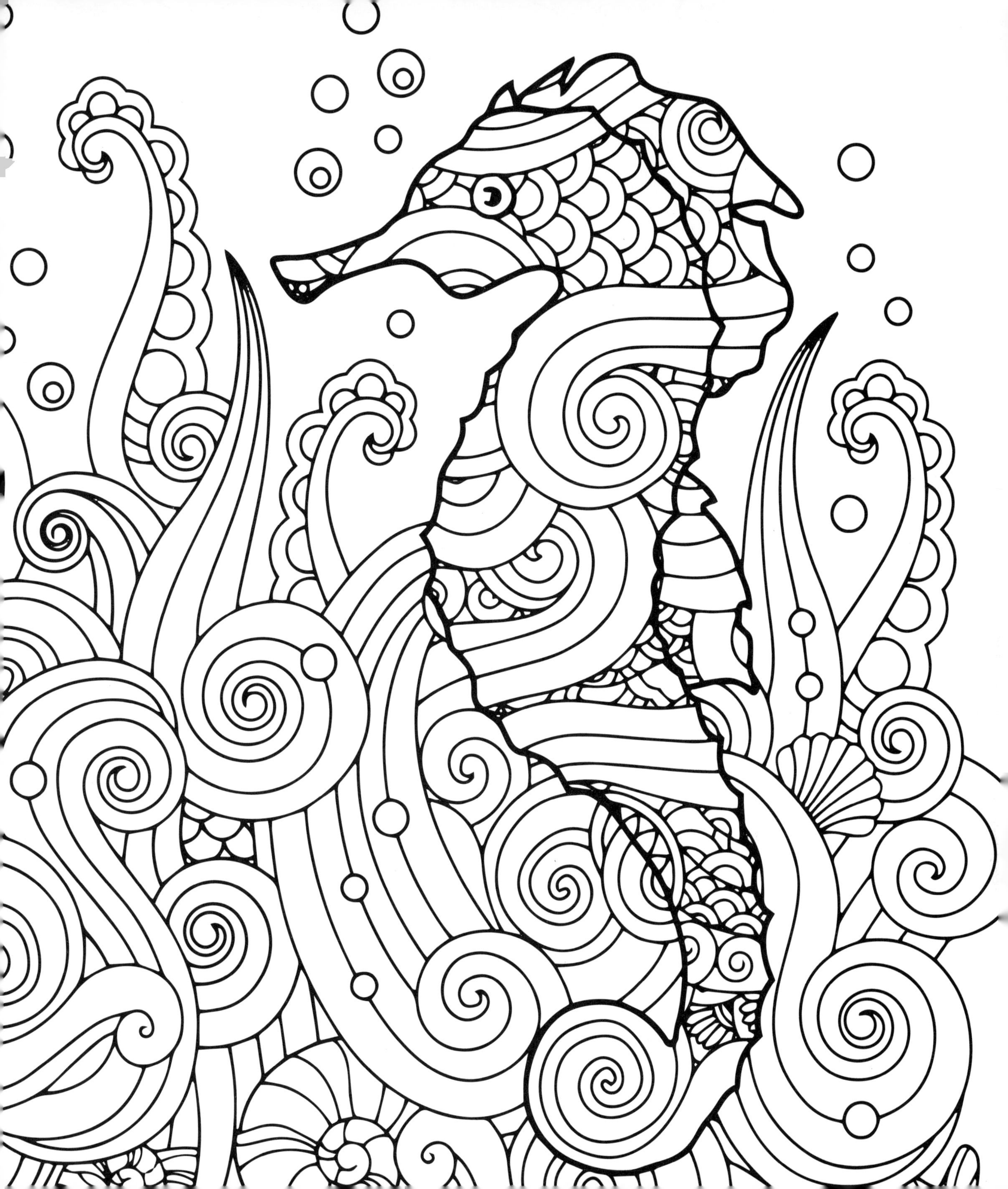

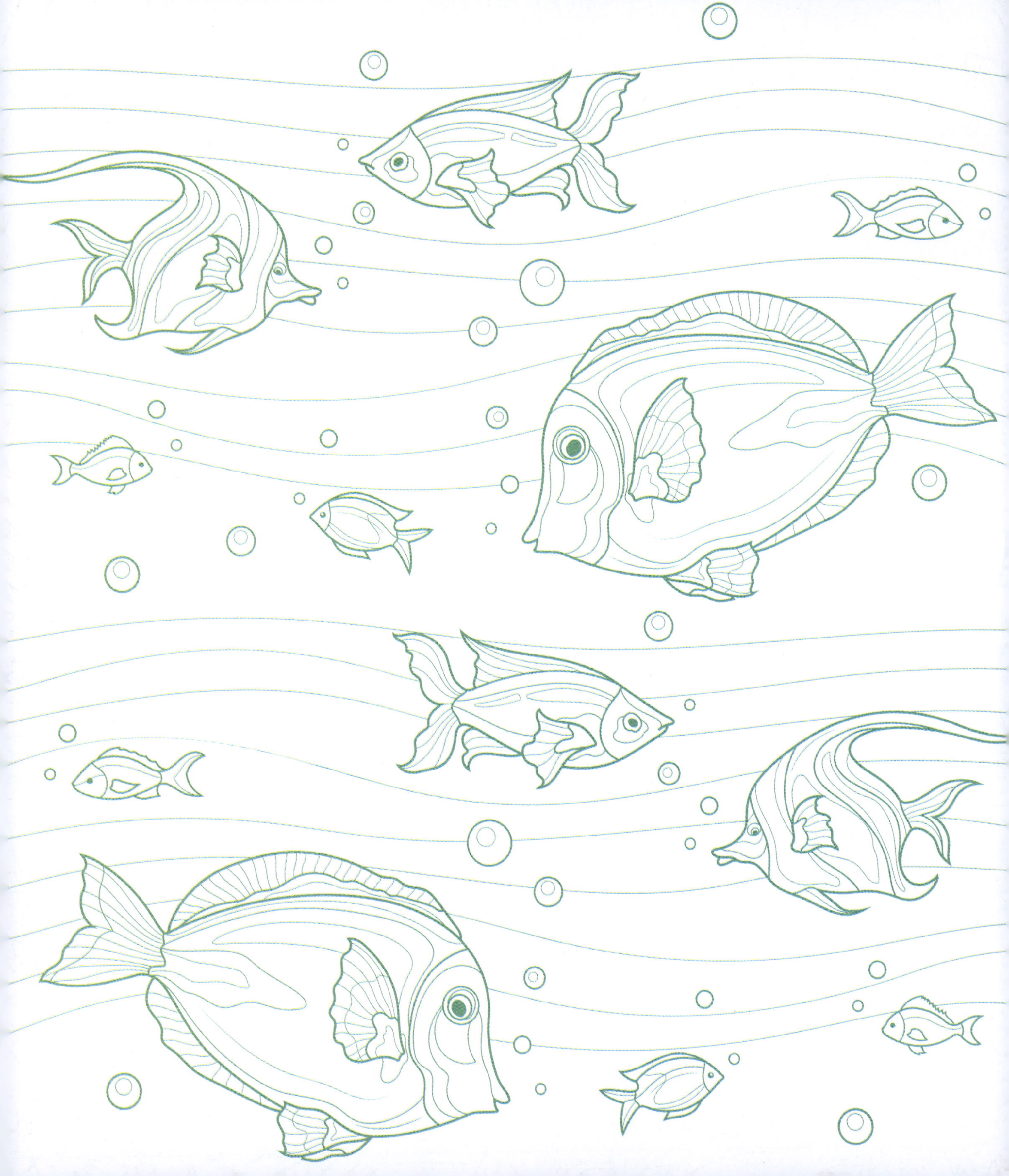

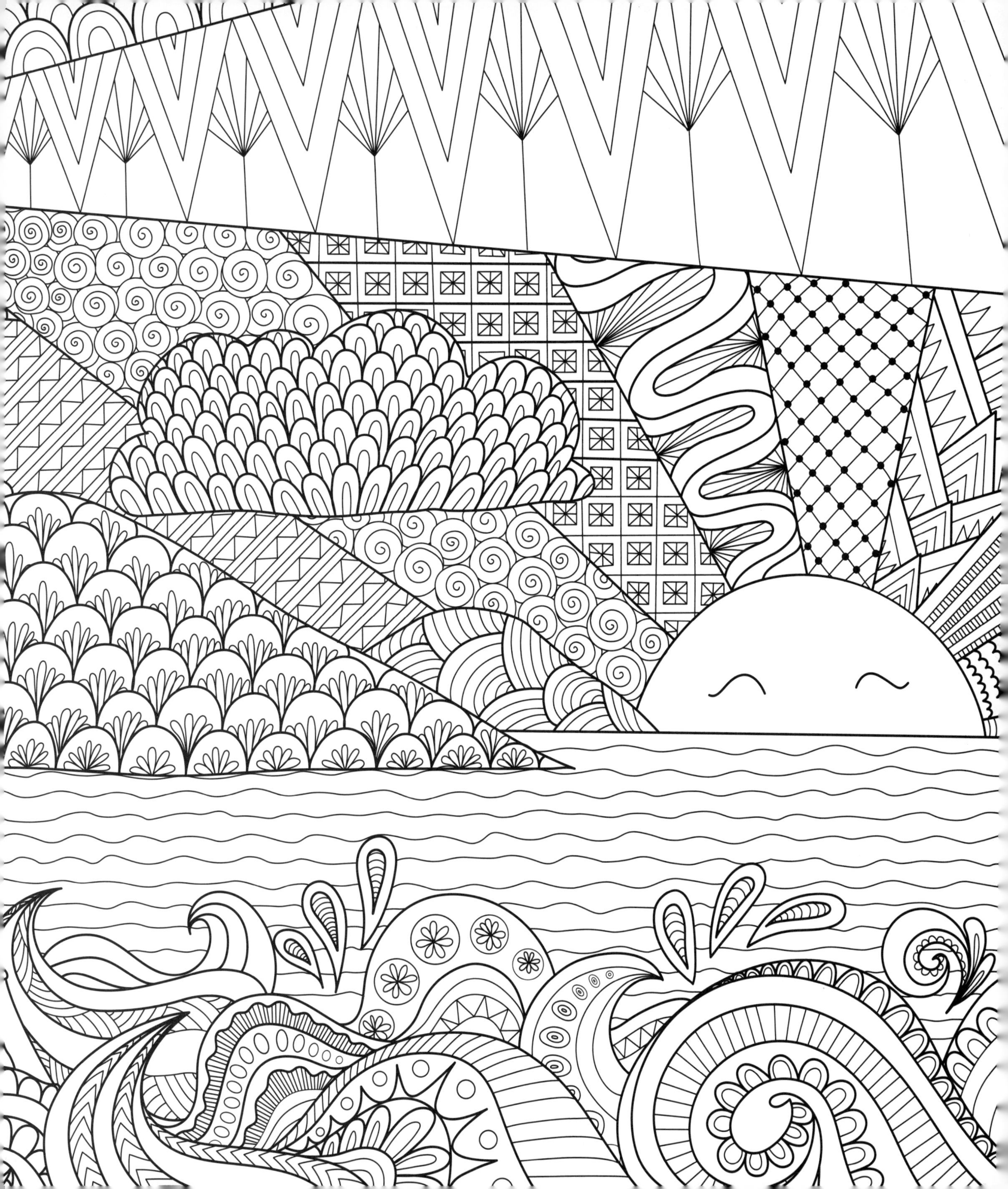

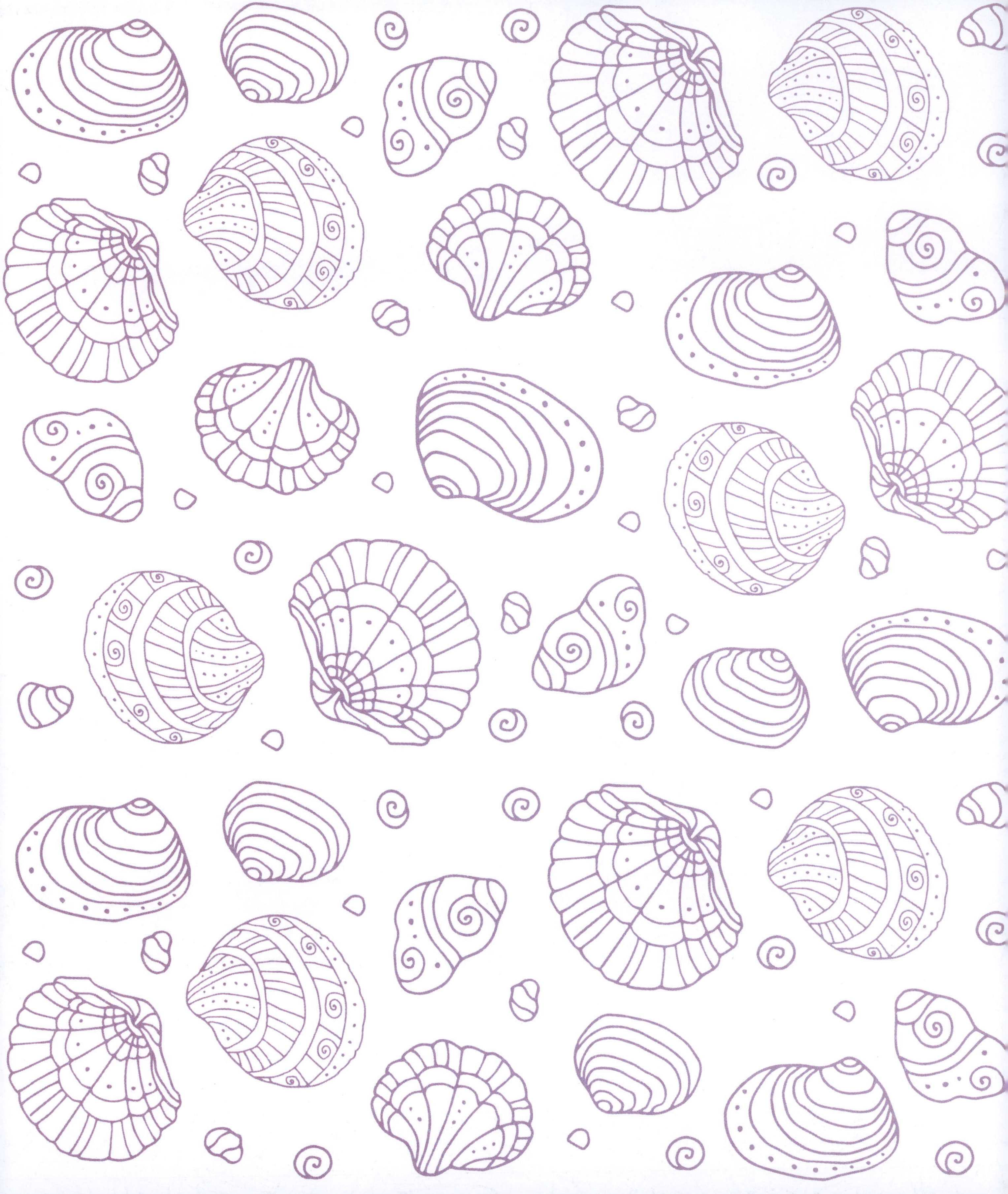

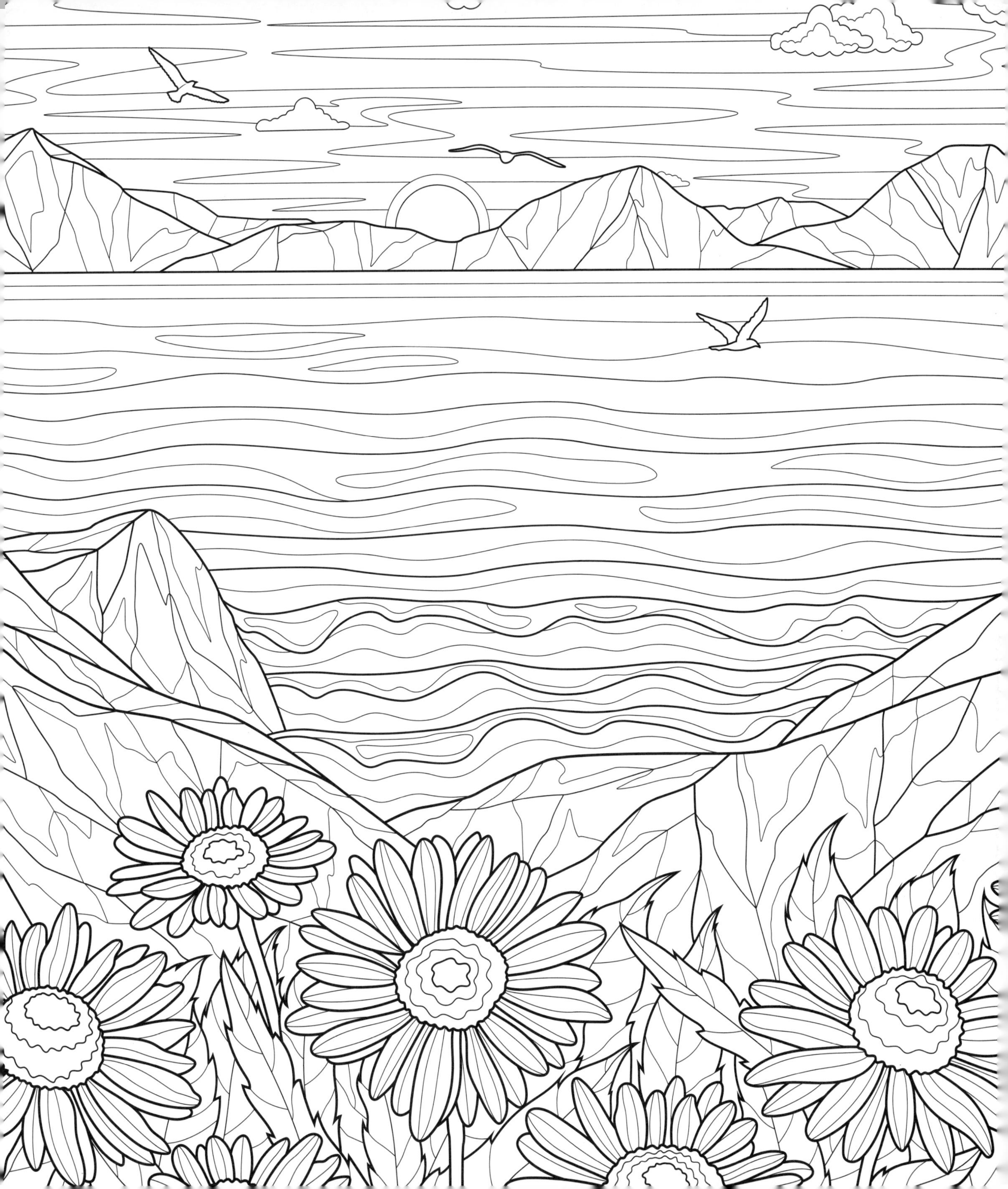

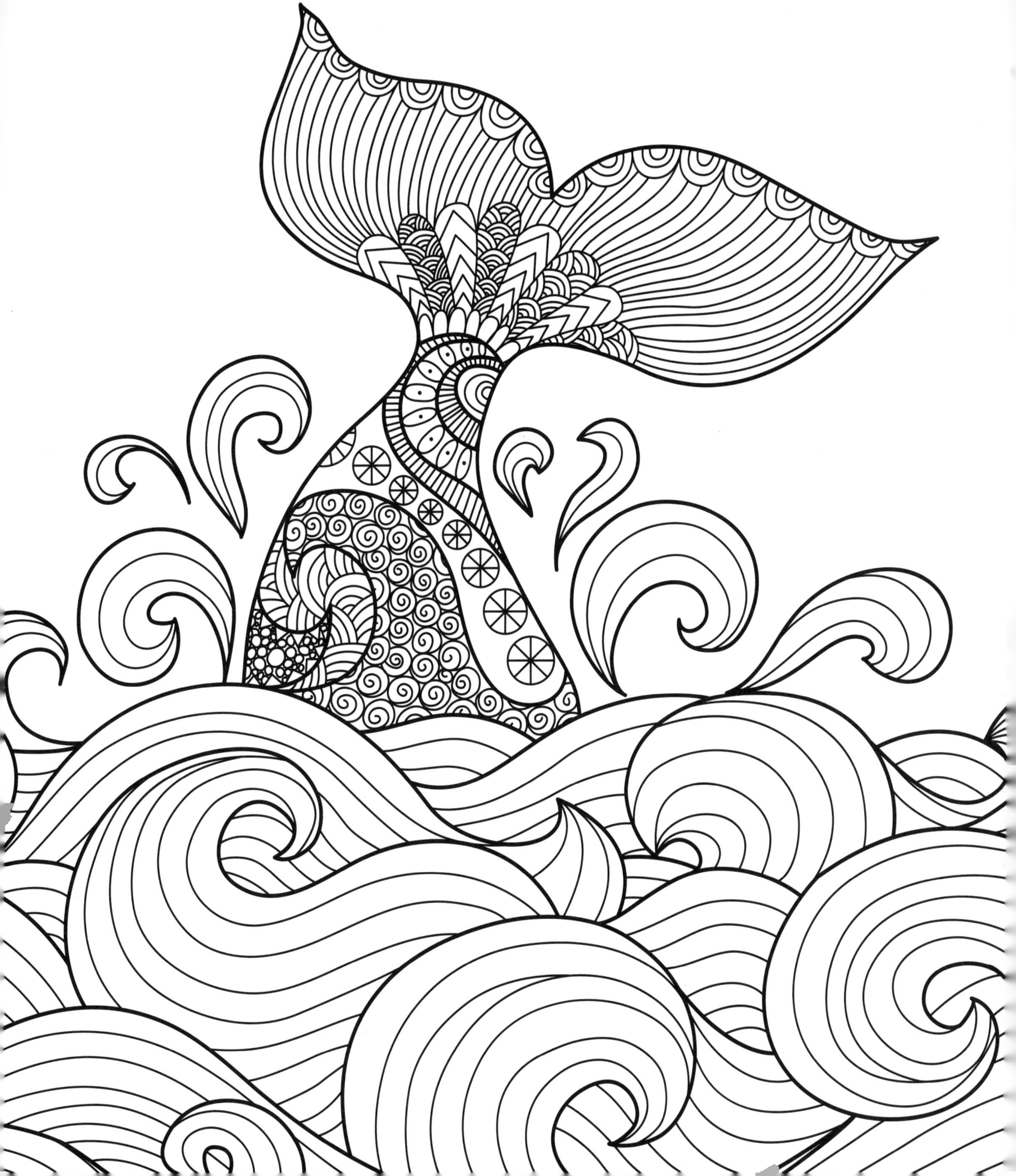

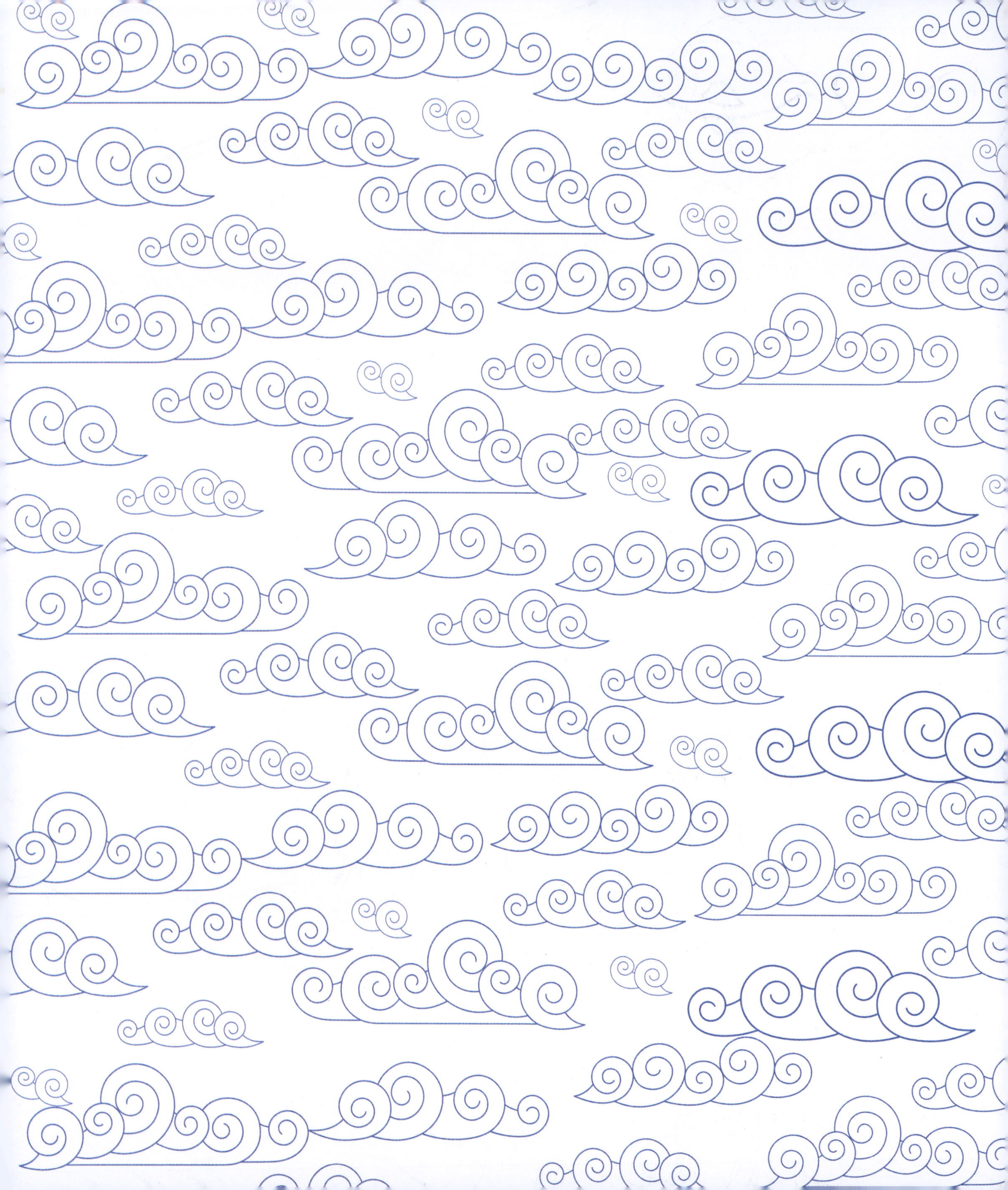

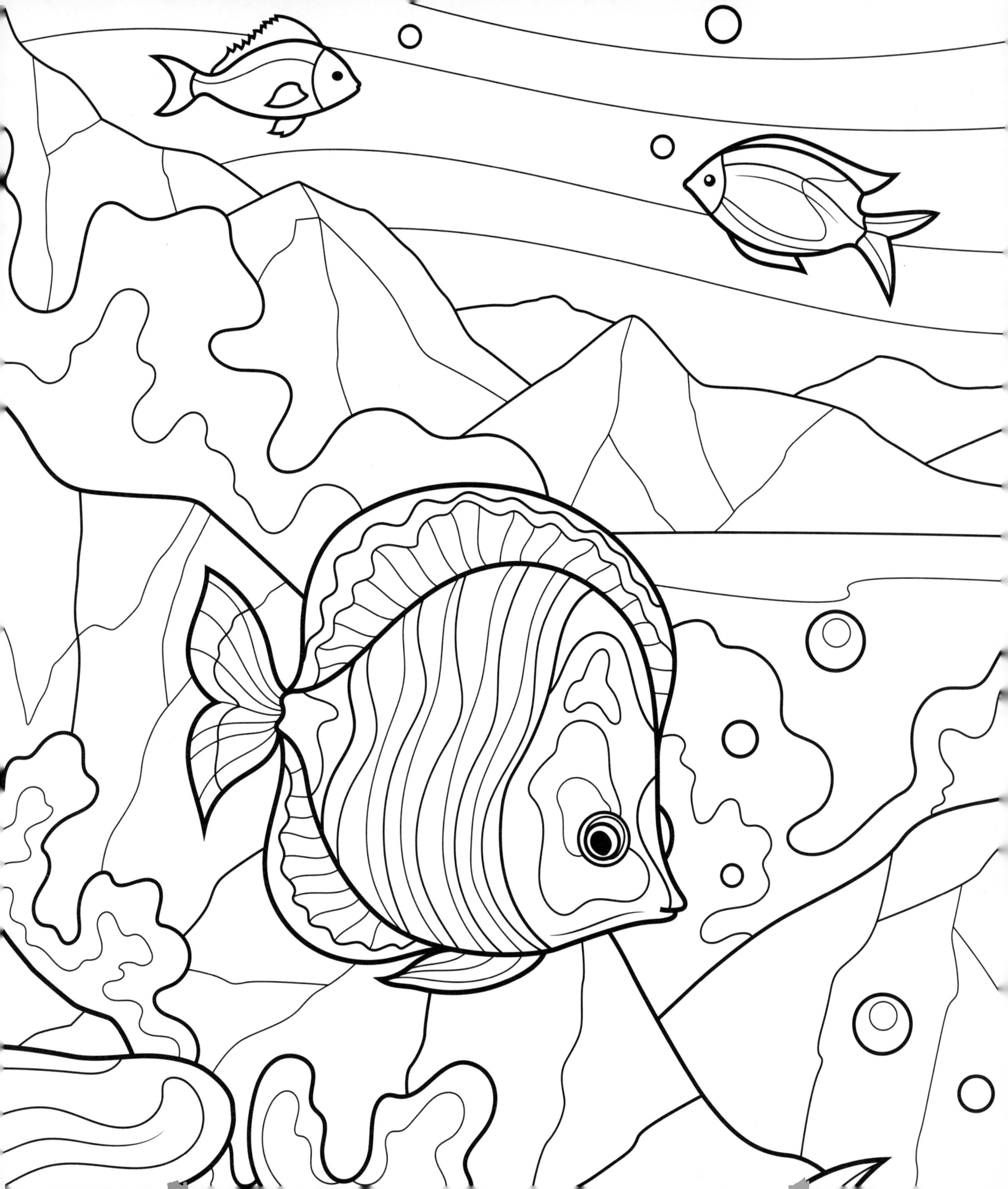

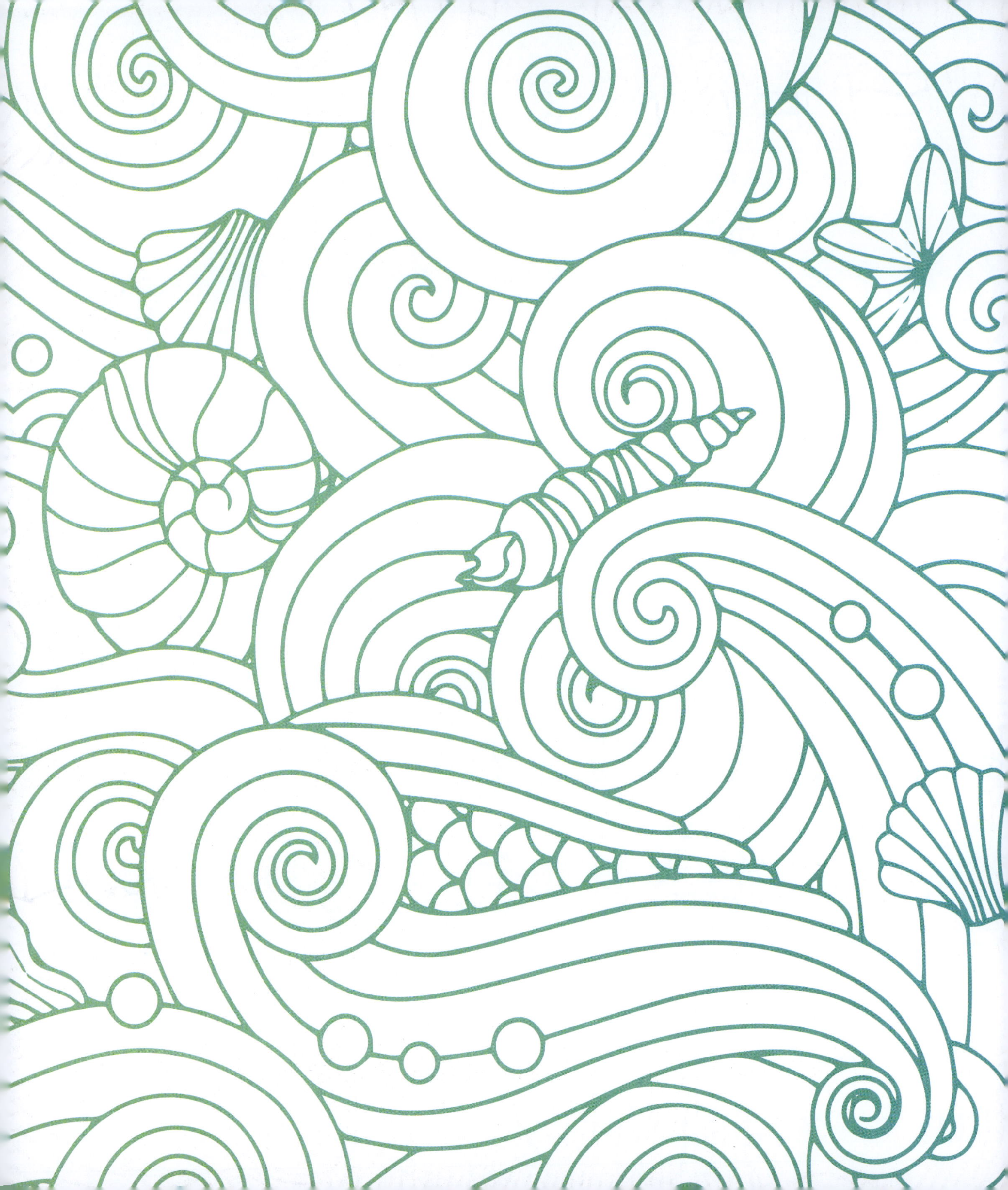

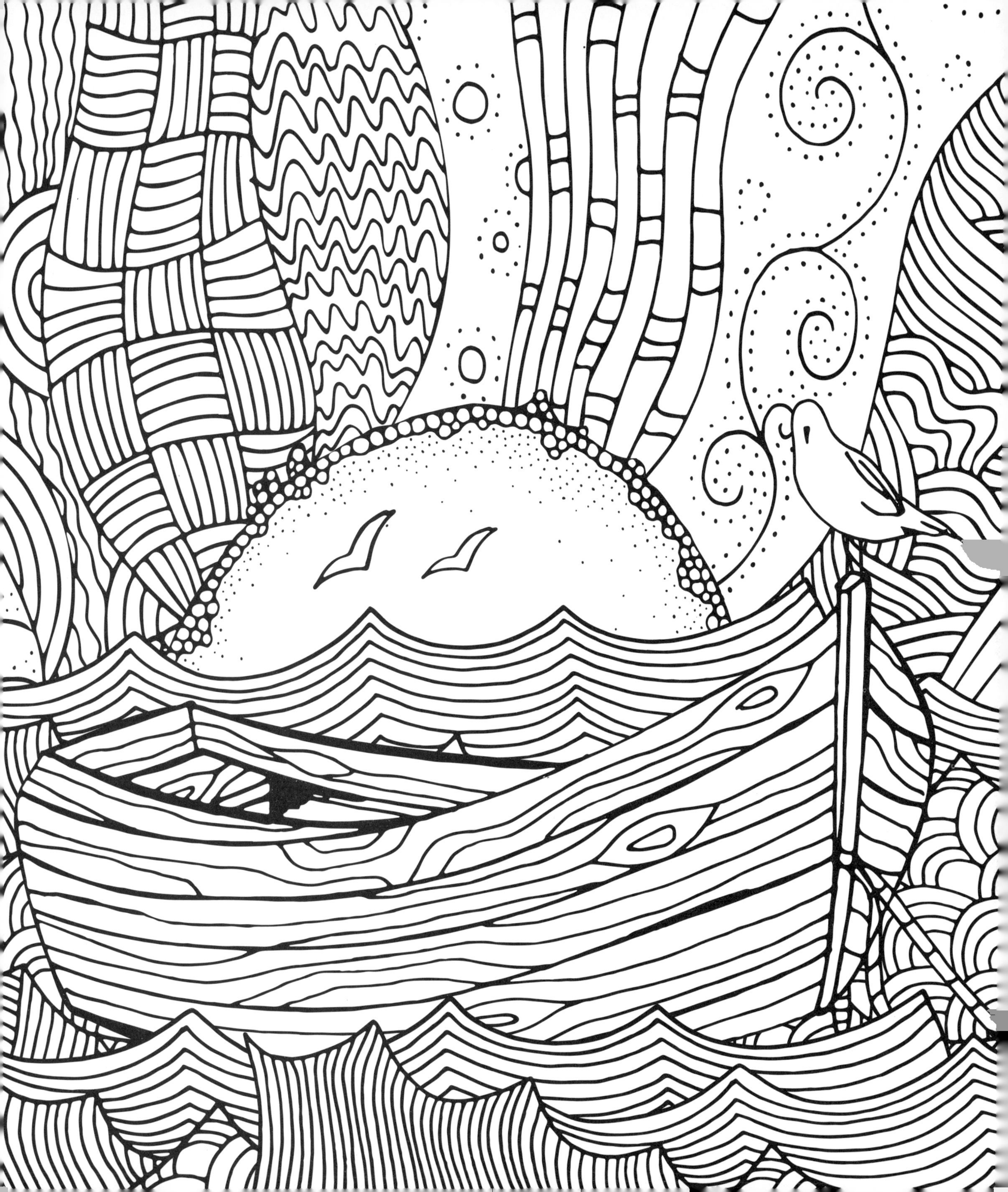

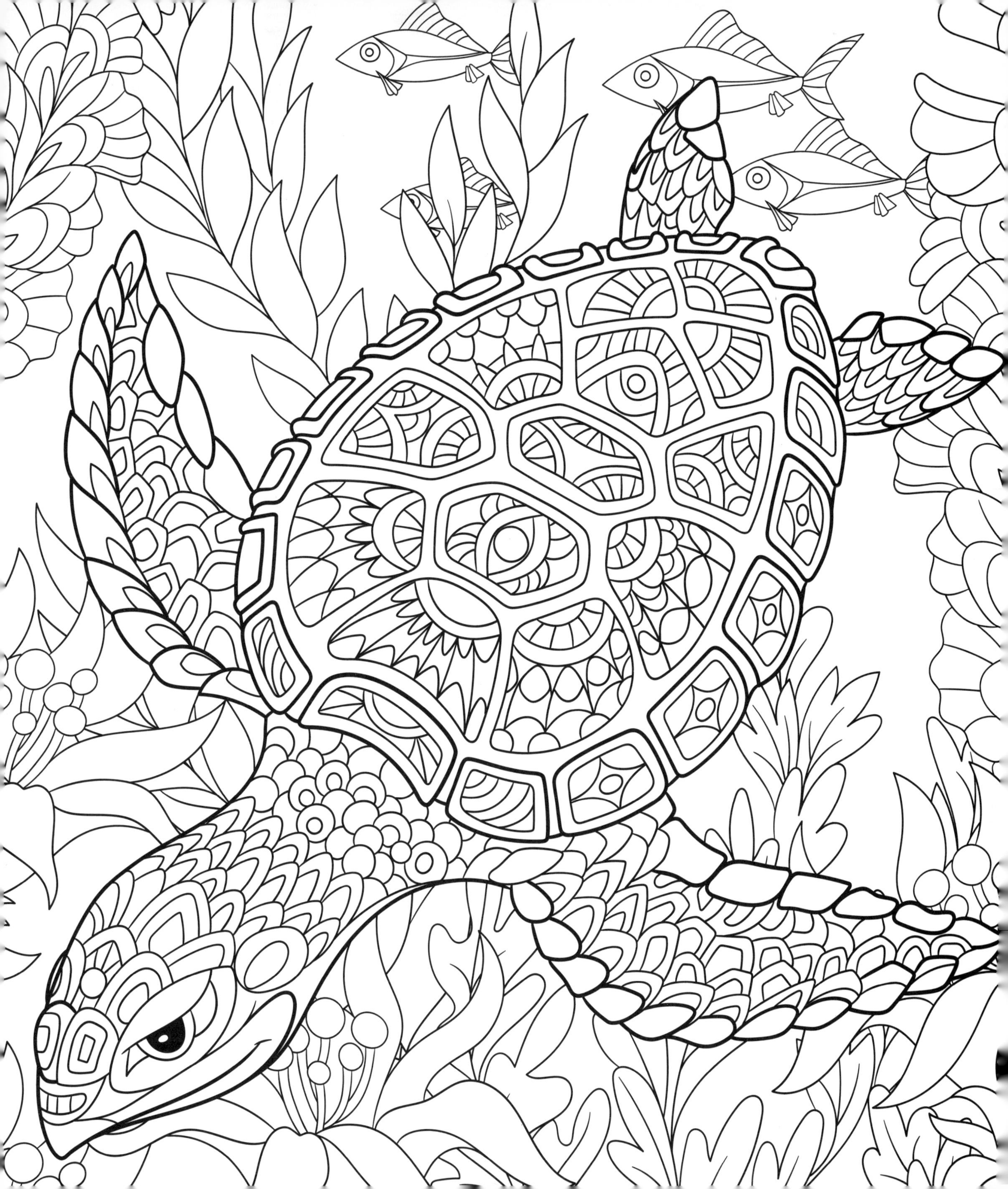

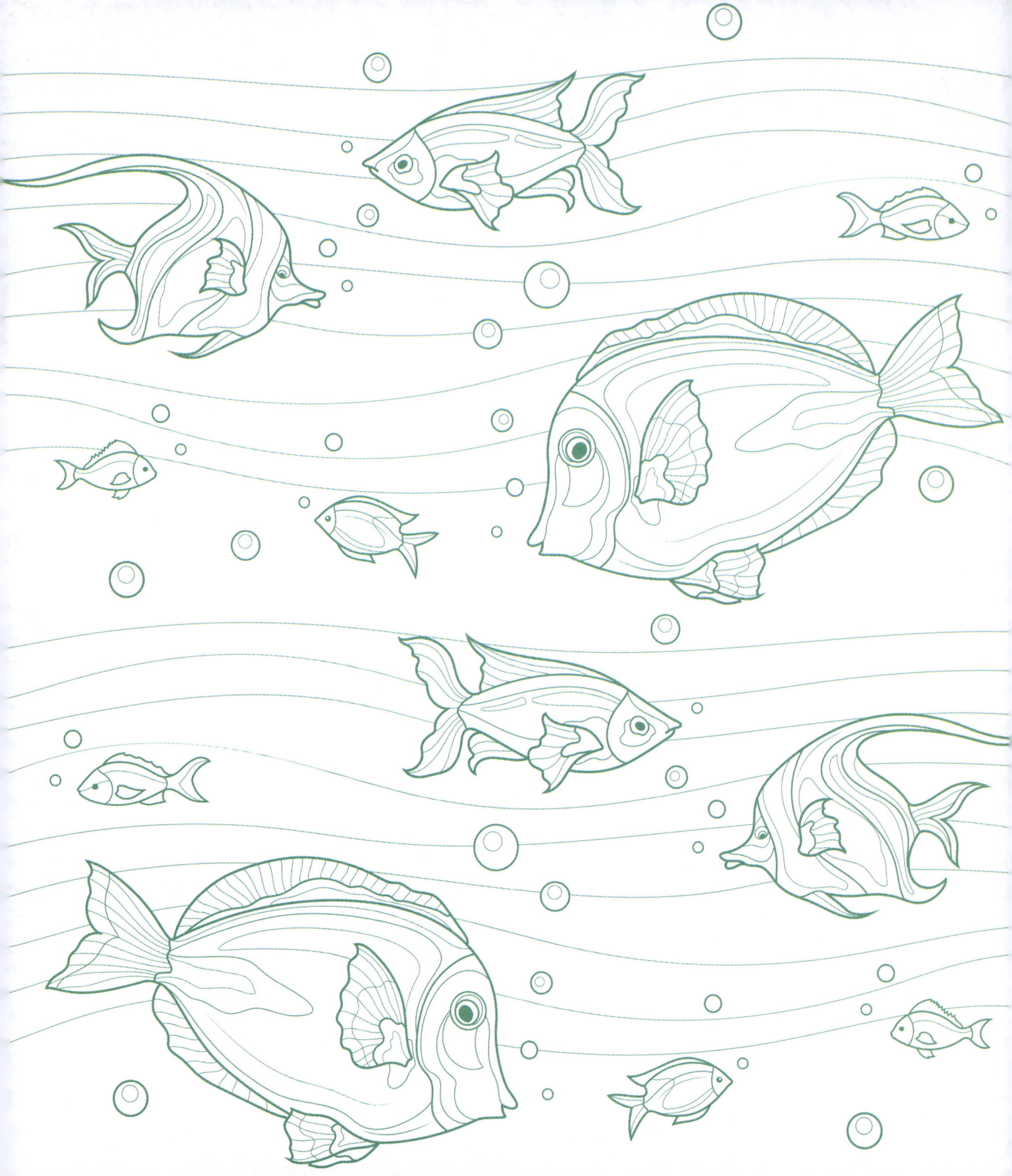

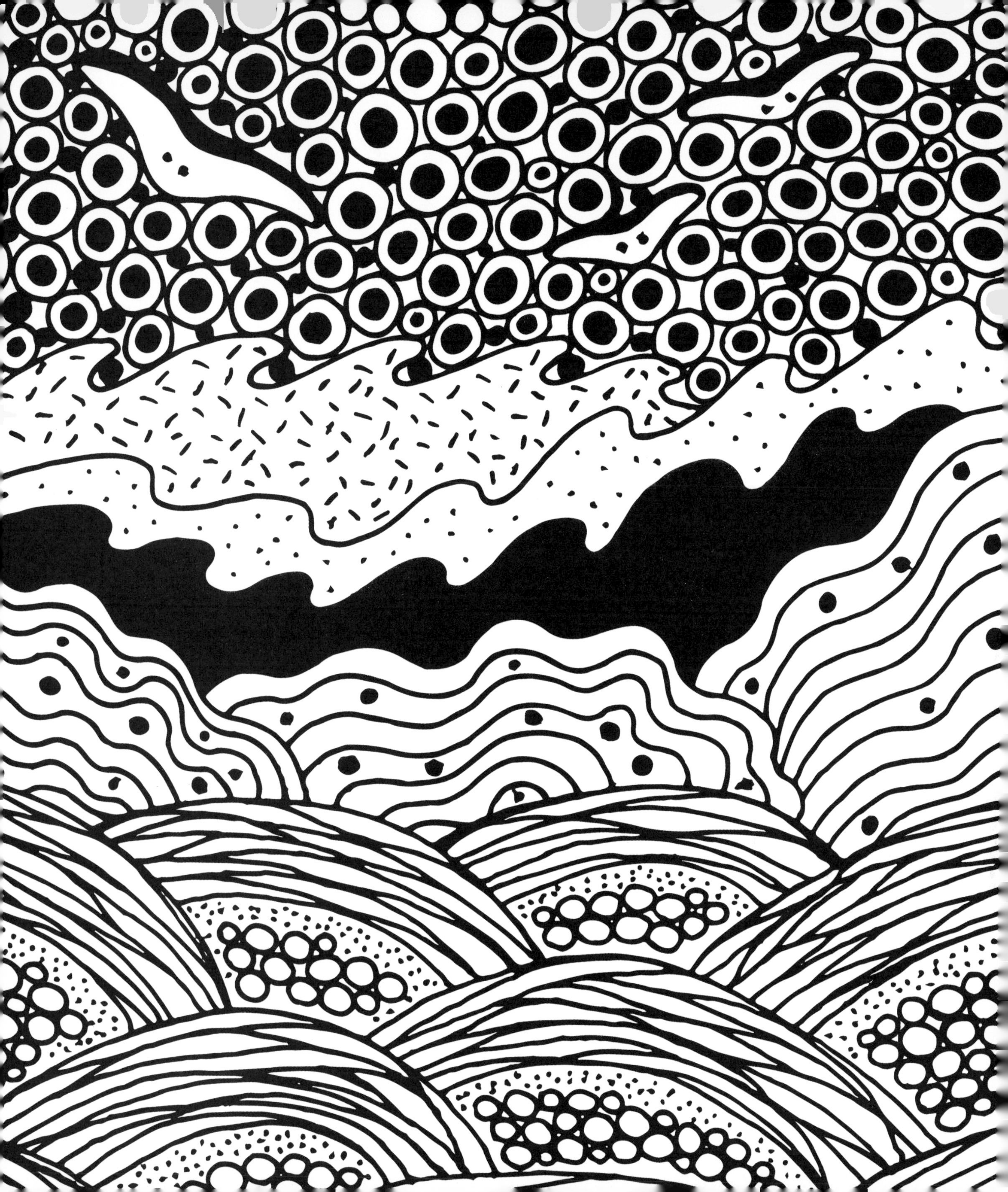

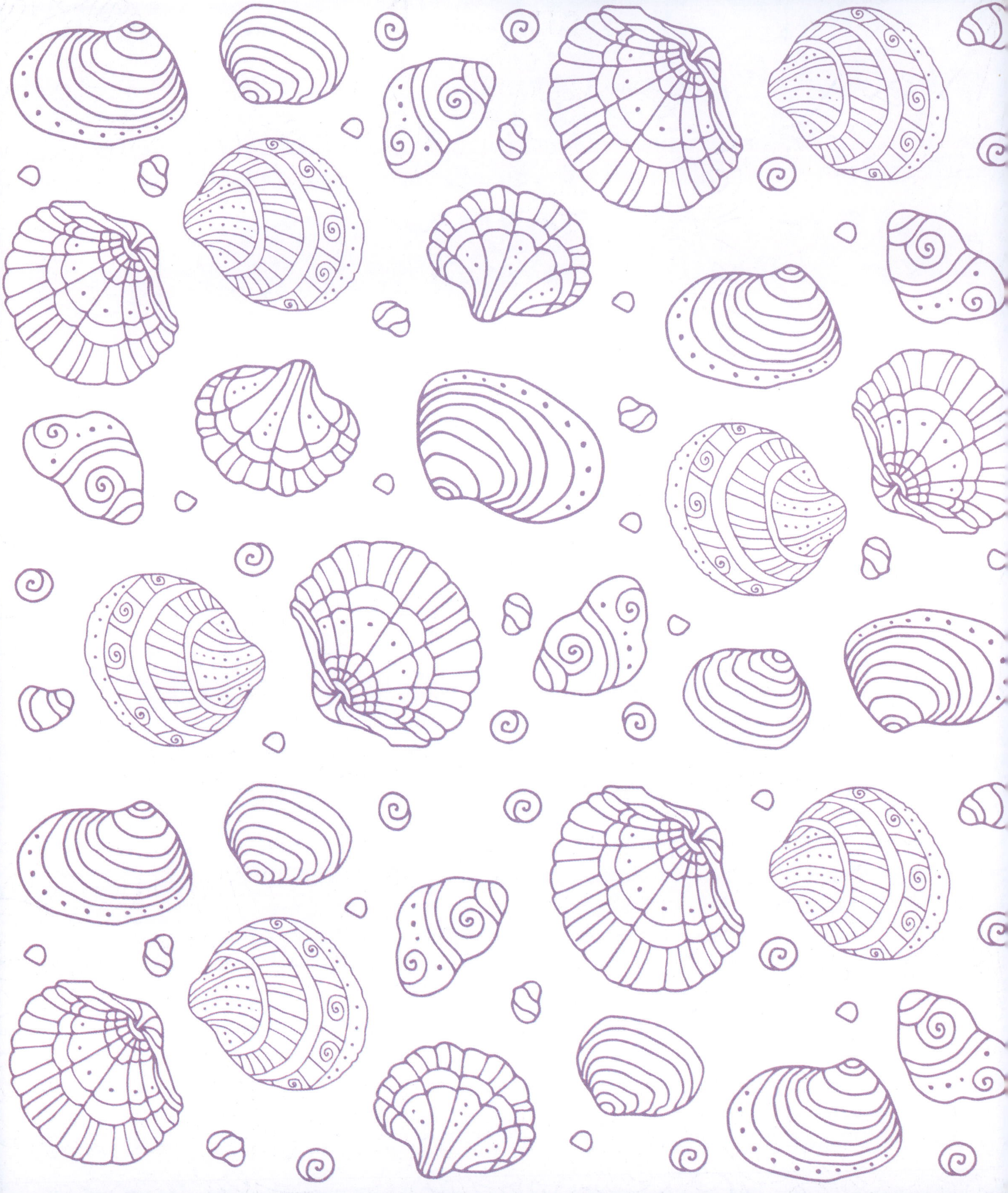

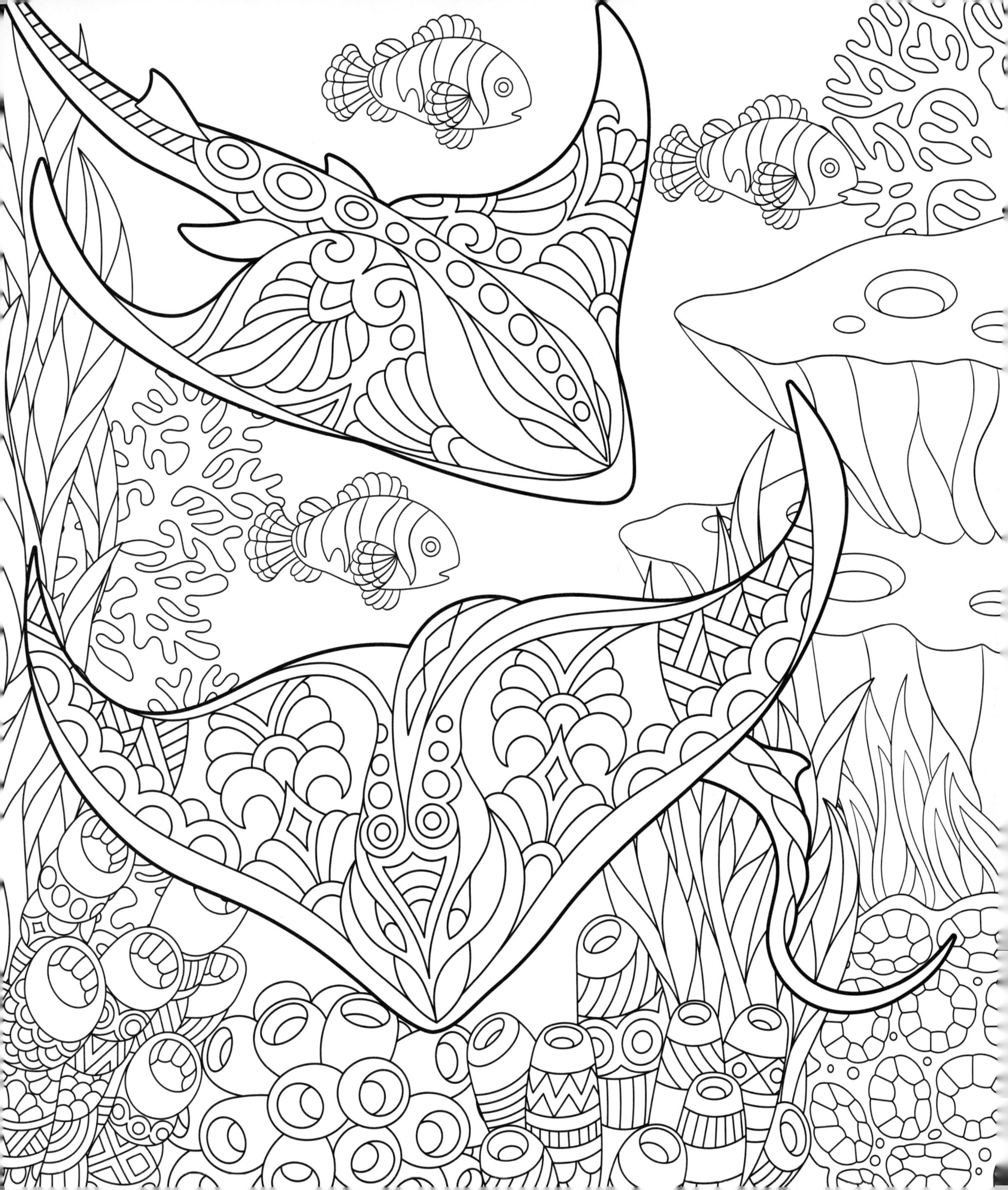

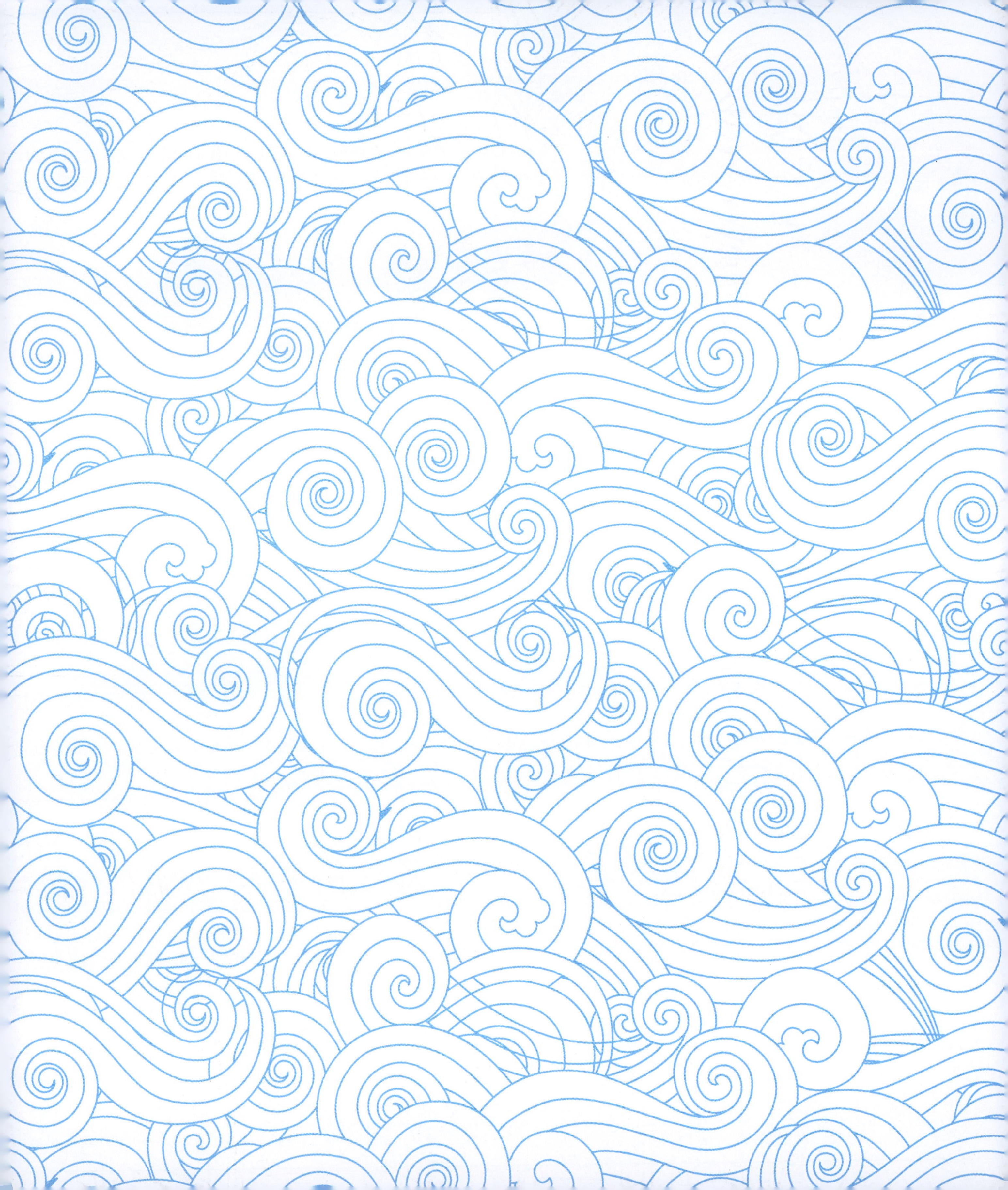

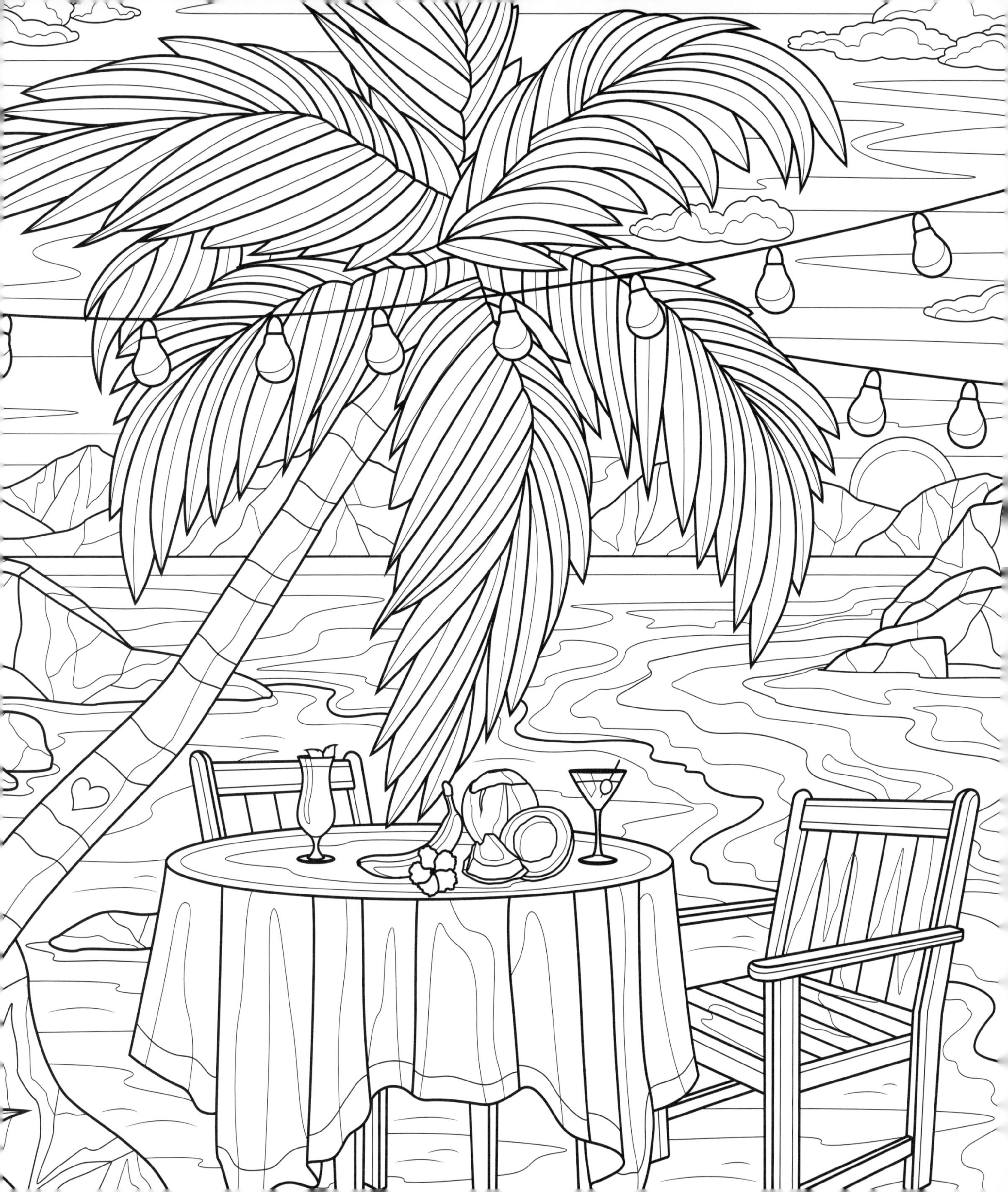

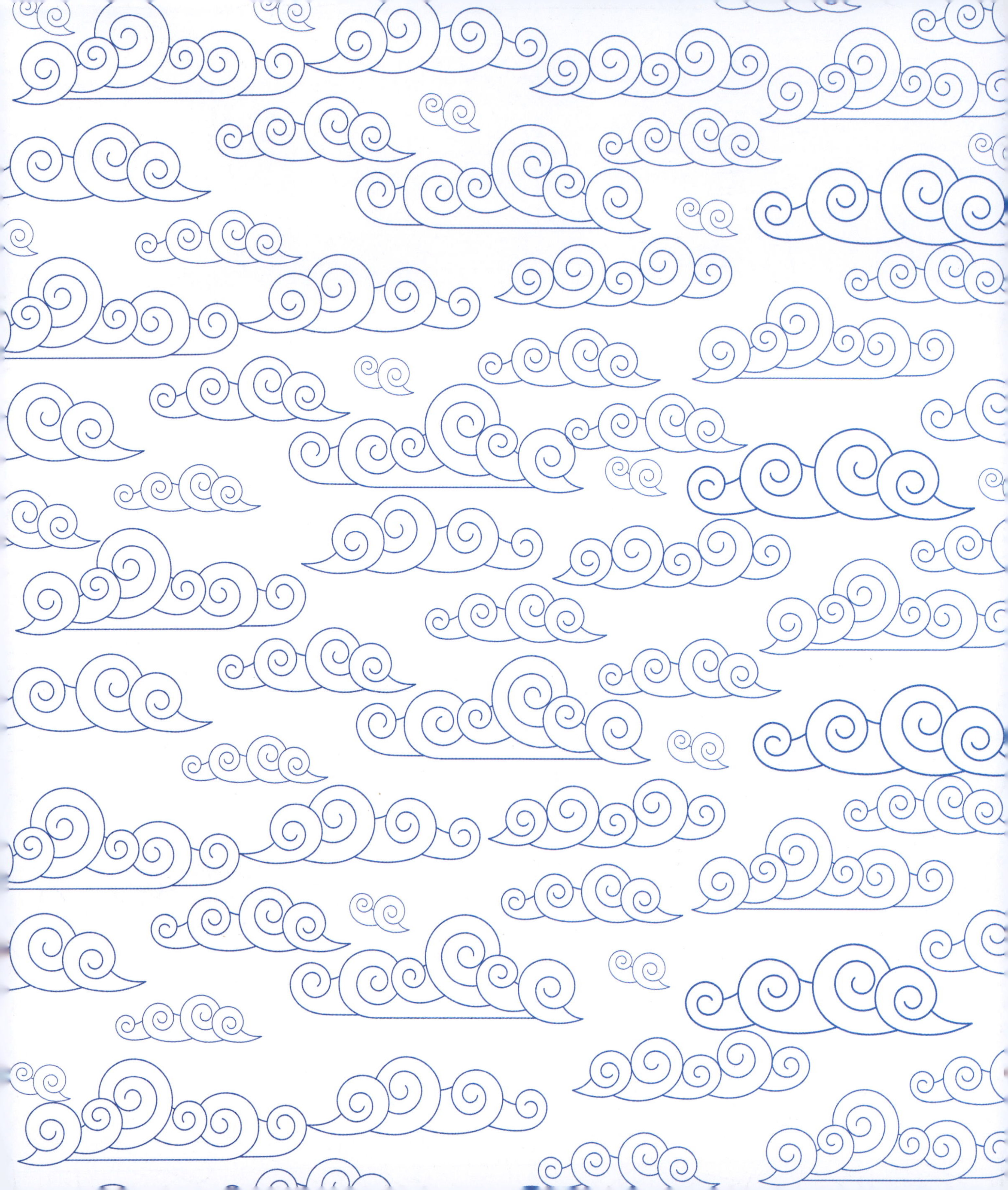

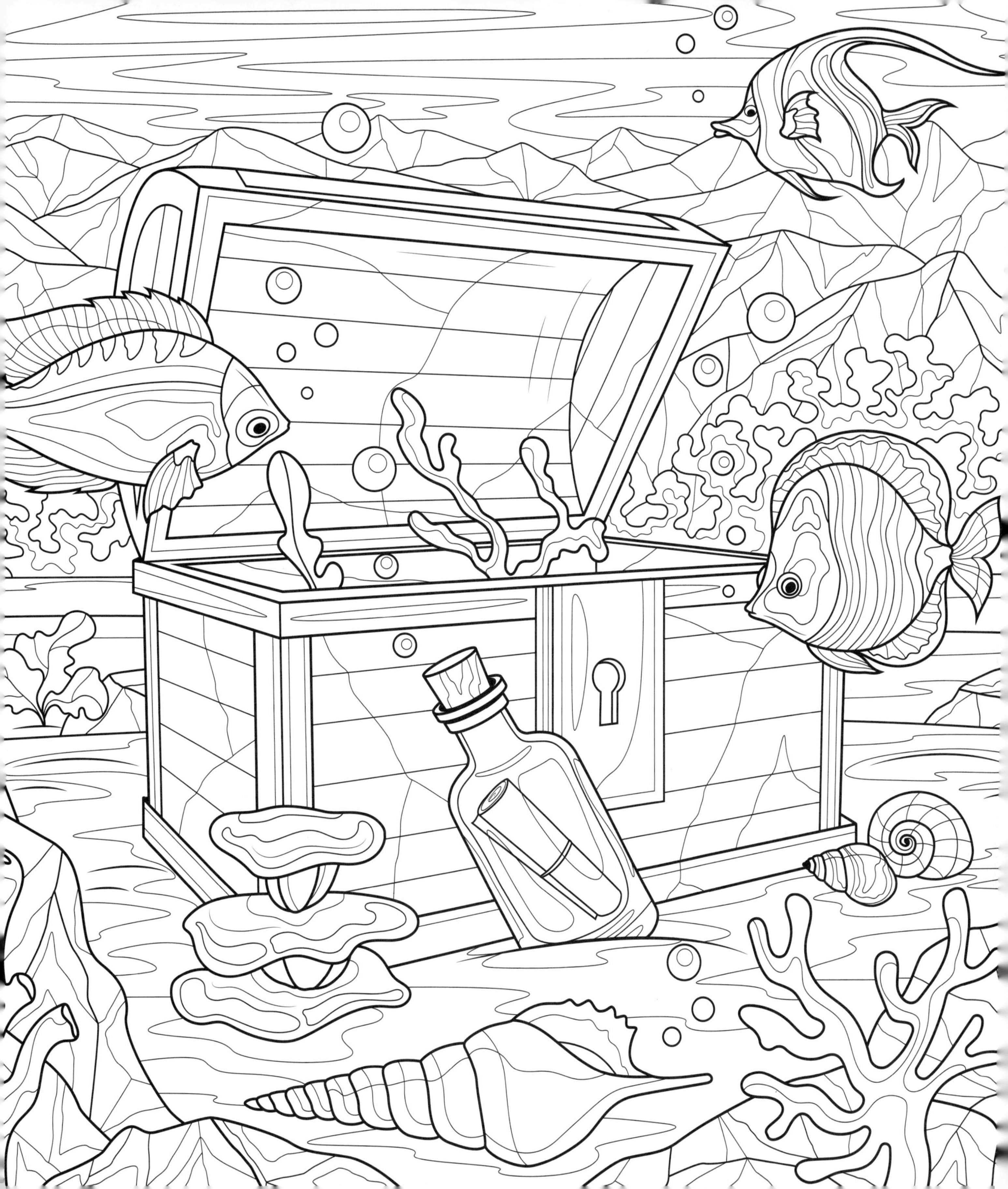

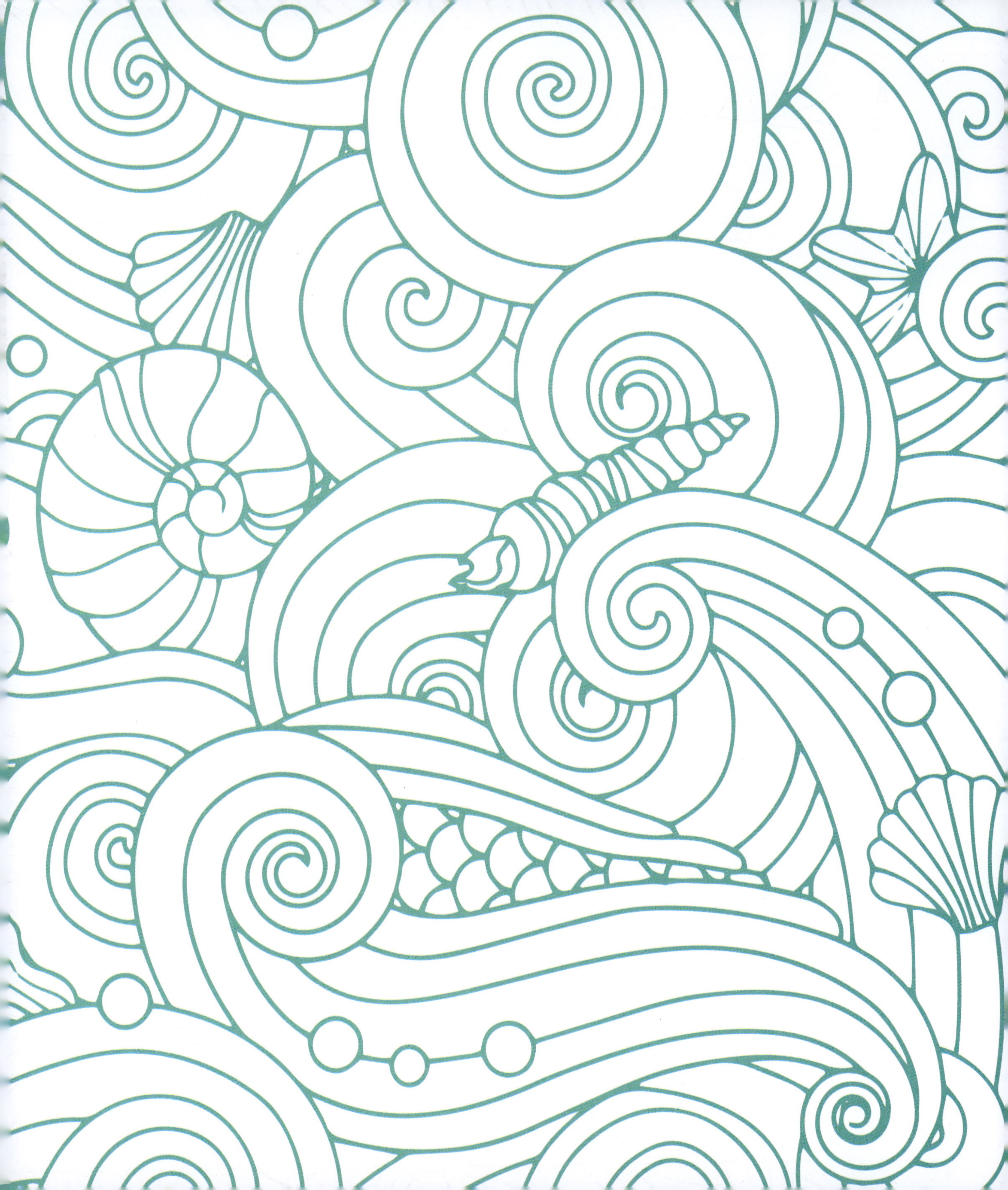

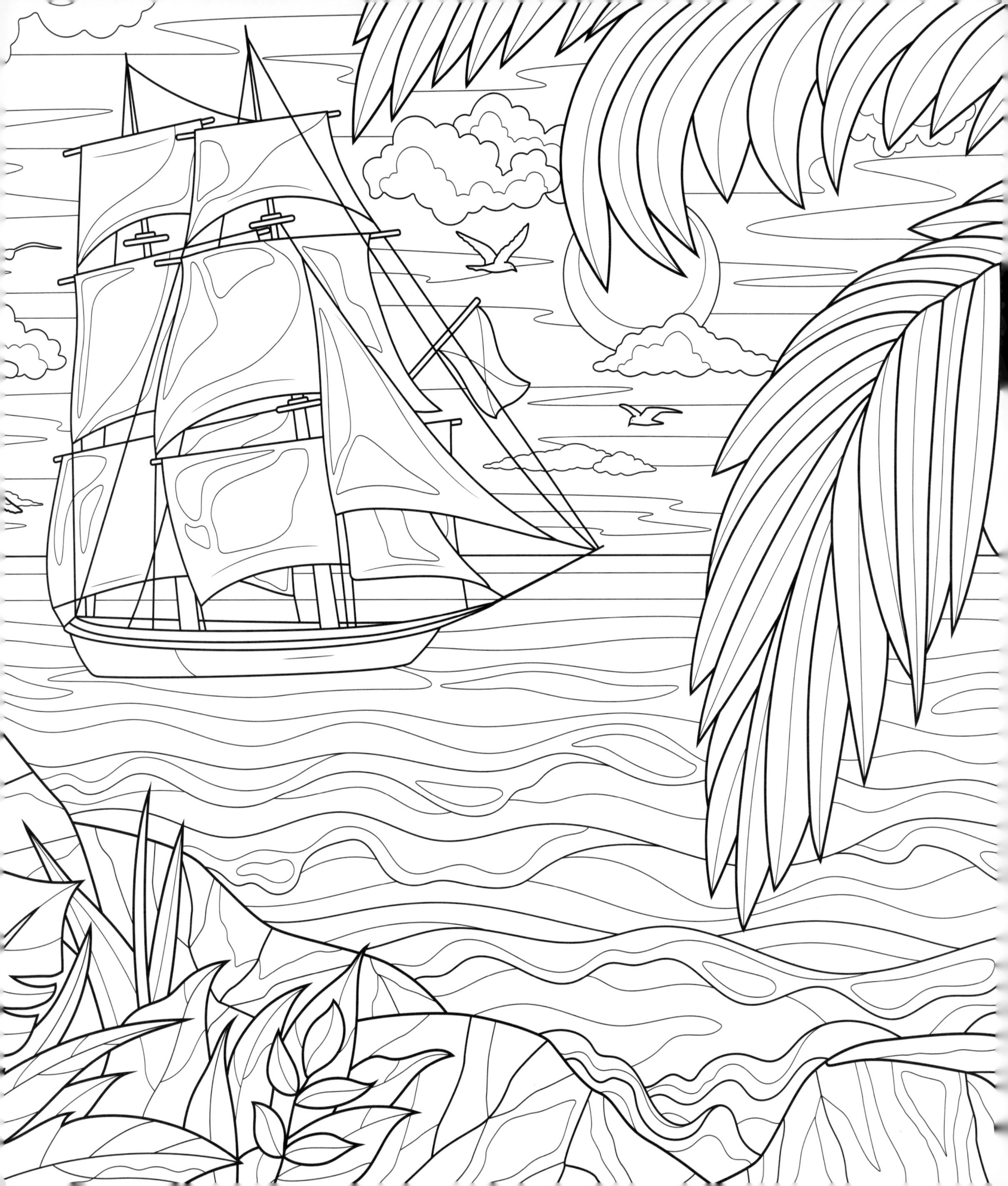

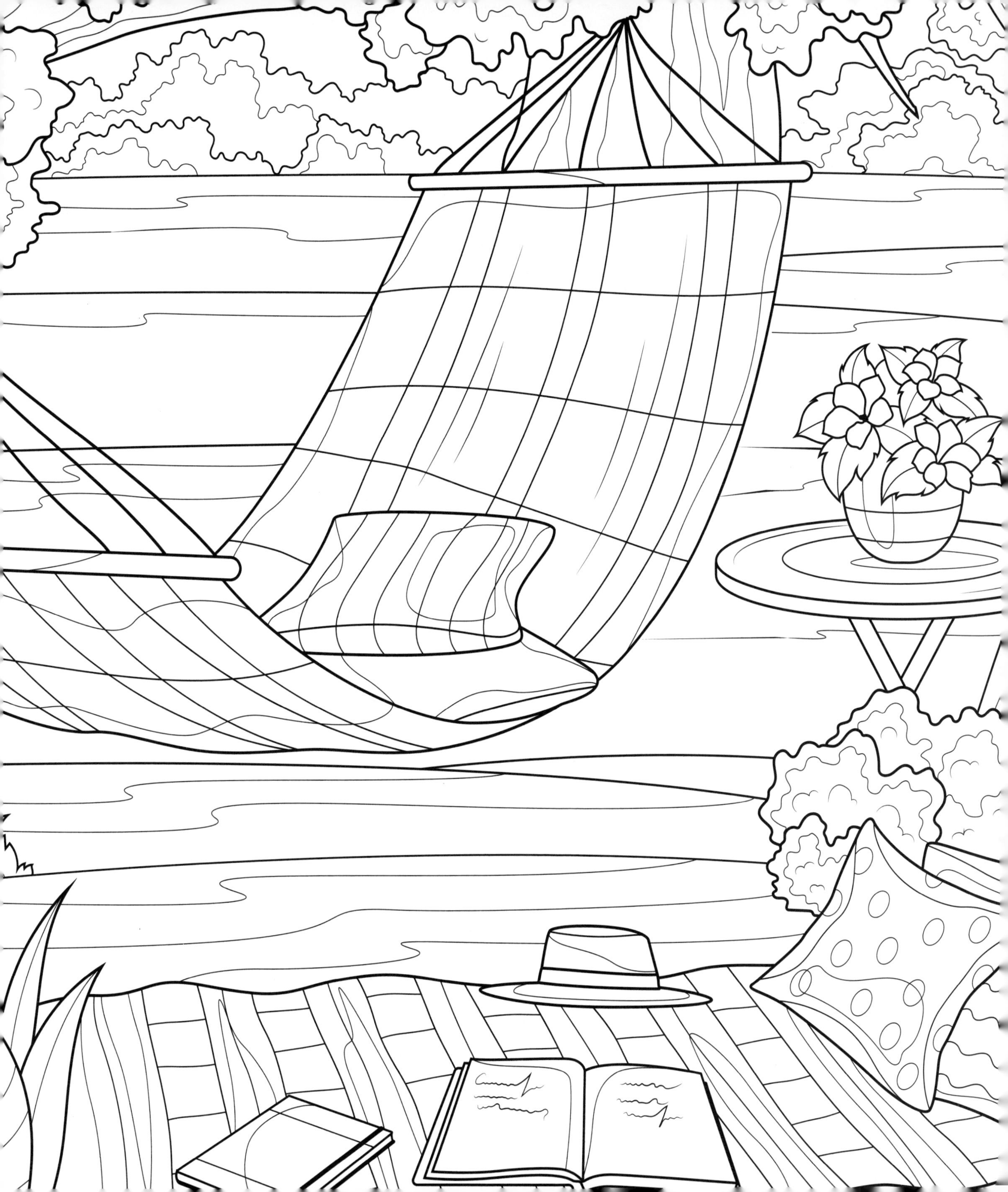

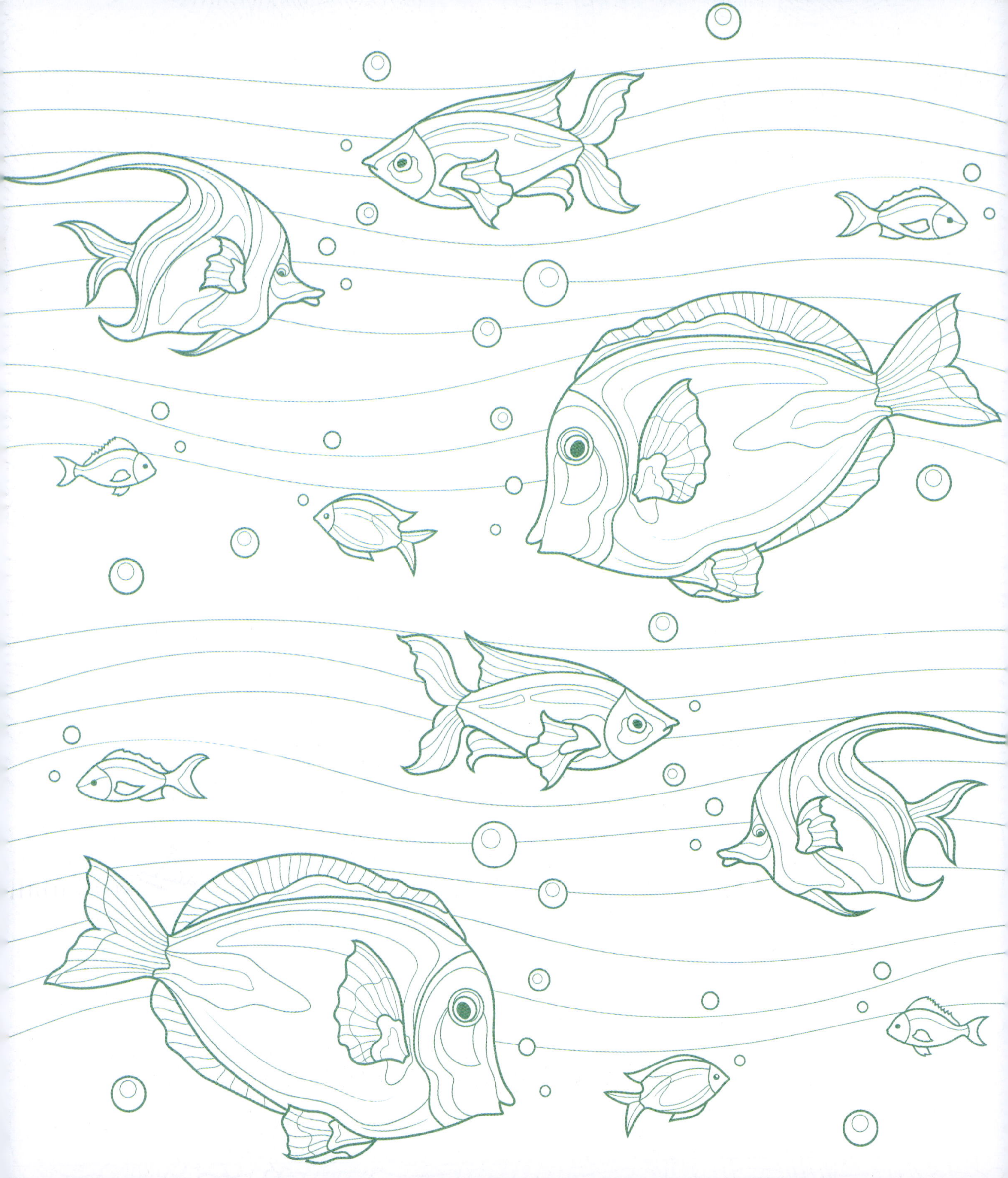

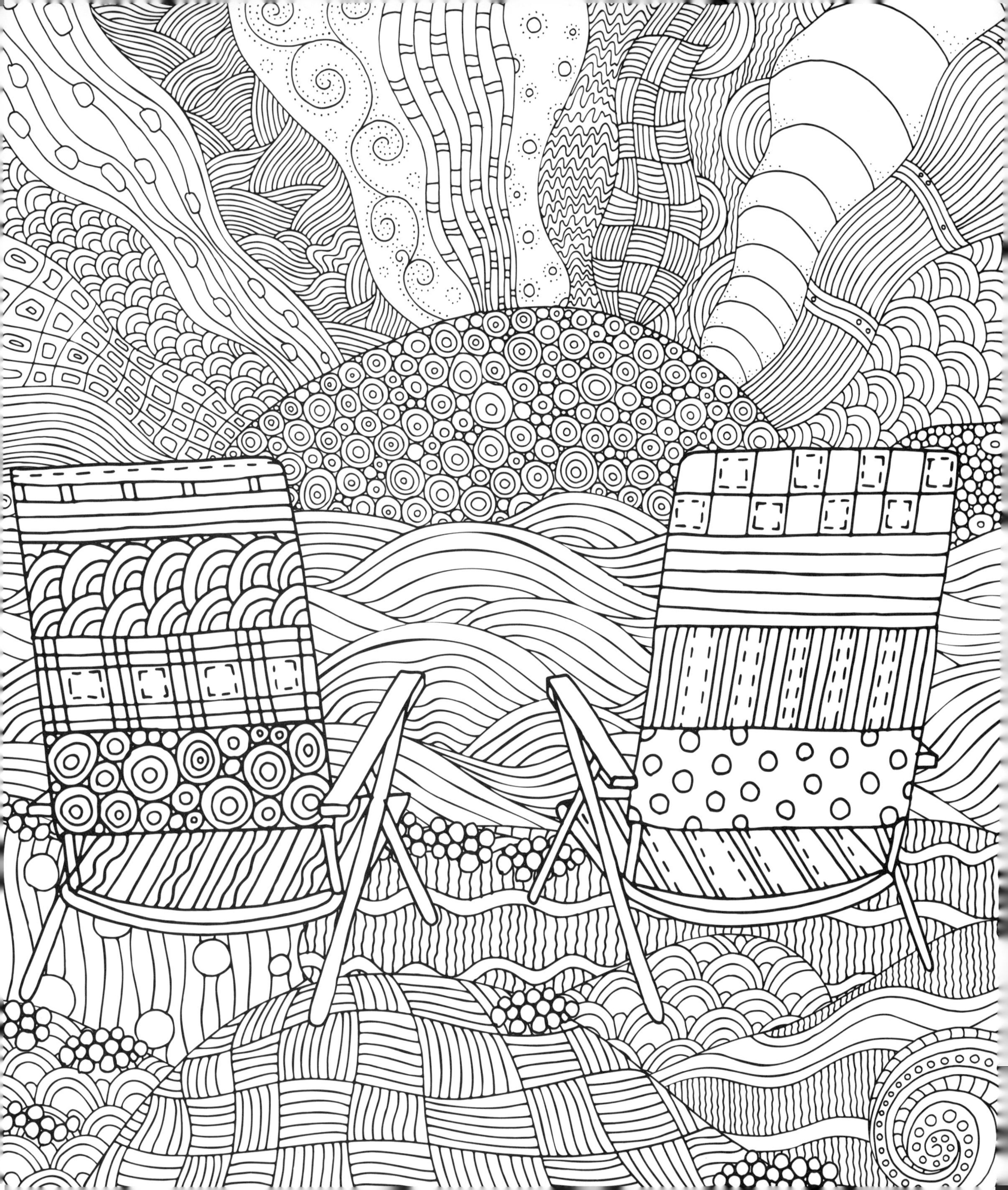

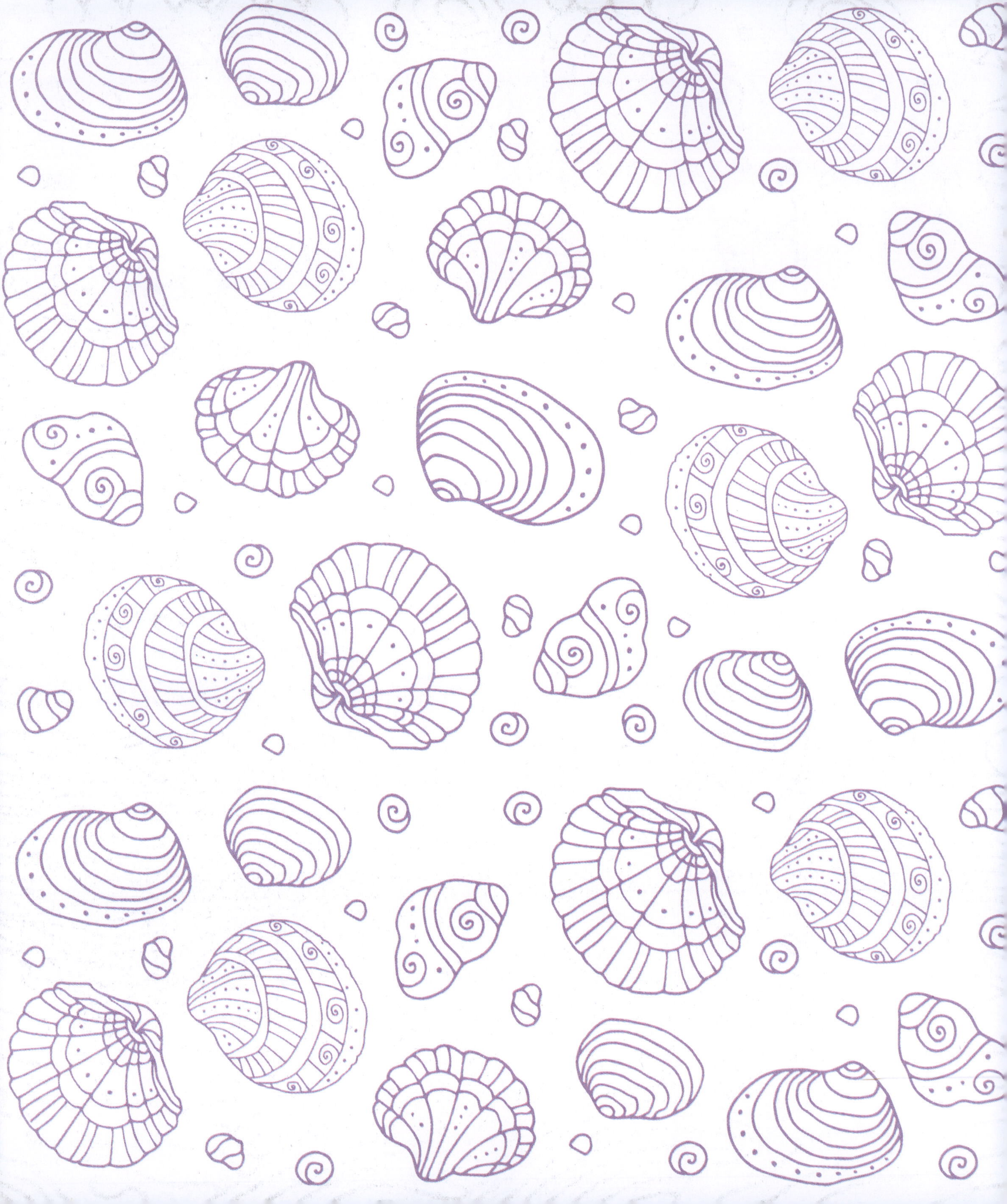

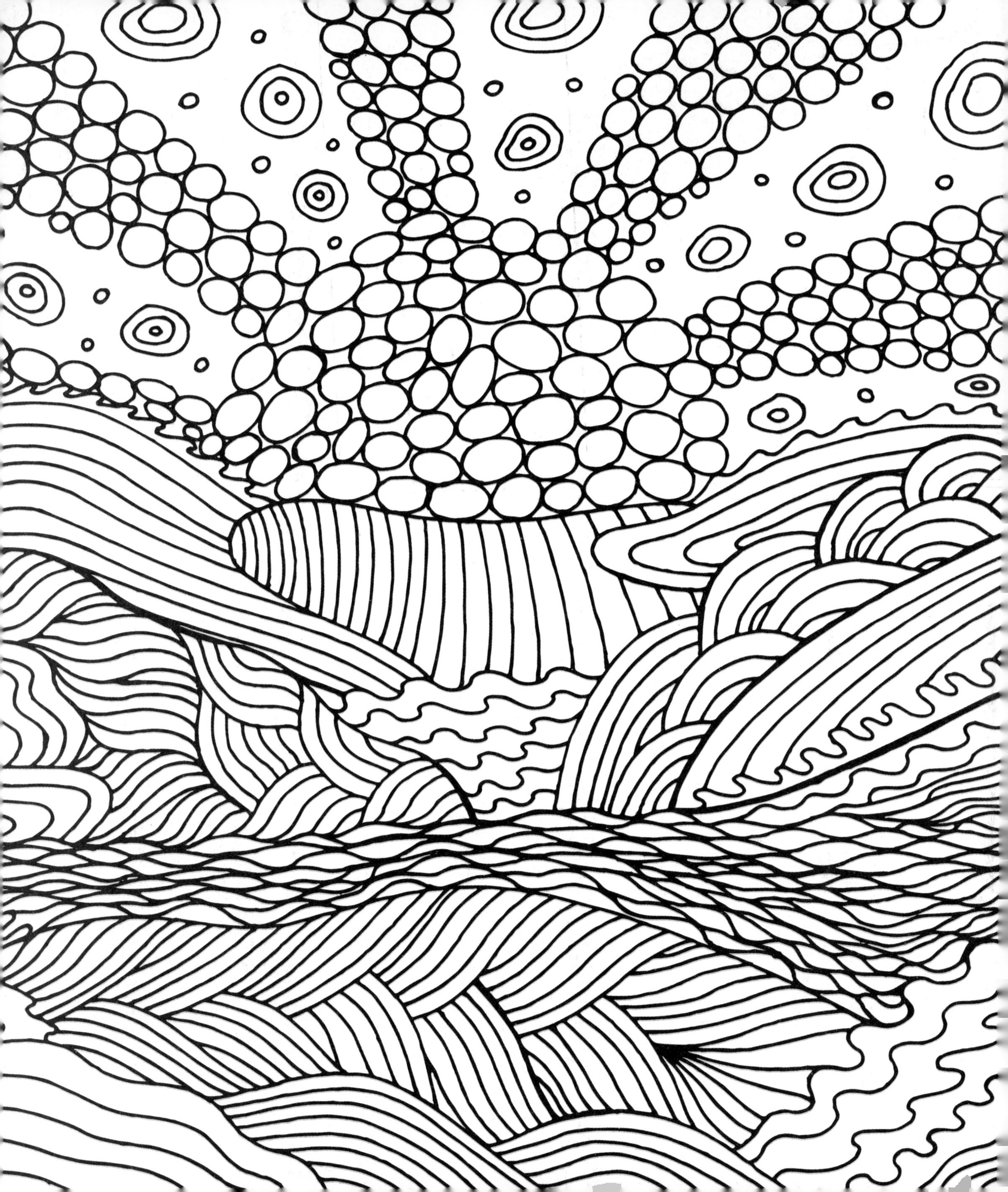

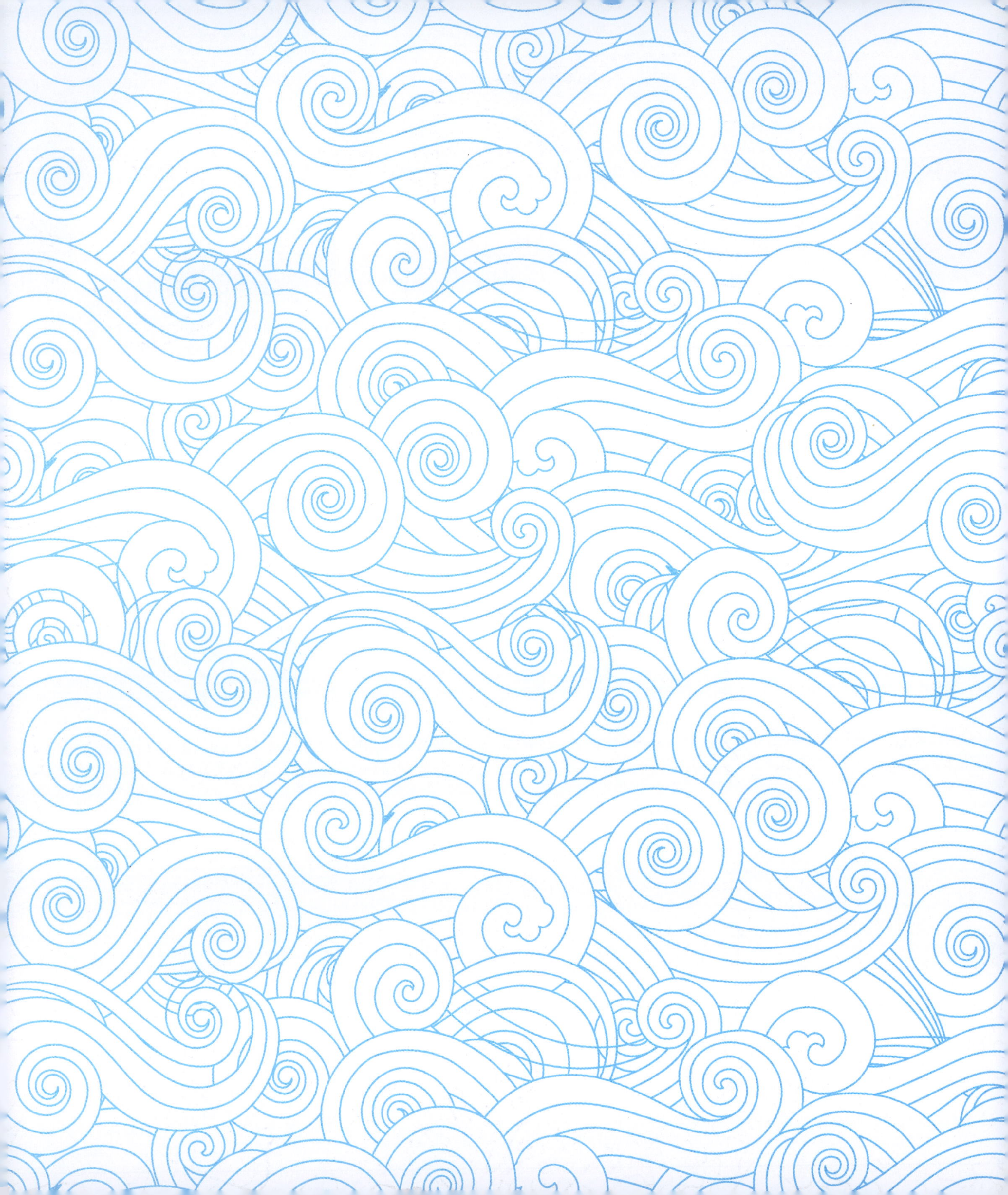

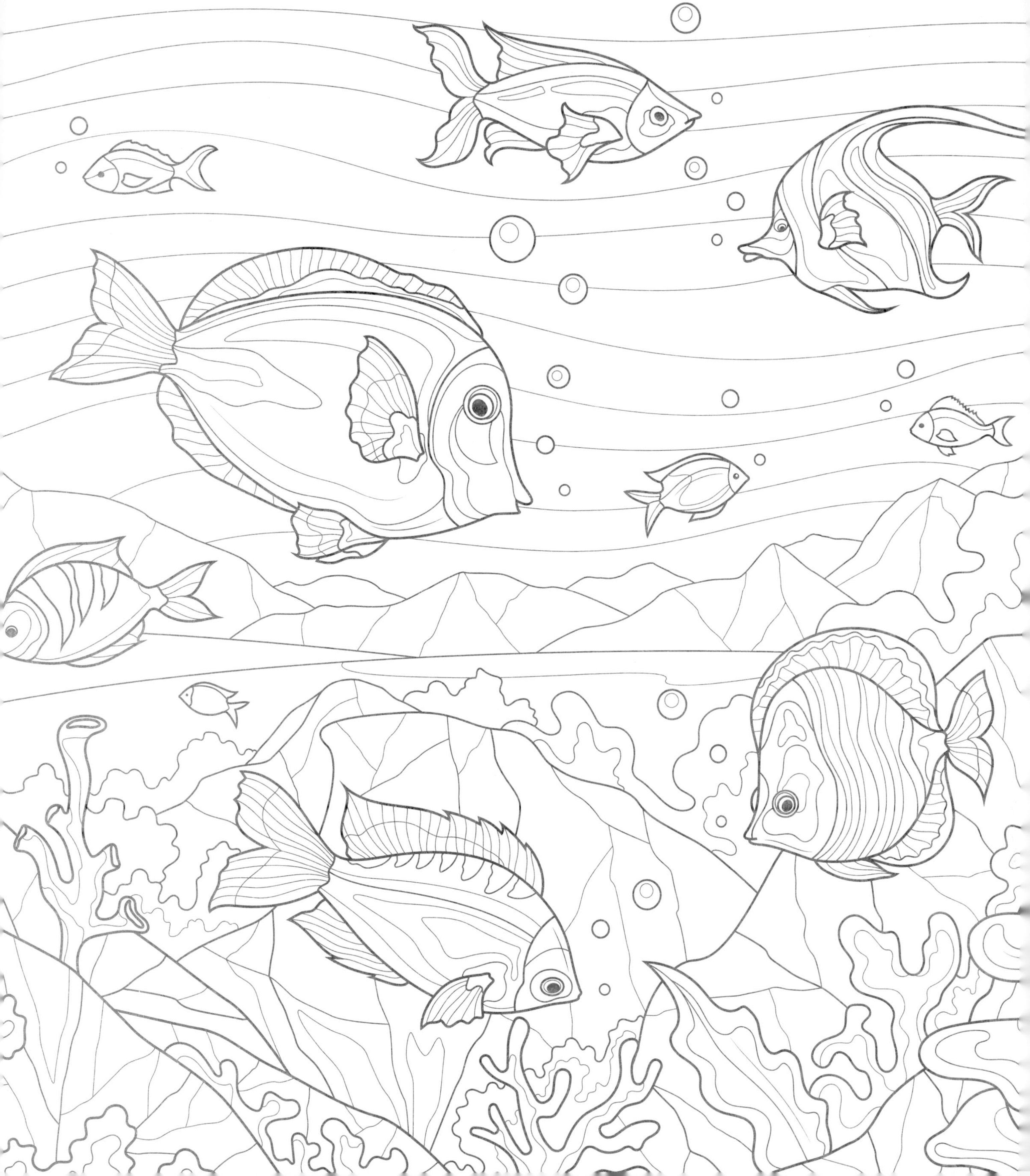

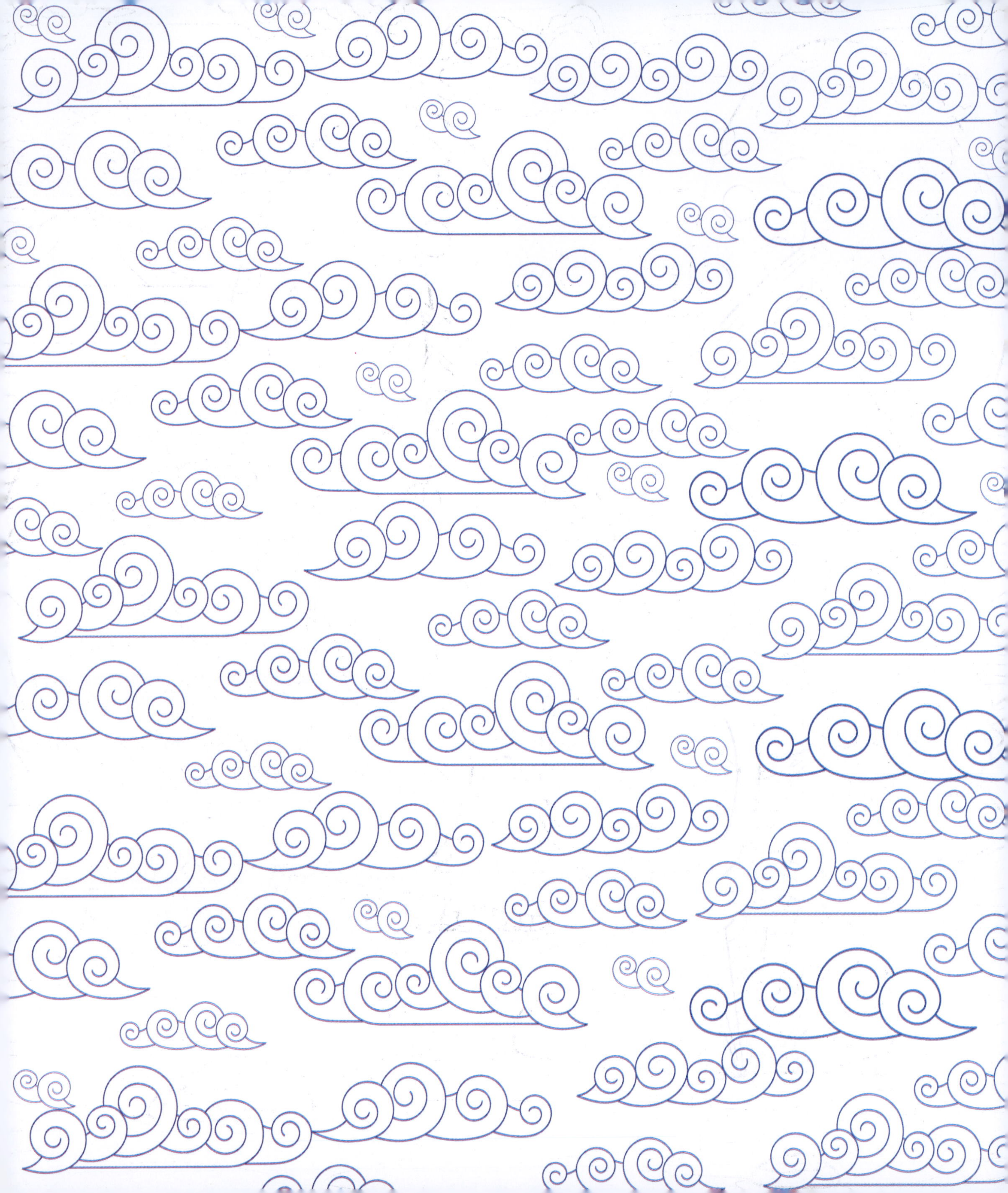

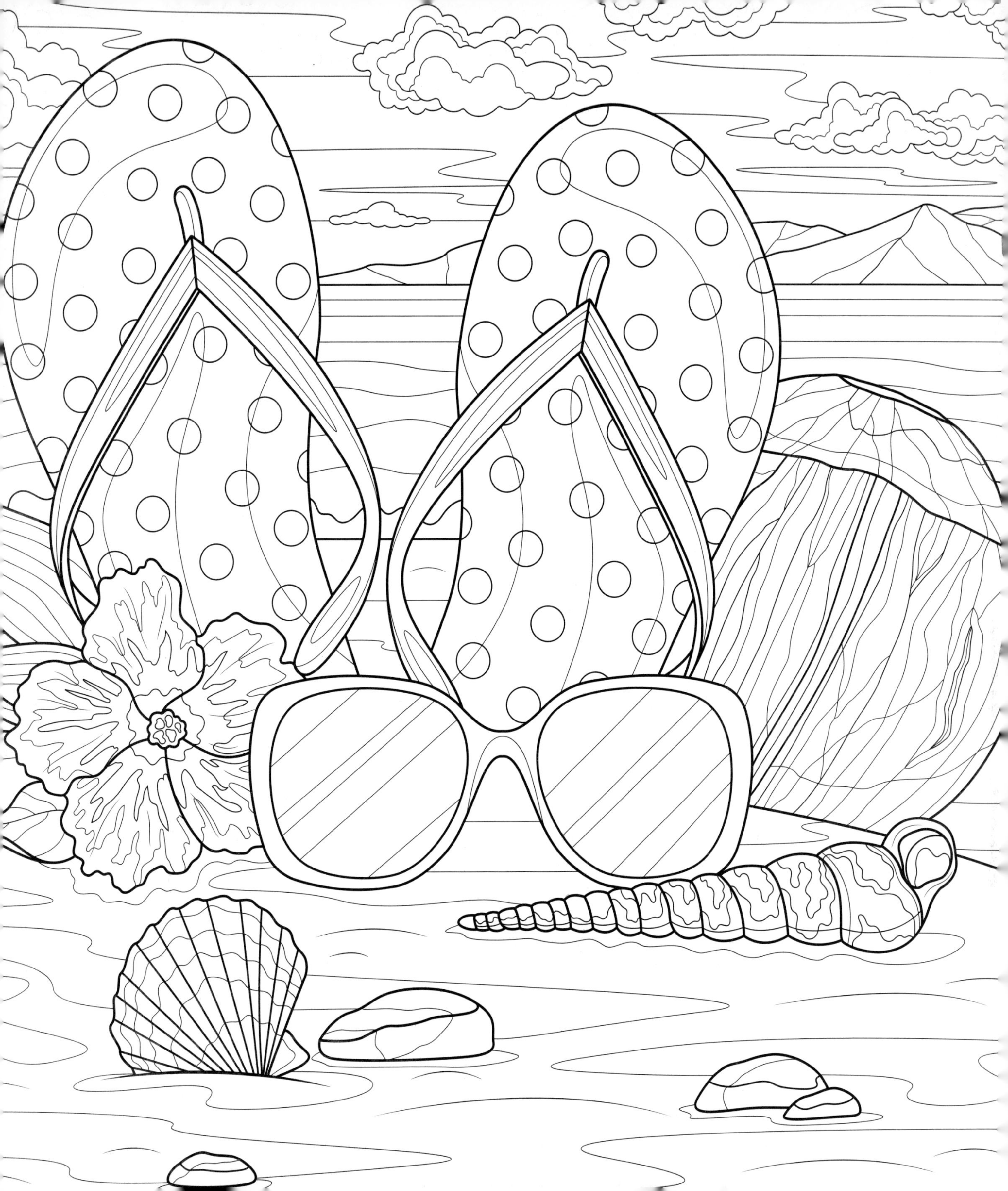

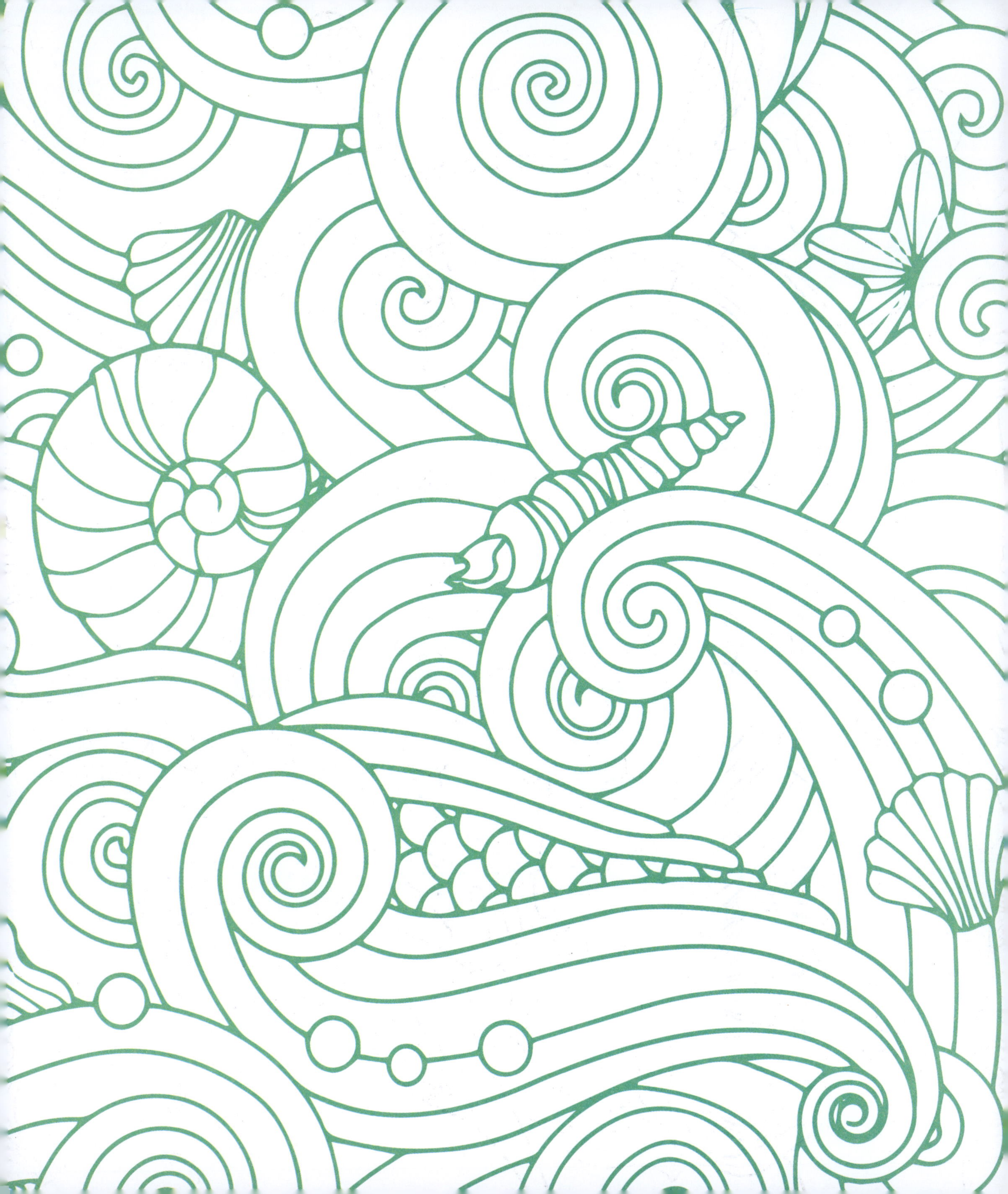

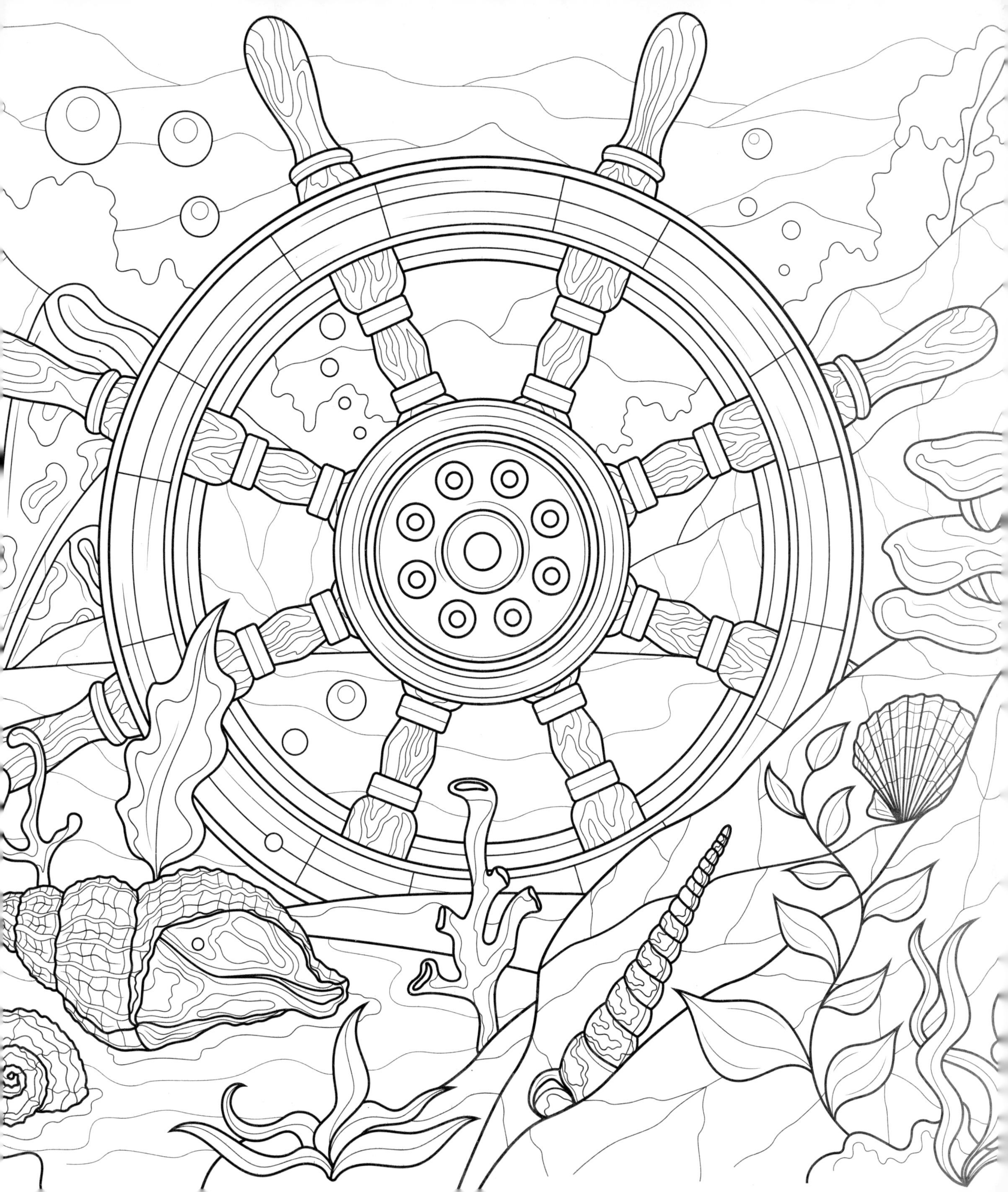

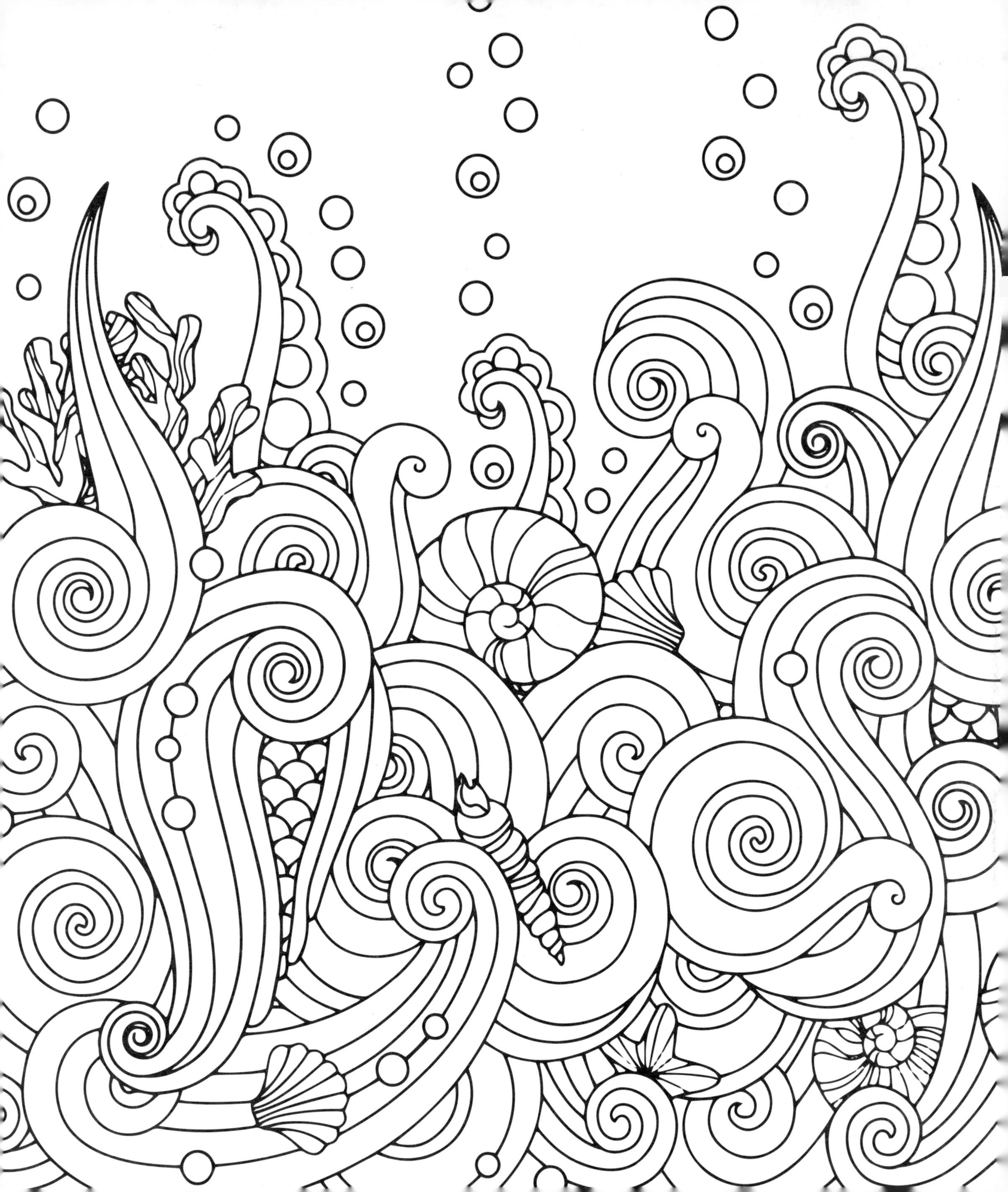

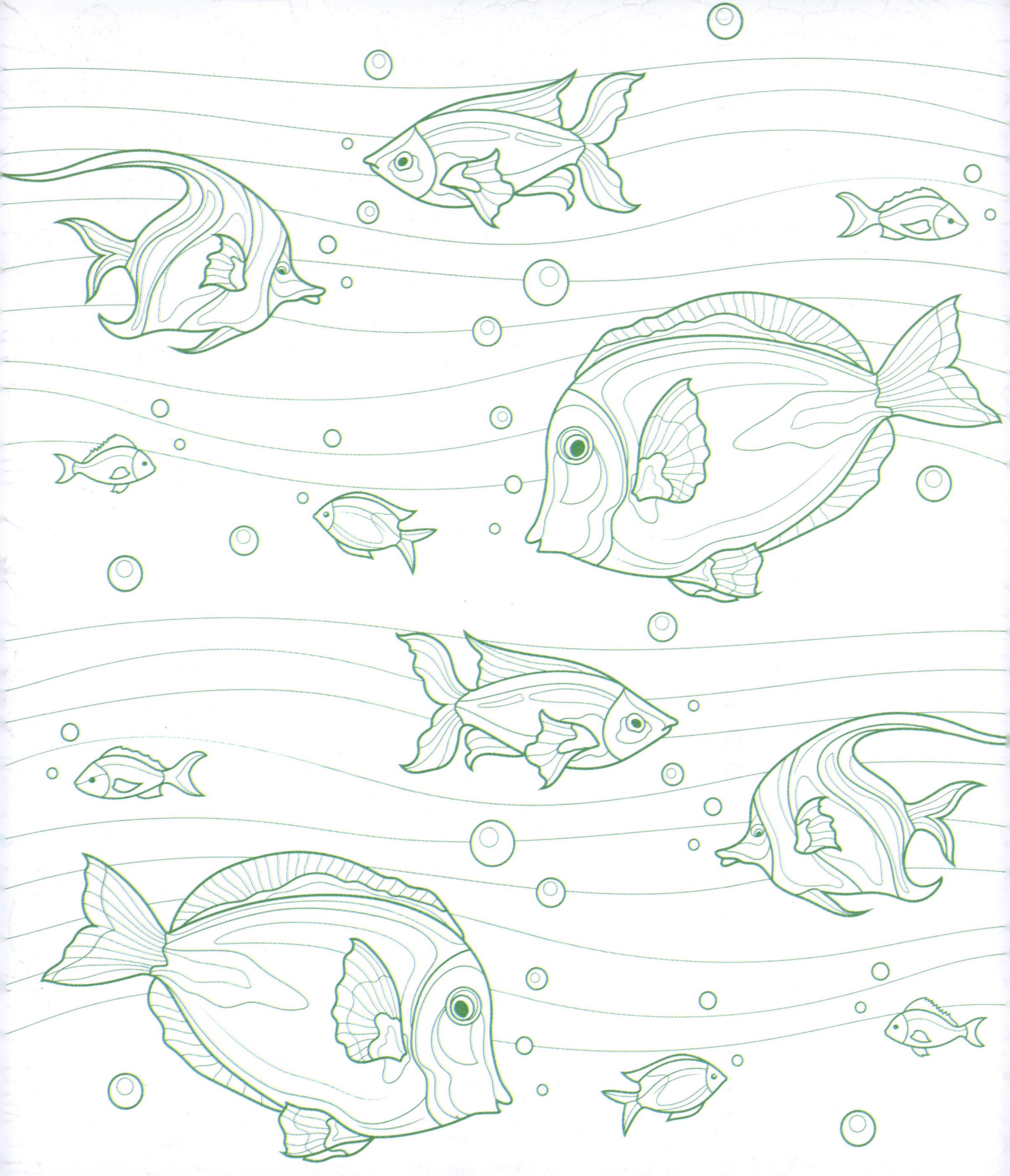

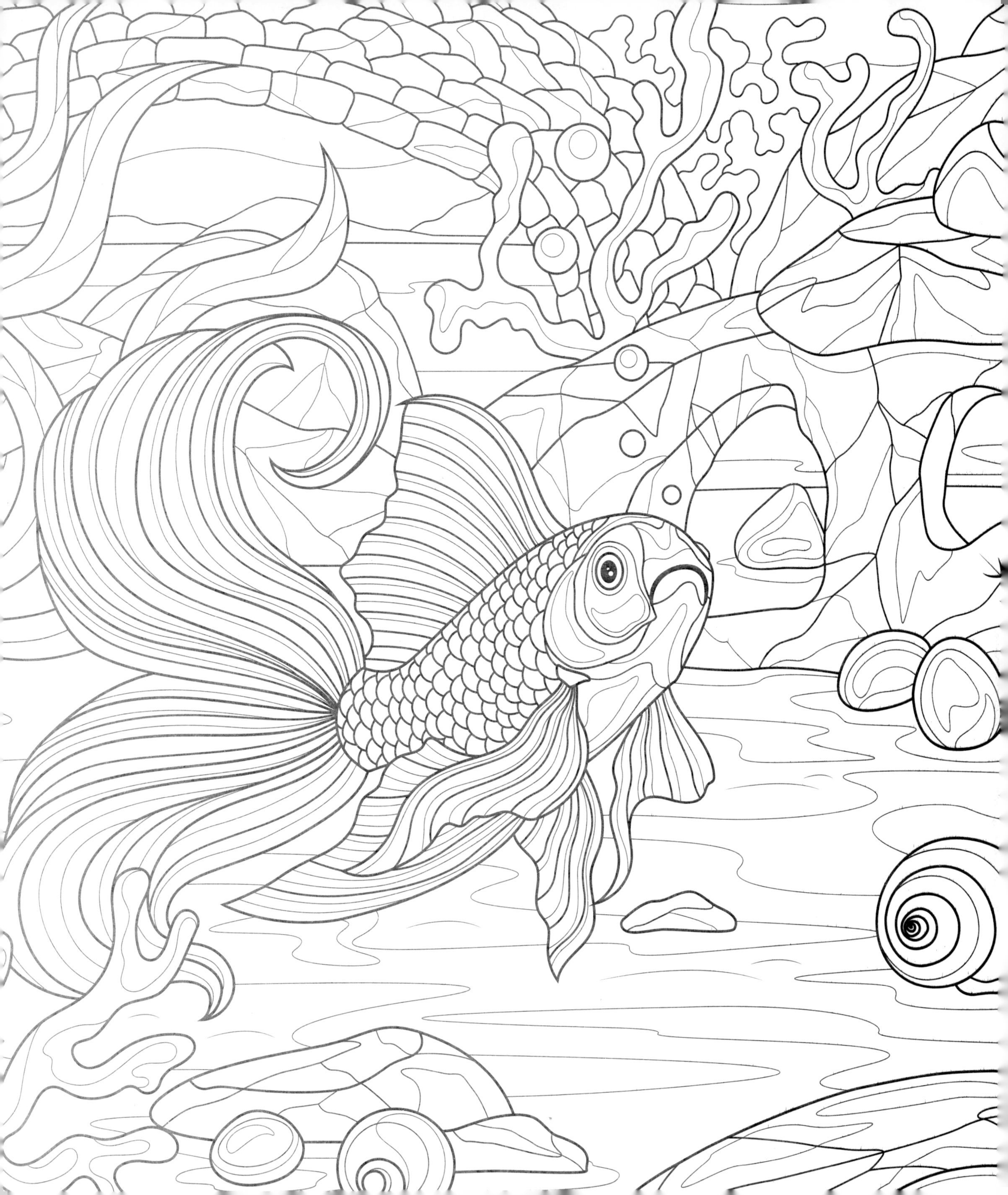

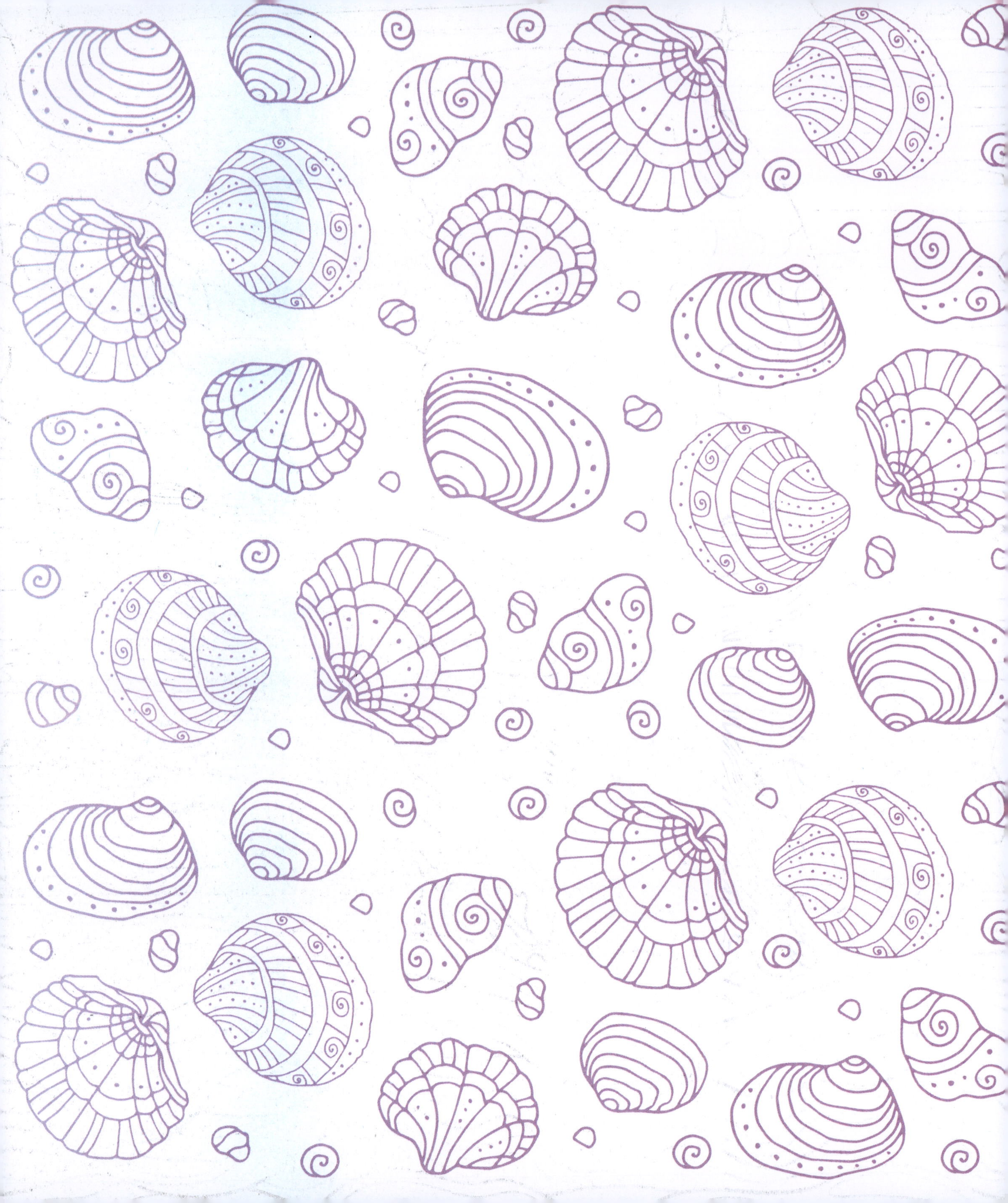

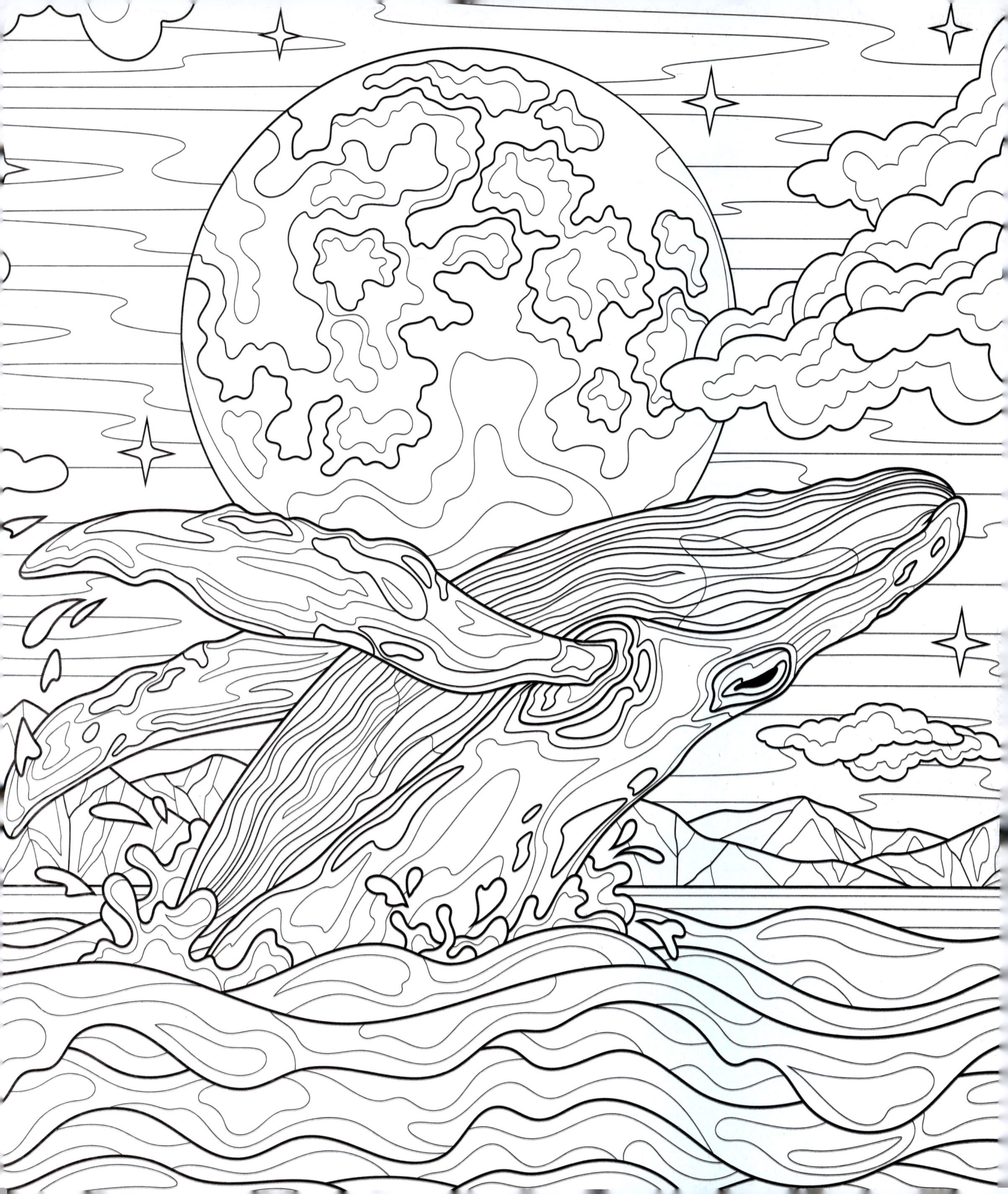

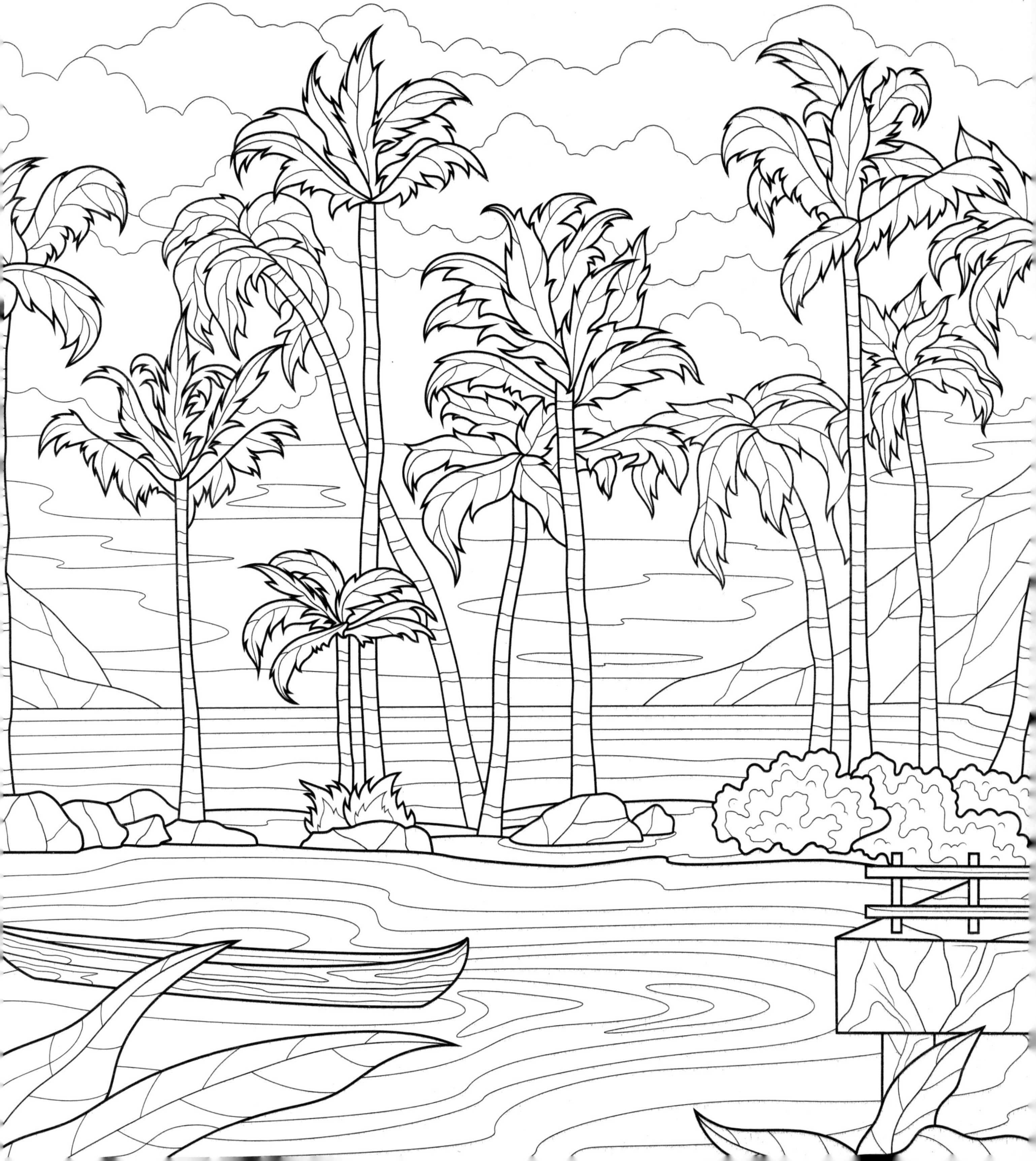